Brewers, Brands and the pub in their hands

Tony Thornton

Matador
9 Priory Business Park
Kibworth Beauchamp
Leicestershire LE8 0RX, UK
Tel: (+44) 116 279 2299
Fax: (+44) 116 279 2277
Email: books@troubador.co.uk
Web: www.troubador.co.uk/matador

ISBN 978-1783065-066

British Library Cataloguing in Publication Data.
A catalogue record for this book is available from the British Library.

Back Cover Images:

Cains Brewery, Liverpool. The Brewery was a real survivor, for many years….
It was founded by Robert Cain, a poor Irish immigrant, in 1858. By 1890 he could afford to build the
Victorian part of the brewery pictured, as well as a number of extravagant Victorian Liverpool pubs, notably
the Philarmonic Dining rooms. After his death and the loss of his driving force Cains brewery merged with
Peter Walker and son of Warrington, eventually to become part of Tetley-Walker. Higsons, another Liverpool
brewer stepped in soon after the merger with Peter Walker to purchase the brewery building, and the right
to brew Cains. In 1985 Boddingtons of Manchester bought Higsons, but within 5 years, sold all of its
brewing interests to Whitbread, who immediately closed Cains. The brewey was sold to Royal Unibrew of
Denmark, and then in 2002 to the Dusanj Brothers before finally closing in 2013.

The Ark, a purpose-built Scream Pub, North Frederick St, Glasgow. The pub of the future? The pub's
website claims that it has the largest sports screen and beer garden in the City.

Dick Jennings, Mill St, Toxteth, Liverpool. A traditional street-corner pub, which was owned by Walkers of
Warrington, which became Tetley-Walker, part of Allied Breweries. The pub was formerly named Woods
House and the Grapes. Its final name was in memory of the pubs' manager during the 1940s and 50s, a rare
honour to be bestowed by an English pub. It closed early this century. (source
inacityliving.blogspot.co.uk2012/11/last-order-pubs)

This book is dedicated to the past, and the memory of the inhabitants of those precious years.

Contents

Introduction

I t is said that the British adult population can be divided into three roughly equal groups; those who use pubs regularly, those who use them occasionally and those who avoid them. If so, then a lot of people have been affected by the profound changes to the nation's public houses. Pub users can see the pub very differently; a community resource, a temple of booze, informal diner, historical footnote, old-boys refuge, the essential scene, surrogate football venue. The myriad of alternatives demonstrate the ubiquitous, versatile and essential nature of the public house in our society.

This account focuses on the fifty years or so from the 1960s until now. In this time we have witnessed a revolution within the licensed trade; the ousting of the dominant big six brewers and their replacement by pubCos, thrusting new organisations which have built up similar vast pub estates.

And whilst some of those pubs have barely changed, others are unrecognisable. They are larger, more open, brash and colourful. Many now focus on food rather than drink as their *raison d'etre*, an unthinkable situation in the past. These changes have happened because their customers have changed. Pubs hold up a mirror to society and, if in tune with those changes, help to shape it.

The book examines this process, the dynamics behind what was taking place and the people and companies involved. It sets this story into the context of what we were drinking and eating in the pub and why, and explores the impact of government interference, licensing and the economy. New concepts and ideas are examined and predictions made as to where the drinks industry is heading, especially in relation to the horrendous and ongoing pub closures.

For almost the entire period covered by this story the underlying theme has been the decline of beer, both in consumption and, inevitably therefore, in its production. All the statistics measuring how much we drink have been heading steadily in the direction of the gutter where they joined with the fate of so many of our old breweries. Suddenly, in recent years, that unfortunate picture has been reversed. Real ale has finally climbed out of its seemingly inevitable decline. A renaissance is in the air, reflected by the exciting rise in the microbrewery. The optimism and sense of anticipation is added to by real ale's exuberant cousin craft beer. And this is bringing with it a wave of noisy enthusiasm from a new generation of drinkers.

The important and refreshing thing is that this process is not being led by huge remote corporations, manipulating and controlling our tastes. This latest revolution is happening from the bottom up, an organic groundswell of individuals at street level, a few brewing, most drinking, and all soaking up the heady new aroma and vibrancy that is spreading into the pub scene. Whatever the outcome of this rousing resurgence the journey promises to be an interesting one.

To epitomise this entire roller coaster ride the controversy keeps coming. The Smoking Ban and its aftermath, twenty-four hour licensing and binge drinking, minimum pricing, and most recently the dispute over the Beer Tie. These are all huge political issues focused on the licensed trade.

The story inevitably addresses many facets of society, the economy and politics. But most of all it is about the pub, and its ability to evolve whist retaining its essential character and atmosphere.

At the rear of the book you will find the Ultimate Guide to Pub Brands, with a unique listing of 149 pub brands. Beyond this the Appendices provide details of our brewers, both back in 1986 and more recent changes.

There are many organisations within the drinks trade who use acronyms because of their long titles. A list of these, and other definitions and abbreviations used within the book, are provided immediately before the appendices.

PART ONE

The Halcyon Years

It is 1967. The Beatles are at the peak of their popularity and shortly to bring out what many regard as their finest album, *Sergeant Pepper's Lonely Hearts Club Band*. The radical thinking hippie generation then spreading their message would have been unimpressed but Britain's brewers were also at the height of their powers. Between them they owned 58,000 pubs; over four out of every five pubs in the country.

Despite this, few would regard the Sixties as the brewers' finest hour. This may have been the era of love-ins, drugs and free expression for the flower children but everyone else had to make do with a pint of Red Barrel. Nevertheless the Sixties drinker must have been fairly undemanding as he drank ever more of this, or any other product which his brewery cared to serve up. Solid dependable working men would drink pints of their favourite brewery bitter in the bar of their local every night.

Yes, the local. Attitudes and social conditions have changed hugely over the last fifty years. The average working man, i.e. most of us in the Sixties, lived without most of the creature comforts that we now take for granted. Inadequate heating, poor decorations and spartan furniture. And an even greater lack of entertainment. The alternatives to the pub for an evening out were not exactly awe-inspiring in the dowdy streets of the Sixties. The local dance hall or cinema on a Saturday night or the chip shop for a meal out. Otherwise an evening out was the local boozer.

Note the reference to the working 'man'. Women rarely entered pubs on their own. Those who did risked inviting questions about their moral rectitude. Pubs were largely a male refuge. Their austere and uncomfortable furniture and fittings reflected this. Things changed a little on a Saturday night when the women would dust down their best

3

frock and accompany their man to the local to sip a few glasses of stout, cream sherry or Babycham.

Given such a captive market the brewers were not exactly falling over themselves to make their premises appealing to their customers. The main legacy to the pub from the Sixties was the formica table-top. Very modern and chic, and with the added bonus of stopping all that spilt beer soaking into the nasty real wood underneath. One other innovation provided the pub with that cosy corporate feel; illuminated perspex signs of one's favourite beer. Great for lighting up neglected corners and providing a stylish little touch from your friendly big brewer.

The brewers were not entirely idle during the Fifties and Sixties. They had been fighting momentous takeover battles to improve their market share. Whitbread owned few pubs in 1945. They acquired 10,282 pubs by taking over other companies between 1960 and 1971. Courage took shape from 200 separate pub and brewing companies during this time, whilst Bass and Charrington rounded off their empire-building by combining in 1967. Ind Coope became Allied Breweries in 1961 after merging with Tetley Walker. In 1963 they added Ansells and Friary Meux for good measure.

Whilst these colossal corporations were adding breweries to their collections like children collect football cards, they weren't really interested in the finer detail of what went on inside their pubs. The brewers made beer. Their pubs were, on the whole, run by tenants. The tenants they chose were not exactly thrusting entrepreneurs; just good upstanding working folk who the brewers could trust to pay the rent and keep pulling the pints to keep the mash tuns at the brewery merrily churning. If the punters wanted a change from an evening stood at the bar drinking bitter then they could always try mild or stout. For entertainment they could choose between darts, cribbage or shove ha'penny. And if they were hungry then there was a wide choice of cuisine to supplement their pint; plain, cheese and onion or salt and vinegar. Food? You ate that at home before you went out.

The Beerage

By the late Sixties, after a frenetic period of takeovers and consolidation over the previous two decades, the brewing and supply of beer was dominated by the big six.[1]

A good example of how the brewers devoured the opposition is the formation of Bass. In 1959 Northern Breweries was created by the merger of the Hope and Anchor Brewery, Sheffield, Hammonds of Bradford and John Jeffrey of Edinburgh. Hammonds had previously taken over The Ilkley Brewery in 1923, The Springwell Brewery, Heckmondwike in 1929, Bentley and Shaw of Huddersfield in 1944 and Seth Senior and Sons of Huddersfield in 1947. Northern Breweries proceeded to swallow up a further sixteen brewery companies between 1960 and 1962 at which point it became United Breweries with 2,750 pubs. But there was no time to draw breath as 1962 witnessed the merger with the large East London firm of Charringtons. Meanwhile Bass, Ratcliff and Gretton had merged with Worthingtons in 1927 to become the largest Burton brewer and in 1961 they merged in turn with the Birmingham-based Mitchells & Butlers. In the 'big is beautiful, anything less is vulnerable' world of the Sixties the two huge combines of Bass and Charrington could not resist each other's advances and combined in 1967, swallowing Liverpool's Bents Brewery at the same time for good measure.

The decisive conclusion of that consolidation can be gauged by the size of these companies in terms of pub ownership in 1960 and then just twelve years later;

	1960		1972
Watneys	4,000	Grand Met.	6,000
Courage	3,500	Courage	6,000
Ind Coope	2,500	Allied Breweries	8,000
Whitbread (umbrella)	2,500	Whitbread	8,500
Charrington	2,400	Bass Charrington	9,300
Scottish & Newcastle	1,700	Scottish & Newcastle	1,700

Like many other industries these rival companies operated along similar lines. Brewing dynasties such as the Whitbreads and Watneys were long established and very wealthy. Most could trace the origins of their brewing activity back several generations to the mid or early Victorian age. Board members tended to be long-serving and were almost universally male, conservative figures from within the industry. During the Sixties, members of the original brewing families were still prominent on some boards, although this did rapidly change during the following decade.

The industry didn't seek or feel the need for innovation. With limited pressure on balance sheets and plenty of spare production capacity, a tendency towards slackness pervaded many areas of the brewers' behaviour. Instead a wood-panelled mustiness prevailed. One of the more critical aspects of this was evident in the value of their huge estates. These included not only their thousands of pubs but also substantial landholdings dedicated to their breweries and distribution depots, some in valuable central locations. These were rarely revalued, which became a serious omission as the brewers consequently had a poor grasp of the worth of their companies. This also masked underperformance when profits were considered as a return on capital

assets employed, or pubs sold based on outdated book values.[2]
However, the lure of getting their hands on pristine and extensive
landholdings with huge redevelopment potential made the brewers an
increasingly tempting target for a variety of business tycoons, property
companies and financial speculators. During the many brewery
takeovers, which become such a regular feature of this story, the
influence of these predators was often decisive.

The brewers wielded power in Parliament and, collectively, were
very influential in political and economic terms. This, combined with
their aloofness and degree of ineptitude, made them appear increasingly
anachronistic in a modern economy. Their size and power, and the
rather eccentric, crusty image, earned the industry the sobriquet of the
Beerage.

To decentralise, to assist in managing thousands of pubs distributed
all over the country, the brewers organised their estates in geographical
regions. They typically used the names of the brewers that they had
absorbed and taken over for their regional operating companies. This
imparted a feeling of continuity and permanence. For example, Allied
Breweries divided into Ind Coope in the south, Ansells in the
Midlands, Tetleys around Yorkshire, Tetley-Walker across the Pennines,
and Alloa Brewery in Scotland. Ind Coope then further subdivided to
keep alive the memories of Benskins in the northern home counties,
Friary Meux south of London, Taylor Walker covering Greater London,
plus Romford Brewery Co and Halls, Oxford and West to the east and
west. Pub signage often also indicated allegiance to these subsidiaries,
which frequently worked out of the former brewery or offices of the
old brewer, still retained in the ownership of the main company. It was
almost as if the departed brewers still existed, providing the new
corporate entity with their eternal blessing and support. The beerage
were savvy enough to foster this illusion.

In the early years, the production of beer dominated. Pub estates
were largely tenanted. A Brewers Society survey of brewers-owned
pubs in 1949 indicated that 83% were tenanted. By 1967 this had only

dropped slightly to 77%.[3] The retail sale of beer was left to others. Free trade departments developed which sold the brewers' wholesale products in premises not owned by the brewery, which became important for some. This side of the business was often frowned upon by brewery elder statesmen as being a little sordid and disagreeable – especially in later years, when large teams of brewery free-trade reps on low basic salaries but high incentives became rather maverick in some of their dealings.

Old rambling and historic brewery buildings, usually on the edge of the town centre, reeked of the unique sweet and sour smell from the cooking of the barley and hops in the brewing process. This sultry odour combined with a timeless complacency to give the brewery a hallowed, otherworldly atmosphere. This feeling of remoteness reinforced the lack of interest shown by the brewers in such tiresome details as the economy, demographic change, or indeed pubs. Head brewers and their immediate team were scientists rather than businessmen. Their only marketing effort was to promote and advertise their beers. And when their customers eventually started to expect a better product, and a more comfortable environment in which to enjoy that product, the brewers, wrapped in the comforting aroma of their Victorian retreats, remained oblivious for far too long.

Despite all their shortcomings, the brewers retained plenty of local respect and goodwill in their home town. The brewery was part of the community, a little like the local football team, and people identified with it and enjoyed its products and shared in its ongoing prosperity. The local brewery not only provided many jobs within its production and distribution processes, it also supplied the golden nectar that the townsfolk would enjoy, regularly.

In 1959 draught beer was king. Only the most sophisticated of us were familiar with the dubious delights of liqueurs, cocktails or even wine. At that time draught beer meant bitter, stout or mild. The bitter was traditionally brewed and pulled. Lager accounted for 2% of the market and the newly developed, pasteurised keg only 1%.

However, big changes were coming. The empire-building of the big six to achieve nationwide coverage meant delivering their beer much further afield. They found that keg beer kept longer and travelled better and did not need to settle before it could be served. And so keg was promoted by the brewers, and quickly grew in popularity. The boffins in their Accounts departments were also alive to opportunity, taking advantage of excise duty being lower for weaker beer.

Marketing companies were employed to dream up trite slogans and corny images to promote keg beer, which were plastered everywhere. Thus Ind Coope's Double Diamond, Whitbread Tankard, Worthington E, Brew 11 and, most notoriously, Watneys' Red Barrel, were blasted into the national consciousness. Even better, as a result of this marketing effort, keg could be labelled as a premium product at a penny or tuppence more than real ale.

This marketing and control of the product supplied to their pubs manipulated drinking habits and saw the brewers' keg sales soar. They reached 8% by 1966, 18% by 1971 and, most phenomenally, 40% by 1976. By that year, keg's continental soulmate lager had also captured 20% of the market whilst real ale had sunk to 14%.[4] Lager was even better news. Accountants could see it sustain a higher price and better profit margin and the marketing men could promote it as the exotic taste of the future, backed up by some memorable and very persistent advertising campaigns. Young drinkers, keen to differentiate themselves from the lifestyles of an older generation, were hooked. The brewers thought they had captured the moon on a stick. They would not have believed it at the time but they had reached the pinnacle of their power and influence. For the big six, life would be largely downhill from this time onwards.

The Pub Tenancy

The method by which the brewers maintained control of their huge estates of pubs was the tenancy system. The brewer owned the freehold of the premises and would let it on an annual tenancy to suitable landlords. The typical arrangement was that the brewer was responsible for structural work and repair, the tenant for internal decorations. The brewer received a rent, but also crucially a Beer Tie so that the tenant had to purchase all beer and other alcoholic products from the brewer, at prices set by the brewer.

The business itself was operated by the tenant, so the brewer had no risk element, but meanwhile was guaranteed, from every tenancy it operated, not only rent but a profit margin from the barrelage supplied to the tenant. It also took a substantial slice of any other income earned at the premises, for example from the letting of upstairs rooms or the new phenomenon of fruit machines. Or 'one-armed bandits', as they were known, for good reason.

The tenancy system had taken root by accident. In the mid-Victorian age the majority of pubs were owner occupied and generally somewhat modest, little more than converted front-room affairs. Brewers were content to secure their supplies to the better public houses by means of trade loans.

The pub industry boomed in the 1880s and 90s with a wave of brewery flotations. These financed new modern breweries and a pub-building boom. Building and modernising pubs has always been an expensive affair. So, when money was required to purchase a pub, or to modernise, the brewers obliged with loans to licensees. Many of the fine Victorian pubs which we enjoy today date from this era and were built with the proceeds from these flotations. The brewers themselves also developed and purchased many pubs during the boom and the idea of brewers owning large pub estates was born.

Alcohol consumption and pub profits rose. Pub prices went through the roof, increasing tenfold and more in a few years, encouraged by frequent speculative buying and selling. During this frenzy, more money was spent on improvements to defend trade whilst new pubs were being opened at a rapid rate. In 1899 the bubble burst. The inflated prices collapsed, many bankruptcies resulted and the brewers, having funded much of the speculation out of their flotations, ended up with considerable bad debt; 28.5% of loans went under by 1903, reaching 40% by 1912.

The result was twofold. By 1914 and the start of war, over 10,000 licensed premises closed. More significantly for the future, 95% of the surviving licenses ended up owned by the brewers, as the only remedy to recover their loans. Whilst some of these properties were run directly by the brewers, they generally found it more convenient to leave the pub business in the hands of the former owners as tied tenants.[5]

Throughout most of the last century the tenancy endured as the bedrock of the licensed trade. The system seemed almost feudal, with some long-serving tenants then passing on the reins within the family, their children naturally groomed as ideal successors. The area manager for the brewery held a crucial position. It was a role that was often filled by retired army officers or similar figures of authority whom the brewers felt they could entrust with their estates, despite their lack of pub experience. Area managers[6] might typically have between fifty and eighty tenancies to control in one geographical patch and would, at least in the first half of the 20th century, be regarded with some reverence. Get on the wrong side of him and your tenancy might be lost. If a tenant earned the disapproval of the brewery then he was probably living on borrowed time.

The tenancy system inhibited investment in pubs. Many brewers had strong local monopolies within their sphere of influence or the towns of other local brewers that they had taken over. In such a case, there was little incentive to spend money modernising when the result would only be to take trade from their other tenants nearby, who might demand similar improvements in turn. Only responsible for internal decoration, if the tenant did require improvements they had to go, cap in hand, to the brewery. Not that the typical pub tenant of the Fifties and Sixties was bursting with ideas or ambition. Most were dutiful and loyal time-servers, making a steady but unspectacular living in their modest and often dowdy pubs. Why bother refurbishing when the interior of its competitors had similar furnishings and fittings, and every pub drew its customers routinely from its immediate catchment?

The time-honoured tenancy system had evolved largely to the benefit of brewers and tenants alike. Without having to worry about day-to-day operations, the brewery retained overall control of the destiny of the pubs. They received a modest rent and the all-important trade tie, obliging the tenant to purchase all of his beers from his landlord, the brewer, and his wines and spirits from nominated suppliers.[7] The brewer took only a passing interest in the pub, provided everything was running smoothly, the rent was paid and the barrelage kept flowing. This enabled a large estate of pubs to be operated by a minimum of people.

The tenant could set himself up in what could be a comfortable business, plus accommodation, and with a certain standing in the community. The cost was relatively low; a small security deposit to the brewer of perhaps a few months' rent, the purchase of the pub trade inventory, its trading stock and a small amount of working capital.[8] Rents were modest and the brewery was there in the background to provide support and advice. In later years the brewers started to operate training courses for new tenants and to teach existing tenants about areas they might struggle with, such as taxation and accounts, and the newfangled ideas of selling food and understanding their customers. Often the tenant had useful sources of additional income, like letting rooms upstairs, function rooms for events or subletting disused garages or bits of land alongside the pub. Good tenants needed little help from their landlord. They were much closer to their customers than the brewer and were therefore responsive to his, generally modest, needs.

But the relationship was not without problems. As time went by, the large brewers became slack in complying with their repairing obligations. When they had to find extra profit to satisfy head office or their City investors, slashing repair budgets was an easy way to improve the balance sheet. And when this happened regularly, pubs started to look very shabby. Tenants resented being totally tied to the brewer for all of their products, particularly if rival tenants, or the free house up the road, were selling what was perceived to be a better range of beers. As barrelage in some outlets fell dramatically during the later years, some tenants had problems in paying their rent or felt duped by the brewery into taking over a declining outlet.

The more successful tenants were also unhappy because tenancy agreements were non-assignable and therefore when time or circumstances encouraged them to move on, they could not sell the business that they had built up, having to surrender back to the brewery who would choose a new tenant themselves. Some tenants felt trapped by this system when they wanted to progress.

The tenancy system endured well until the Seventies and Eighties when the first cracks appeared. The old school of dedicated tenants who were content to run a modest pub for a lifetime were disappearing. Many were ageing and no longer needed the increasing hassle involved in dealing with more demanding and aggressive customers, or serving food and having to employ external staff in the process, or the growing burden of accounts and red tape. Meanwhile, all of a sudden, the brewers wanted their pubs back.

There had been debate within the big brewers as far back as the 1950s regarding taking more of their pubs back into management. For example it is recorded in the 1955 Whitbread Annual Report that Colonel Whitbread stated;

> *"Personally I deplore the trend towards the management of public houses but it is the result of changing trading conditions… "*.[9]

Generally, as a result of such attitudes there was little change at that time. But by the 1970s, pressure was building on the brewers. In seeking to recover possession, Watneys and Bass in particular acted rather insensitively, simply issuing block notices to quit on large numbers of tenants. The tenants formed themselves into groups to oppose these, and ended up by taking the fight to Parliament, with 2,000 of them protesting outside it in July 1973. The Brewers Society got involved to defuse the situation, mounted a publicity campaign to protect the brewers' image and drew up the 1974 Code of Practice. This clarified that the brewers could still secure possession on economic grounds but protected the tenants a little by laying down a procedure for this, and a right to modest compensation.

The Code of Practice, if anything, accelerated the transfer of pubs from tenancy to management. The brewers rapidly expanded their managed house teams and focused on running pubs themselves. Properties which were long-established as tenancies were transferred to management. In the course of a decade or so the tenancy lost its role as forming the nucleus of the brewers' estates and became a neglected sideshow. The brewers may have still had more tenancies than managed houses but all of the attention, and investment was channelled into the latter. Irrespective of the compensation, or even offers of alternative pubs or a position as a manager, tenants became disillusioned by this situation and the threat that if their trade was too impressive they could be next. Meanwhile other tenants were simply leaving, due to falling trade and disenchantment with the industry.

Marketing

I t is now the end of the Seventies. Liverpool Football Club are almost unbeatable, Michael Jackson has taken over from the Beatles and McDonald's, Pizza Hut and punk rockers have arrived on the high street. But Annie Walker is still running the Rovers Return and many of her generation are there with her. Try as they might to keep their heads buried in the sand, the brewers could not fail to realise that the consumer age had arrived. In the early Seventies, their industry was hit by the equivalent of a plague of locusts. CAMRA, the Campaign for Real Ale, founded in 1971, were initially viewed as a bunch of cranks and upstarts when they had the audacity to demand better beer. Within a few years they had convinced the public that what they did NOT want was Watneys and that there was an alternative to keg beer.

Not only this, but Britain had been gripped by a social revolution. Colour vision had come to the masses to replace the old streets of grey. New clothing and cars and lifestyles. People went out to restaurants, and cinemas and nightclubs; not just in London and Manchester, but all over the country. Young people wanted to discover these new alternatives instead of the old bland pubs which their parents used. Customers deserted pubs in droves and beer sales sank faster than the popularity of the Sex Pistols.

The brewers' complacency slowly disappeared and they finally reacted. To compete with the threat from the off-licence, the discotheque, free trade pubs, the rapidly growing fast food chains and a host of other counter-attractions they realised that pubs needed to make themselves appealing places to visit. They had to improve service standards and change their style. With the size of investment needed to bring their pubs up to date, the brewers ran their new showpieces under management, directly by themselves.

The brewers started to embrace their brave new world with enthusiasm. The mantra 'We are retailers' was repeated regularly at meetings and conferences to convince everyone involved of the fundamental change in attitude that they had to achieve. Smart-talking whizz-kids and dynamic young executives with experience elsewhere in leisure or other business fields were recruited to inject new ideas and mastermind running the growing managed house estates.

But the change in attitude posed a challenge due to the presence of the source of the brewers' lifeblood, the brewery. The brewers' use of barrelage as the most critical measure of performance was perhaps the best tangible illustration of this. Because of the dominant presence of the brewery, the focus remained on turnover rather than profit. Pub refurbishments that were not heavily geared towards beer sales were less favoured. This approach slowly changed but it took time to shake off such instincts.

As the number of managed houses increased, whole new departments of personnel, accountants, surveyors, stocktakers, technical support and marketing appeared. The change which had the most significance for pubs was marketing. Marketing people were typically young and confident, and bursting with new terminology, demographic studies and radical ideas on how to transform dingy old pubs into exciting new licensed outlets.

One of the most common techniques which they employed was Categorisation.[10] Categorisation was an analytical model used to target pub investment to the right markets and analyse pubs' performance. It was important in the days before branding when brewers operated large mixed estates. These are the generally accepted pub categories;

A) COMMUNITY PUBS

These normally trade from a well-defined, tightly-drawn catchment area. This is the typical local, often found on the council estate, in back streets or sometimes in villages.

B) DESTINATION OUTLETS

These pubs enjoy a particular characteristic which enables them to attract custom, normally on a regular basis, from a wide catchment area. The destination value is of three types, either;

- Environmental – i.e. pubs which have an attractive location, over-looking a river for example.
- Intrinsic – there is something within the pub which attracts people such as historic features
- Developed – the pub owners provide something which draws customers from a wide catchment i.e. a good food offer or music, entertainment etc.

C) YOUNG PERSONS MEETING HOUSES (YPMH)

These can either be design-led i.e. the owner has deliberately invested to attract such custom or adopted in which case young persons use the property through a process of evolution.

D) MULTI-FUNCTIONAL

There are a number of possibilities. They may trade differently from session to session i.e. lunchtime and evening, they may be cosmopolitan, attracting a wide variety of customers at the same time, or they may be poorly targeted.

E) BUSINESSMANS

This is normally a town or city-centre pub whose trade is concentrated into lunchtimes and early evenings.

F) PARASITES

Pubs whose custom is dictated by their position. They trade off a transient non-regular audience. The most common example is road-houses, large pubs alongside main trunk roads. Other examples are seafront pubs or those close to a sporting venue. A pub on the high street which trades primarily to passing shoppers will also come under this group as do pubs next to a railway station or within an airport.

With the assistance of such marketing techniques, and their newly assembled teams, the brewers set about refurbishing their growing managed house estates. They at last started to throw some of their pots of accrued wealth back at their pubs. Suddenly there were colourful pubs and food pubs and disco pubs and all sorts of other themed pubs. What we did not see were good pubs. This was to prove a false dawn on the new era that the brewers were bravely embracing. Many a good old Victorian boozer had its guts ripped out as vulgar decorations and brash lighting were installed. The jukebox and fruit and gaming machines became common and pool tables made an appearance.

Brewers even ventured beyond the packet of crisps in attempting to satisfy peoples' appetites. Unfortunately their taste in conversions were no more appetising than the anaemic shepherd's pies, dehydrated meat and two veg, and curled-up sandwiches that they were serving up from the ubiquitous and ugly new glass display cabinets. In most towns, the best pubs were those developed by individual entrepreneurs who fitted their premises out with more panache and had a better feel for customer needs. As the brewers took more and more pubs back from their tenants' it became evident that their newfound enthusiasm for refurbishing and running these pubs far exceeded their ability to do so.

John Young, Chairman of Young's, the London family brewer, commented on the trend in an annual report to shareholders;

> *"Pubby pubs is what we at Young's shall strive to preserve, confident that they will long outlive the gimmicky pubs which invade town life today. The current mania on the part of some brewers to gut their premises and concoct a stage set, be it a Mississippi show boat, the inside of a bus, tram or smugglers' cave has become so frenzied that decorators don't seem able to ruin pubs fast enough. I see a danger that one of our greatest heritages may be spoiled or disappear through the onslaught of gimmickry, just as many of our traditional beers have disappeared."*[11]

The process did no harm to Young's, and most similar small family brewers whose pubs remained as a refuge of tradition and common sense, increasingly appreciated by customers for their excellent beers in the face of the misguided behaviour of their larger rivals.

Community Pubs

C ommunity pubs were being undermined even eighty years ago. During the residential building booms of the 1930s, licensing magistrates required that new 'improved' pubs were built to a rigid formula, open plan and easily policed with large gardens and forecourts. The brewers were permitted to splatter numerous road junctions and new urban highways throughout Britain's new suburbs with what became the recognisably standard style of 'brewers Tudor'. The price they paid, at the insistence of the magistrates, was the surrender of the licences of two or three existing pubs in town and city centres.

The brewers were happy to play this game. Their new showpiece premises, the first new wave of pub-building since Edwardian times, were highly revered at the time. They were able to draw on the surrounding middle-class populations and could command substantial trade with a monopoly over large residential areas. In particular the brewers were ridding themselves of run-down 'problem houses' often serving deprived and low income urban communities.

Despite this process, and the consequent bulldozing of many backstreet pubs, the community market remained the backbone of the brewers' estates. But the brewers came to realise that this was a shrinking market, reflecting Britain's industrial decline and changing social structure. Community pubs are typically in either the backstreets of larger towns or on large housing estates. They are the rambling, dilapidated Victorian palaces with three or four bars, and weeds and shrubs growing from the roof. They are the ghastly flat-roofed, Sixties boxes dwarfed by adjacent tower blocks, scarred by graffiti and with a large vacuous expanse of concrete at the front, or the little street corner pubs hidden away in the swathe of terraced housing at the back of the railway line. Attractive they are not.

The disposable income of many community pub customers was at a premium whilst these people wanted space in which to play pool or dominoes, sit and contemplate life over a half of Guinness or chat to the landlord. Most did not appear to match the image which the brewers were anxious to create. So the community market represented to the brewers a declining backwater, a retrograde reminder of their past that they increasingly wanted to escape from.

There was also a practical element which the brewers disliked. Community pubs rely, to a much greater degree than other types of pub, on personal relationships to drive turnover. Customers want and expect to discuss the meaning of life or at least have a brief exchange with the 'governor'. And in tough pubs a robust experienced character who can control the punters is essential. Thus the quality of a landlord in a community pub makes all of the difference between success and failure. This is not desirable when the brewery could spend substantial sums on refurbishment and see the project fail because they installed the wrong manager. Or, even worse, got the right manager who then departed after two months because a rival operator recognised his talents and tempted him away to a nearby pub. Relationships between customers could be a further critical factor beyond the brewery's control. A group of punters might fall out over a trivial personal matter with the result that some of them transfer their loyalties to the Spotted Dog down the road, reducing sales by 10 or 20% at one disastrous stroke.

The new style pubs that the brewers increasingly committed their future to were driven more by tangible assets than personalities. If the manager of these outlets were to change, most customers would not notice the difference. The brewers therefore learned to invest in projects which were more predictable, and commensurate with the philosophy and needs of a corporate entity.

But there are good reasons for protecting the community pub. Community Britain has been steadily undermined for many years. Sixty years ago people knew many of those living in the same neighbourhood. They worked together and they frequently joined together in their social lives; in recreation, at church or in the local shop or pub. These institutions and activities have become increasingly marginalised from normal lifestyles. People now have few opportunities to meet and get to know those who live nearby. The situation has been exacerbated by greater mobility and the decline of the extended family. As countless social studies have demonstrated, community life has disintegrated across much of Britain. What such studies have also addressed is the consequential loss: increasing psychological problems due to the feelings of isolation that can arise, greater crime rates, and, amongst lower socio-economic groups, increases in poverty levels and more reliance on the state due to the lack of support from neighbours during difficult times.

One of the last bastions of community life was therefore the pub, a place where local people could still meet and congregate, fully justifying the term 'community pub'. Furthermore a very high proportion of pubs in the 1980s were community pubs, well over 50% of the country's entire stock and in excess of 90% of pubs in many urban areas. Given the lack of alternatives, the pub had inherited a leading role in maintaining a little of the threadbare fabric of community life in contemporary Britain.

Unfortunately, the larger brewers had lost all interest in such altruism. For them the community pub sank to the bottom of the pile, the most undesirable and neglected part of the estate. 'Community' pub became almost a term of insult; the pubs you didn't want to deal with other than to sell off. The place where the great unwashed drank.

This attitude was reflected in rationalisation programmes by the brewers, weeding out particular types of property for sale or closure.

Where the latter took place, the effect could be fairly devastating for those concerned. One of the earliest and most notorious examples was the ruthless Grand Met purge of Norfolk. Having acquired all three local brewers, Bullards, Steward & Patteson and Morgans, to give themselves a virtually absolute local monopoly, they proceeded to rampage through the county closing one after another village pub. Their justification was this;

> *"Norfolk has been overpubbed for many years. Rationalisation was necessary. The national average of drinkers per pub is 700. In Norfolk it is 500-600, often dropping as low as 350. Not enough for a profitable pub."*[12]

They had little to lose as drinkers in the new dry villages would end up having to travel to another Norwich Brewery pub (Grand Met's flag of convenience in the area), such was their local stranglehold. And those were the lucky ones. Many villagers, especially pensioners, had no transport; bus services were frequently inadequate. They could thank Grand Met's rationalisation for taking away their daily routine and the heart of the village community. Grand Met meanwhile didn't care to explain why they bought so many pubs in the area if trade levels were so unsatisfactory.

Eighties Vulgarity

Brewery executives commissioned plenty of marketing reports during the 1980s. They reflected the size of the retailing challenge that faced most medium and large brewers. Many had by now been raiding their tenanted estates for some time. The top tenants were steadily bought out, the pubs transferred to management and money invested heavily to improve trade. Some progress had been made on the out of town pub-restaurant side, notably Whitbread with Beefeater whilst Berni Inns, Chef and Brewer and Toby were other examples of brands which had become established through maintaining consistent standards. But in-town pub refurbishments lacked style, and were often poorly run and aggressive. They dated very quickly.

This was the era of the notorious 'Fun pub' or 'Pub-Eighties' which is a suitable metaphor for the numerous attempts at conversion of urban pubs. This was often achieved by brusquely forcing them into the 'young persons' market by installing sound and light systems and hoping that the pub could function like a discotheque. Hideous decor, bulbous fitted seating, garish lighting, awful music and aggressive bar staff were obligatory. Poor design and lack of operating standards ensured that these refurbishments rapidly died off, at great expense to the brewers.

Grand Met were, typically, the most radical in their approach with their 'open house' concept. This was a misguided attempt to reposition many of their large community estate pubs into a variety of sports, food and music bars. The concept adopted the lowest common denominator of appeal to the mass market; pubs were renamed with one syllable only; hence the Kings Head would become 'Kings' and names like Palms, Flints and Brooks predominated. The one-syllable approach was often reflected in service standards, such was the ambience created. The overall result was that many of the older community drinkers retreated elsewhere, to be replaced by younger locals. Many of the pubs remained stubbornly as community pubs, albeit branded ones.

In contrast to Open House, the Eighties could also be regarded as the pub market's library and conservatory era. Do not be tempted to think that the brewers were embracing a modicum of culture. Conservatories almost became *de rigeur* for pub extensions. A nice idea when it first arrived, but highly tedious when every other suburban pub sported its own incongruous and over-sized greenhouse. No-one ever thought of adding a few plants for some reason. The library influence came from the practice of decorating at least one internal wall with rows of books, often identical and sometimes even with blank pages inside. Again a reasonable idea, provided that the books were genuine, but sadly done to death.

The pub 'modernisation' carried out by the brewers in this period were generally uninspired and repetitive; at their worst vulgar and contemptible. The change in approach needed to underpin the superficial changes in pub names and decor hadn't generally been effective. The brewers spent the Seventies and Eighties attempting to catch up with and understand trends rather than becoming part of the process that creates them.

Amongst this frenetic scene of pub refurbishment, one area of stability was the traditional real ale pub. This market was monopolised by free houses because tenants were restricted to their brewer's brands, and brewers were still not sufficiently perceptive and flexible to enter this market. The one or two pubs in a town which offered a good range of real ale were well rewarded for their efforts, with many drinkers trekking for some distance to enjoy elusive tastes not available elsewhere. Such customers were not restricted to the CAMRA connoisseur either; many session drinkers made the effort of seeking out these pubs because of the better range and quality of beer on offer, compared to their local. In London and the south, northern beers, even brewery standards like Tetley's, attained a cult status of superiority, bordering on the irrational. Samuel Smith's in particular exploited this, spending large sums to buy pubs in London where they could sell their highly-revered brews direct to an adoring drinking public.

Meanwhile, as fast as conservatories were going up, internal dividing walls were coming down. Brewers liked their new pubs to have big open spaces and only one bar; they were easier to staff and thus cheaper to run. Visibility and therefore control was improved and the process maximised drinking area. The marketing men supported this process by advising against attracting two, often distinct, customer groups into the same premises with two separate bars. To them, trade in the newly refurbished lounge would be prejudiced by the old pub regulars, still frequenting the public bar. Pub categorisation did not encourage a pub to sit in two separate boxes at the same time. Unfortunately, many well-loved and intimate little snugs and smoke rooms were wiped out as a result. Frequently the public bar was the victim, with its regulars evicted to an alternative pub nearby that had not yet been modernised.

The brewers' performance at this stage would seem to deserve a slight adaptation of the refrain generally attributed to Samuel Johnson;

"Your pub designs are both good and original. Unfortunately those which are good are not original and those which are original are not good."

Perhaps kinder words were merited by a concept which emerged towards the end of the Eighties; the cafe-bar. Allied Breweries adopted the idea with great gusto in the form of Muswells, Whitbread had its Henrys, and Bass came up with Drummonds. Bordeaux cafe society had come to Battersea and Birmingham. Numerous media articles appeared applauding the manner in which Britain was transforming itself into a cosmopolitan, sophisticated society as reflected by these cafe-bars. But was it? By the start of the Nineties, as quickly as the yuppies disappeared, so did their venues. Whitbread sold the Henrys chain to Greenall's, Muswells was broken up and sold off whilst Bass just gave up with Drummonds. How could the cafe-bar, which had supposedly captured the spirit of the age, die off as quickly as flared trousers had a few years earlier? Was the growing sophistication of the English pub-goer, which the media had promoted so loudly, really so cosmetic and ephemeral?

The demise of the cafe-bars was partly due to shortcomings in their operation; food didn't take off consistently at Henrys; Muswells were popular but overall turnover was mediocre, whilst Drummonds was little more than a pub pretending to be something else. But the main reason that the brewers abandoned the exercise was pressure and distraction from elsewhere. That pressure was the Monopolies and Mergers Inquiry into the beer industry. The end of the Eighties marked a distinct watershed for the licensed trade.

PART TWO

The Heavy Hand Of Government

The MMC Report

On the 4th August 1986, Gordon Borrie, then Director General of Fair Trade, referred the supply of beer to the Monopolies and Mergers Commission. Until the MMC reported in February 1989 there followed arguably the most intense and thorough investigation into an industry that has taken place. The MMC literally scoured the country, looking into every aspect of the licensed trade from every possible angle, noting the views of hundreds of interested parties along the way.

The document that they produced at the end of their deliberations was long and tedious; 303 pages of close-set type and a further 198 pages of appendices for good measure. But within the pronunciations and calculations, the statistics and submissions a fascinating account of the licensed trade in the mid-Eighties emerges. The MMC analysis broke the brewers down into three sub-groups; the big six nationals, eleven Regional brewers of medium size and forty-one local brewers. It also identified many tiny microbrewers that it considered to be relatively insignificant.[1]

Some of the facts regarding the industry as recorded within the MMC report as at 1986 are worth noting;

-UK beer sales of £9 billion, over 2% of gross domestic product.
    This was the equivalent of 29,068,000 barrels.
-Lager increase from 4% of the market in 1967 to over 45%.
-Draught sales very high at 77% of total beer sales, with the highest

equivalent in any overseas country being 47% and generally much lower than this.

-84% of beer consumed within on-licensed premises. (The 16% drunk at home was very low by international standards comparing with Belgium and France at 57%, Germany 60%, USA 80%.)

-The number of full-on licences grew from 75,283 in 1966 to 80,364 in 1986, an increase of 7%. Note that not all of these were pubs as perhaps 5-10% of these were wine bars, restaurants with a full-on licence and hotels.

-Brewers owned 46,000 pubs, an estimated 62% of UK pubs. (45% of the total were owned by the big six.)

-There were some major regional and local imbalances in ownership. As a result, in 6% of local licensing divisions one brewer owned at least 50% of all full on-licences and in a further 26% of local licensing areas, two brewers together owned at least 50%.

-The big six managed between 27% and 38% of their estates (as opposed to letting them as tenancies).

-The average trade in a managed house was 564 barrels, significantly higher than the average tenancy at 296 barrels. (A barrel is 288 pints or thirty-six gallons)

-In the period 1982 to 1985, the big six committed in capital expenditure an average of £74,400 on each managed house but only £11,200 average per tenancy.

- 53% of free houses were in rural areas, compared with only 31% of brewer-owned pubs.

-In terms of brewing (as opposed to share of pub-market) the big six supplied 75% of beer sales, the Regional brewers 11% and the Local brewers 6%. The remaining 8% was supplied by non-pub owning brewers like Guinness and Carlsberg and from overseas.

-The average price of a pint of draught beer was 83.6p. Free houses were most expensive at an average of 85.8p, managed houses 83.5p with tenancies, cheapest at 82.6p.

-The duty on a typical pint of bitter was 18.1p with VAT adding a further 9.4p.

-The price of a pint had risen from an average of 13p in 1973. In real terms, taking the movement of the retail price index into account, beer prices had risen 20% higher than this index since 1973 and 15% higher in the eight years since 1979.

-Regional variations in beer price in bars were as great as 30% between the most expensive area, London and the cheapest, the West Midlands.

-Lager was, on average, 10p a pint more expensive than bitter.

-Profit for the big six brewers averaged £245m each per annum. The 11 Regional brewers averaged £15m whilst the Local brewers made a more modest £1,658,000 each on average. This represented an average increase in profits of 14.9% over the previous year.

-Wholesale profit per barrel for the brewers was calculated by the MMC as an average of £30.41 in managed houses, £28.16 in tenancies, £3.48 when supplied to national accounts like supermarkets, £19.51 for sales to free traders who had a loan-tie to a brewer and £10.46 to untied free houses. (The brewers had refused to divulge these figures which they regarded as being very sensitive.)

-The top four brewers in the UK (not the 75% big six figure above) had a total of 58% of market share of beer sales compared to 99% in Japan, 98% in Australia, 95% in Canada and the Netherlands, 93% in France, 90% in Denmark and 73% in the USA.

Having gathered and analysed all of this and much more, the MMC announced their preliminary findings and asked for feedback on a number of options that they were considering for the industry.

Although the dry, formal language of the report is typical of the civil service style, the message between the lines was clear. The MMC were forming a very unfavourable impression of the brewers and particularly the big six nationals. Whilst the brewers were stressing the paternal relationship which existed with their tenants, the MMC comments imply domination, manipulation and neglect.

The evidence from drinks wholesalers portrayed the big brewers as possessive bullies, prepared to exclude deliveries to any wholesaler who did not follow their restrictive rules. Guinness appeared to be nervous that they too could be shut out of supply arrangements if they stepped out of line. Bulmers, the cider manufacturers, listed twenty-two brewers (some of substantial size) whom they used to supply, but after take-over by another brewer from the 1960s onwards, had been excluded because the new owning company appointed its own preferred (i.e. owned) supplier. CAMRA also weighed in with accusations of dark deeds relating to brewery closures, domination of the free trade market and manipulation to expand lager sales at the expense of bitter.

The Consumers Association appreciated the opportunity to air its views. In particular it made accusations of brewery manipulation of free houses through trade loans. They suggested that as a result, competition from free houses was often an illusion. There was an implication that the big brewers' control extended into their smaller brethren through trading agreements for lager and packaged beer which the smaller brewers did not produce for themselves. And they hinted at an informal price cartel in wholesale beer supply to the free market and national accounts. The Consumers Association summed up its concern with;

"The brewers… might continue to offer a range of drinks most convenient and profitable to them, with only minor adjustments to accommodate changing consumer tastes."

The Brewers Society, the trade association that acted for the brewers, was busily rebutting all of this evidence and claiming that the system should continue because the pub was a unique and cherished institution, that the brewers' share of the market was reducing and that the brewers always acted responsibly and judiciously. The MMC response, hinting darkly about the brewers' excessive influence, was;

"Throughout our inquiry we were struck by the vigour and thoroughness of the Brewers Society's response to the many questions we asked and the points we put back to it. There is no doubt in our minds that the Society is formidably effective in championing its members interests."

After the arguments and debate had ebbed and flowed for many months the MMC finally published its report. It found that there was a 'complex monopoly' in the licensed industry. This rested on the definition that 'a number of companies were conducting their respective affairs in a way to prevent, restrict or distort competition'. The monopoly was proven (to the MMC) because the brewers controlled their tied estates and a large chunk of the free trade sector through preferential loan ties which restricted the ability of licensees of 90% of British pubs to offer for sale brands of their own choosing. The ability of other brewers and wholesalers to freely compete to supply beer to such outlets was restricted.

The MMC justification of their findings proceeded through the following arguments;

Through the tentacles of direct ownership, the Beer Tie for their tenants, and preferential loans for free houses, the brewers had guaranteed control of a dominant proportion of pubs.

Because there was over-supply in the brewing industry (attempts to measure utilisation generally conclude that the breweries were running at between 73-77% of capacity on a national basis) this implied that production was not at its most efficient and thus that beer prices were higher than they needed to be.

Because there was an element of discount applied to tenants' rents and to the loan interest on free trade loans, this had to be recouped in some way and that full undiscounted wholesale beer prices were the only means available.

The brewers maintained their dominant position on the supply side because they also controlled the retail side of the business. This excluded any new brewers who might wish to enter the market because they would not have access to sufficient market share to justify the high entry costs. Thus the only entrants had been brewers with trading agreements giving them access into a major estate e.g. Heineken-Whitbread, Castlemaine XXXX-Allied.

Their dominant position in the retail market was maintained by the difficulty of obtaining new licences because these are restricted by licensing magistrates by the 'need' argument. This prevented any outsiders building up a sufficiently strong retail position to be able to buy beer at any great discount. The MMC thus contended that this prevented consumer choice entering the market through price and product competition. They contrasted the position with the off-licence market, where licences were easy to obtain and where the market was changing. Supermarkets and other independents had entered the arena and were claiming a substantial market share, with the brewers, in some cases, withdrawing.

And so the brewers were accused of acting against the public interest. The incriminatory mood of the MMC was demonstrated as they amassed the following list of nine activities which they found to be pursuant to the brewers exploiting their monopoly position against the public interest. For good measure, they also suggested that the Office of Fair Trading look into the supply of amusement machines in the future in view of the enormous profit being milked from this source by the brewers.

Charging high wholesale prices and thus forcing high retail prices
    on the market.
Charging higher prices for lager than is justified by production and
    advertising costs.

Maintaining regional price differences which were not justified.

Limiting the independence of tenants in order to maintain the monopoly.

Operating their tied estates and loan ties in order to reduce consumer choice.

Excluding competitor's ciders and soft drinks from their managed and tenanted estates.

Offering tied loans for the supply of beer and thus restricting choice.

Restricting independent wholesalers.

Imposing ties or restrictive covenants on the sale of licensed outlets.

In order to address this malaise and protect the consumer and brewery tenants, the MMC felt that drastic changes were needed in the industry. These could only be achieved by a total restructuring. They considered recommending, as was the case in some European countries, that brewers be prohibited from owning any pubs. It seems that they would have recommended this option if they had not been concerned that the smaller brewers might not survive. Instead they proposed an ownership and control limit of 2,000 pubs for any brewer, which would reduce the influence of the big six but not affect the smaller brewers. This would involve 22,000 pubs being sold off by the industry giants.

Other recommendations were that tenants be given the protection of the Landlord and Tenant Act rather than rely on the Brewers Society's own code and that the brewers not be allowed to tie any further free houses through loans or impose restrictive covenants or ties on sales. To encourage wholesaling, they wished to see wholesale price lists with prices and discounts for all customers, and brewing duty reduced on small brewers.

This was far from the end of the issue. The MMC formally presented its recommendations in February 1989, and it was then up to the Government to decide whether to adopt the proposals. Initially Lord Young, the minister in charge at the Department of Trade and

Industry, stated famously that he was 'minded' to implement the recommendations.

The Brewers Society, having lost the argument with the MMC, now recommenced lobbying the government on behalf of its powerful members with even greater intensity. Bank-rolled heavily by its leading members the Brewers Society took the arguments to the public with a huge pro-brewery campaign. It may have also suggested to the government that it would be unwise to bite too deeply into a hand that fed it. Many of the brewers were large contributors to Tory party funds. As well as strong representations from the brewers, Lord Young was also encountering considerable all-party opposition. A total climb-down from being 'minded' would have been too blatant a surrender, and whilst the Brewers Society was still howling with protest when the revised proposals emerged in July 1989, the result was probably a relief to the occupants of the oak-panelled board-rooms in London and Burton-on-Trent.

The number of pubs that the brewers would have to lose would be halved from the original proposal. In other words, each brewer would have to dispose of half of its number of licences in excess of 2,000 and its cap set at this level (specific to that brewer) in the future. When Parliament finally endorsed this limit, and introduced the Beer Orders in December 1989, the brewers were given almost three years to comply. With 11,000 pubs to sell, the sale of the century was about to start, or so it seemed.

Catalyst For Change;
Verdict On The MMC And
The Beer Orders

The pub industry of the mid-Eighties was far from perfect; the brewers, acting as a cartel, used their position to maintain their supremacy and their profits; customer needs were poorly catered for; the tenancy was under siege due to the growth of the managed estates. But there was no crisis, whilst some encouraging signs existed that pub refurbishment was at last improving. And new pub operators were appearing, developing chains of bars to compete with the brewers and provide much-needed customer choice.

One can perhaps understand the MMC reaching the conclusions they did. The brewers, acting in concert, had undoubtedly controlled and manipulated the industry for many years. But if they dictated matters it was largely in a benign manner, in which all parties had a stake, and therefore something to lose. It was significant that pub tenants, one of the groups who the MMC were most concerned at protecting, were fairly muted in their criticism of the brewers and the system. Other than seeking greater protection in landlord and tenant matters, tenants-stream organisations were largely happy to preserve the status quo. Equally the smaller brewers, who it was suggested were exploited by the big brewers over lager and packaged beer supply, were almost unanimous in supporting the big brewers' case.

The Brewers Society accused the report of being 'a charter for chaos within the industry'. They had support from one dissenting voice within the MMC panel who felt that the recommendations were 'an unnecessary leap in the dark'. Reaction from the big six, like the Brewers Society, was predictable but comments from the smaller brewers are interesting to note. Boddingtons, who were destined not to survive the report by more than a year or two, stated;

> *"The recommendations are seen as excessive and failing to match the intent. The effect is likely to fragment the industry. Those with large estates may separate from their brewing activities."*

Young's suggested that small brewers should be relieved at the recommendations, whilst Fuller's were unhappy;

> *"We feel there may be advantages, but mainly disadvantages. Introduction of guest beer is likely to be a long term problem; if larger competitors introduce a major national brand the smaller houses would be unable to compete with heavy advertising campaigns by the bigger brewers."*

Interestingly, in view of subsequent events, some of the regional brewers were more pugnacious; Greene King stated prophetically that it was;

> *"Well placed to avail itself of such opportunities as may arise"*

whilst Wolverhampton & Dudley saw:

> *"Tremendous opportunities if the MMC proposals are enacted."*[2]

The MMC detected a monopoly and claimed that they had a desire to protect the position of tenants, wholesalers and external drinks suppliers. But the whole focus of the investigation was on price and consumer choice and the need to reduce one and widen the other. So, with hindsight, what did MMC and its changes achieve?

In terms of beer prices, little changed. Prices continued to rise at similar rates to previously. The enquiry had also concluded that regional variations in the price of beer, and the premium cost of lager, were not justified. But no action was taken to address these discrepancies and both vagaries have remained. And if price was of such great concern, then why not recommend that excise duty be frozen?

Perhaps the only positive impact from MMC is that there was a genuine widening of product choice for consumers. Guest beers became widespread in the big six brewery tenancies, and tenants gained a free hand in deciding what non-beer products to stock. Free traders gained an unfettered choice of what they would sell. And many pubs started to stock a wider range of real ales and other products.

The Consumer Association carried out research to which the MMC supposedly gave great credence in their report. The research indicated that the price of beer had almost no influence on the choice made by the consumer of where to drink. 6% of those questioned in the survey mentioned 'availability of the right beer' as a factor in choosing a pub, but there were five other factors which were of greater overall importance to the consumer. Thus in attracting custom, price seemed to be largely irrelevant and beer range of minor significance. The more important factors revealed were location, atmosphere, availability of food, going where one's friends went and service. These are concerned with pubs rather than beer. So why was the MMC so obsessed with beer prices and choice?

The MMC also concluded that because licensing was restrictive and wholesale prices to the free trade too high it was impossible for competitors to build up retail chains in competition with the brewers. But at the time of their report such chains had existed and new ones were developing. An alarming oversight by the MMC was to underestimate JD Wetherspoons. The company was significant enough in 1986 to provide a submission for the MMC report. Even though

Wetherspoons explained that it was possible to build up a retail chain and that they had no problem with the existing brewer wholesaling system, the MMC chose to ignore this evidence because it undermined their arguments.

The ongoing growth of Wetherspoons, achieved by organic growth, has shown this aspect of the MMC reasoning to be flawed. Wetherspoons predecessors never became substantial because a brewer had always stepped in to purchase before they grew to any significance. By the Nineties these pub chains were numerous and growing in size and influence. These entrepreneurs had identified significant gaps in the pub retail market and were exploiting such opportunities. This process had commenced prior to MMC and was relatively unaffected by its impact. The sites which these companies have developed were mainly conversions of other property and the availability of existing pubs was largely irrelevant to their growth.

A reflection of the futility of MMC's intervention was that they acted to break up a monopoly of six brewers who controlled a 75% market share. Within twenty years this had become an industry dominated by a big four producers, who shared 76% of beer volumes.

One of the most authoritative studies of the effect of the MMC was carried out by the Regulatory Policy Institute.[3] In January 1994 they published their findings which claimed that the analysis of the MMC was seriously flawed, that the brewers had incurred massive costs as a result of the Beer Orders, and that the cost to consumers was £500m over three years. The structure of the industry would, they concluded, have changed in any event as a result of decline in beer consumption and an increase in demand for food. The only beneficiaries they could identify were the new pubCos and brewers without estates. They felt that the tenancy had suffered seriously and that the ultimate cost was three pence added to the cost of each pint.

The MMC intervention was most flawed because it didn't consider the overall, and fairly obvious, impact of its intervention. It was not interested in comprehending exactly what made the brewers tick and thus how delicately balanced the dynamic of brewing and selling beer was. The brewers had built up their huge pub estates and secured the tenanted elements of them with a Beer Tie, not because of an egotistic urge to be big, or for pure profit reasons. The main driver in their anxiety to expand was the primeval urge to ensure their own survival. And for their breweries to survive they needed the guarantee of long-term tied sales from substantial pub estates.

Brewery capacity utilisation was assessed by MMC at between 73 and 77%. With the enforced sale of a substantial part of their estates this utilisation would almost certainly reduce. The MMC analysed the business model of the brewers and so would surely have gained an insight that large brewery operations would start to become unprofitable if the large pub estates were divorced from the brewery. Their calculations showed that sales to independent outlets where there was no Tie were at a profit per barrel of around £10.50 per barrel compared to £28.16 on sales to their own tenancies and £30.41 when sold in to their own managed houses. So without the critical mass of an owned pub estate the brewer could only recoup this trade from free-of-tie pubs by selling beer to them at a much reduced profit. When dealing with large pubCos this profit margin would reduce further because of the pubCos' ability to demand a substantial discount. The impact on breweries up and down the country was obvious. The MMC was thus happy to gamble blindly with the future of the industry, by sowing the seeds of destruction for the big six, although it had little idea what would follow.

Even more than the enforced pub sales, the most critical change arising from MMC was the attitude of the brewers. They were obliged to consider the long-term impact of declining beer volumes, brewery profit and the potential for further political interference. Their single-minded focus on the brewery as being almost the entire reason for their existence was shattered by the imposition of forced sales. They now had to consider the alternatives. They had been dragged from the sanctity of their cosy boardrooms and forced to take a long hard look at themselves and the world about them. That world, containing thrusting new pubCos, rapidly expanding pub retail chains and a demanding, questioning stockmarket would never be the same again.

Churn;
Creation Of The Pub Companies

On 19th December 1989 the Beer Orders finally came into effect. By the deadline of October 31st 1992 the big six had to sell 11,000 pubs between them. This represented a rate of ten pubs a day throughout this period. Nearly one in six pubs in the country were subject to a forced sale, to be removed from the clutches of the big brewers.

There were two ways of complying with the regulations. The obvious one, as adopted by Allied, Bass, Whitbread and Scottish & Newcastle, was to sell off sufficient bottom-end pubs to comply with the limit. The alternative, because the regulations only applied to brewers, was to retain their estate and to cease brewing. Typically, Grand Met chose this radical alternative and worked with Courage to implement it. Grand Met had already, partly in anticipation of the findings of the MMC, set up Inntrepreneur, a pub leasing company which sought to realign the traditional brewery-tenant relationship. Under this highly vaunted scheme leases would be assignable, and therefore of value, to licensees as they could sell them. More responsibility and freedom was given to lessees, who were in some cases released from the Beer Tie, but paying a higher rent in return. Inntrepreneur sought to find a new breed of business-like pub landlords who would be financially astute and sound enough to take on such responsibility.

Courage, by this time, was no longer part of the beerage. It had lost control back in 1972 when Imperial Tobacco had purchased the brewer with all of its assets. In 1986, when Imperial was in turn taken over by the Hanson Group, Courage was swiftly unloaded to Elders, the Australian brewer famous for Foster's lager. Unshackled by sentiment or tradition and having a brewing background, the idea of a breweries-for-pubs swap appealed to Courage's new owners. At the time of MMC the Courage estate stood out in contrast to the other majors with only 8% of its pubs run under management. During the Eighties, seventy or so of its best sites had been converted by Imperial to Harvester, which was then sold to Trust House Forte. After this, and exposed to the upheaval of takeover, little effort had been made to modernise or theme the company's pubs. In truth the estate was increasingly bedraggled in appearance, its distinctive golden cockerel on its pubs almost a guarantee of neglect.

For Courage the pub-swap would satisfy the MMC, unburden it of the demands of running its pub estate and in the process make it the nation's second largest brewer with a 20% market share. It was significant that Grand Met, like Courage, was not a member of the traditional beerage, having acquired both Trumans and Watneys breweries in hostile takeovers in 1972. Brewing and pubs were a modest part of the overall and fast expanding Grand Metropolitan empire, led by the tenacious Max Joseph. Under his control, the company adopted many innovative and aggressive business practices. Grand Met led the retail revolution within the trade, showing a regular commitment to breaking new ground. This must have created anxiety within the beerage, but some of its more radical ideas were eventually adopted elsewhere in the industry.

Grand Met had rationalised its breweries following its takeover. Industrial relations problems had continued as a result. Grand Met were consequently very happy to wave goodbye to this part of their business. Given their philosophies, and under the pressures imposed by the Beer Orders, the logic of the breweries-for-pubs deal made a lot of sense to both sides. And therefore, in February 1991, Grand Met briefly became the largest pub operator in the country with 8,550 pubs, and all of Grand Met's brewing interests were transferred to Courage.

By the terms of the agreement, 6,830 of these pubs became the dominion of Inntrepreneur. Courage gained supply agreements which these operators would have to subscribe to until April 1998. The principles of Inntrepreneur were sound enough to convince the rest of the big six, because Allied with their Vanguard lease (1,700 pubs), Whitbread with their Pub Partnerships (2,200 pubs) and Bass with their 1,400 LeaseCo all converted their surviving tenanted estates to lease agreements. This trend was partially foisted on them by another mandate of The Beer Orders, which brought all lettings of pubs in line with other business tenancies controlled by the 1954 Landlord and Tenant Act. As pub tenants consequently gained security of tenure, the brewers lost their ability to manage their tenanted estate so as to promote better tenants to bigger pubs, remove the poorer ones and recover good traders for management.

By granting leases the brewers acknowledged this loss of control but gained compensation from higher rents and avoiding responsibility for maintenance. Grand Met through Inntrepreneur granted twenty-year assignable leases[4] and claimed that they attracted a better quality of business-minded tenant and achieved lower turnover rates as a result.

The quality of licensee they attracted remains open to debate. What is established fact is that Inntrepreneur suffered a string of acrimonious disputes with their lessees, mainly regarding the Beer Tie for years after. Perhaps these were a result of their finding business-style operators who, unlike their former tenants, were prepared to argue their case all the way to the courts. The arguments unfortunately raged on for the rest of the decade, in the media and in the courts.

As Inntrepreneur became autonomous its activity and strategy appeared to be increasingly muddied. Unravelling what was happening seemed on a par with attempting to understand the plot of a disjointed murder mystery. The complicated story involved wrapping massive packages of pubs in a tangled series of legal documents and transfers. Meanwhile Grand Met and Courage, who started the whole chain of events, slipped quietly away from the scene, retaining a 1% nominal interest and, presumably, a huge sense of relief to be spared involvement in the ensuing confrontations. Grand Met confirmed its complete withdrawal from the industry in November 1994 with the sale of Chef & Brewer and the rest of its managed estate of 1,654 pubs to Scottish & Newcastle. Elders retained their interest for only four years longer, when they sold the Courage brewing business, ironically also to S&N. Two of the big six had completed their exit strategy.

Some harsh facts of life might have been learned from these departures. Elders demonstrated the difficulty of survival in the unique melting pot that was the UK pub market for a brewer when it was cast adrift from its pub estate. Grand Met, despite the involvement of highly respected management like Allen Sheppard, and their barn-storming and largely successful approach to tackling a range of food and drink businesses, were never entirely comfortable with the pub trade. They wished to transform it as they had done other businesses but were too impatient to understand the deep-rooted culture involved. In attempting to pioneer a 'retail' approach to the business they were the first of many brewers to fail. Unlike most of the others they did manage to extricate themselves with their reputation and finances relatively intact.

Whilst Inntrepreneur attracted most of the attention, other pub leasing companies (pubCos) were being created from the brewery sell-offs. The challenge to the other four members of the big six was to sell large numbers of low-trading pubs quickly. Individual pub sales would have been too slow, whilst prices would have become depressed. The situation may have looked bleak. Who would be interested in buying several thousand mediocre and neglected brewery tenancies? The brewery reorganisations which resulted from MMC provided the answer. Many brewery executives were either losing their jobs or were happy to depart from the tumult if the right opportunity arose. They knew the business and in most cases knew the pubs as they had been managing them for years. All they needed was finance to acquire worthwhile packages of pubs at bargain prices. Their employers seemed prepared to send them on their way with the ultimate leaving present; a few hundred old pubs. In return, the brewer had more confidence that beer supply and any other ongoing agreements would be honoured by their ex-colleagues.

The pubCos thus appeared overnight as the new owners of a package from one of the brewers. Enterprise was started on its way with 368 Midlands pubs sold by Bass; Century Inns took 185 pubs from the same source; the Pub Estate Company relieved S&N of 230 pubs, Sycamore Taverns, run by Allied old boys, took 296 pubs from Allied; Discovery acquired its estate from Whitbread. It will not be too surprising to note that the main beer supplier for these new chains was generally the original owning brewer. This was not what the MMC had in mind when it insisted that the big brewery estates be reduced in size to widen customer choice. But, in the circumstances, who could be blamed for taking such pragmatic action?

Even after the sufficiently drastic pruning of their estates to comply with the Beer Orders, the brewers continued selling. Bass, having sold 1,400 pubs in both 1991 and 1992, sold a further 723 in 1993 and more the following year. All of the capped brewers estates were reduced well below the limit set by the Beer Orders. This seemed logical as it gave a comfortable zone of manoeuvre in looking at opportunities to acquire new high volume outlets. But after a time, the process of slicing off a few hundred more pubs from the bottom end of the estate became habitual for the brewers. They seemed to thrive on the need for a continual 'churn' of their estates and the constant review process which accompanied it.

Until MMC the dominance of the brewery and its need for a large tied estate had been an unchallengable 'holy cow'. But MMC had broken the spell, and tradition and sentimentality had gone out of the window, along with the Tory party donations. And so the big brewers casually and routinely lined up package after package of disposals as a catalyst to transforming their company. Any opportunity was not wasted on the new pubCos, which eagerly awaited the next disposal like hungry dogs at their masters' table.

The pubCos were an unwanted by-product of the MMC. Spawned in such a manner, they lacked beauty or grace; the modest and utilitarian pubs they owned were matched by the spirit of the companies which ran them. With an entirely tenanted estate, deliveries largely still coming from the former brewery-owner, and other technical services available to be bought in from the same source, a basic pubCo package of a few hundred pubs could be managed by a handful of people working from a small rented office. But credit must go to some determined entrepreneurs who inherited these outcast pubs and worked hard to turn them into profitable businesses. In many cases management of the pubs improved compared to the brewery era. Money was made available for urgent repairs and redecoration. Ugly and faded swing-signs, often indistinguishable between the Queen's Head and the Duke of York, were replaced.

The poorest trading outlets were rooted out and sold off by the pubCos, new tenants were recruited to replace disenchanted landlords and, in some cases, small but significant elements of their portfolios were developed as brands. Examples included Pubmaster's chain of Tap and Spiles, a traditional real ale pub (which reached about sixty in number) whilst Discovery started to expand its chain of Seamus O'Donnell's Irish pubs.

Magic Pub Company, run by serial pub-entrepreneur Michael Cannon, seemed to be the masters of building brands out of limited material, 282 pubs sold by S&N in May 1994, to create Rat and Carrot, the town centre 'fun pub' and the Hungry Horse pub-restaurant. Hungry Horse was a rare and adventurous example of a small operation challenging the brewers in an area which they previously dominated; building pub-restaurant chains. The purchase of Magic Pub Co by Greene King in June 1996 for £197.7m was a surprise to many. The potential of Hungry Horse may have sealed Greene King's resolve to buy and accounted for the impressive price approaching £800,000 per pub.

By the mid-Nineties, due to rapid consolidation and rivalry, the pubCos had to transfer attention from their new pubs to the art of survival. As the market became established with more pubCos the price of a package of leased pubs rose. The original sales by the brewers in the uncertain and recession hit market of the early Nineties were at around £110,000 or £120,000 per pub. This had risen to a norm of up to £150,000 per pub by 1997. The victims of these takeovers and mergers, who had picked up a package in the early Nineties, could therefore console themselves with a profit of £25,000 to £30,000 per pub. This represented a tidy profit when selling a few hundred pubs acquired five or six years previously. It certainly sweetened the impact when a small group of directors shared a profit of a few million pounds. Most of the takeovers were conducted in a harmonious and decisive manner as a result.

A thorough consolidation took place. In late 1997 there were around 7,000 pubs in the pubCo sector, excluding the Inntrapreneur groupings. The largest outfits were Pubmaster with 1,615 pubs followed by Enterprise with 1,150 and Inn Business with 512. There were twelve companies with over 100 pubs, seventeen more with over fifty pubs, and forty-four owning eleven to forty-nine. Enterprise bought the 300-strong Discovery chain in April 1997, having already picked off John Labatt retail. During 1996 Inn Business acquired the 134-strong Marr Taverns for £19.75m and 216 pubs from Sycamore Taverns for £30m.

As they flexed their muscles in these contests of strength, diligently knitting together long lists of pubs in humdrum towns up and down the land, some of the older heads running the pubCos may have been reminded of their involvement in the brewery mergers from thirty years before. The sector was unglamorous, dealing as it did with others' cast-offs. Most media attention was focused on the simultaneous growth of the managed branded pubs and the high street circuits. Few realised the huge significance of what was taking place at this time with the growth and consolidation of these pubCos.

But powerful and substantial investors were taking note, and weighing up the opportunities involved very carefully. A fluid market of high value property represented an ideal medium by which huge amounts of investment could be set up as finance deals, to appreciate in value or float on the markets. The limited management required, together with the spread of the investment over a large number of component parts, often a thousand or more individual pubs, scattered all round the country to lessen dependence on one area, made the investment even more attractive. The money men didn't care what the pubs looked like, but they approved of having solid property assets with a regular base income of rent plus the margin from the supply of beer. Opportunities to squeeze extra value also existed, either from increased rents, selling off non-operational parts of the pubs such as surplus land, or by supplying a wider range of non-tied products to those tenants to gain additional margin.

Foremost in the process, perhaps inevitably was the rump of the Inntrepreneur estate. This had appeared to splinter into three distinct elements, known as Phoenix, Spring Inns and Inntrepreneur. But, in 1997 these were suddenly reunited in the control of Nomura, the Japanese investment bank. Having gained confidence from various rulings supporting the validity of the Beer Tie, Nomura's next move in December 1998 was to launch the Unique Pub Co. This consisted of all the 'good' pubs out of the 4,000 pubs they had acquired. These 2,600 pubs, all leased, some multi-let to corporate operators like Yates and Regent, and all subject to the Tie, would be floated on the stock market. The remainder, the so-called Pegasus Portfolio, were earmarked either for disposal, were free of the tie or were amongst the 400 pubs still involved in the long and bitter litigation over the Beer Tie. In 1998 Nomura revealed its financial muscle by acquiring a further 1,180 tenanted pubs from the struggling Greenalls.

Before then the upstart Punch Taverns caused a minor sensation when it secured the purchase of the former Bass leaseCo pub estate in 1997. Punch was set up by Hugh Osmond, one of the founders of the imaginative Pizza Express chain. The Bass acquisition provided a national coverage, regional offices and administrative staff with sound working experience within the industry, as the entire company was sold as a going concern. Osmond had, in a very short time, moved from obscurity to becoming an influential figure in the industry.

Two years later further shockwaves greeted the news that Whitbread were to pay £2.5 billion for the entire managed estate of Allied Lyons pubs and had signed a three-month exclusivity agreement. Punch immediately stepped forward as rival bidders. The money men weighed up the deal and Punch offered £2.66 billion. Both sides raised their bids. When Bass lent their support, it seemed Punch had achieved a knockout blow. Bass were not interested in the Allied estate as a whole, but were attracted by the prospect of cherry-picking the top pubs. The idea of thwarting Whitbread, their long-term rivals, must have also played its part. With this backing Punch offered £2.925 billion, compared with Whitbread's top offer of £2.88 billion. Despite this the Allied Domecq board still favoured the Whitbread offer. They claimed that it had more certainty and an earlier completion date by two months. Possibly they just favoured another member of the beerage.

Whitbread looked like winning the day until Stephen Byers, Trade and Industry Secretary, stepped in and referred the bid to the Competition Commission.[5] As the City watched, enthralled at this epic battle, the potential blocking of the deal by the C.C. proved decisive. Whitbread effectively withdrew and Punch finally got their deal and 3,600 pubs. The price equated to an impressive figure of over £750,000 per pub. This reflected the high quality nature of the estate (2,000 of which were managed houses containing a number of brands and a lot of high-value London pubs).

Bass must have enjoyed picking through the spoils and took 550 properties most suited for conversion to its retail brands. They had to de-brand the Big Steaks and Firkins amongst these as the brand names had become the property of Punch. For their part Punch confirmed that they would be running 2,000 or so pubs under management and would be developing their own brands for this purpose.

The sale of a third large and impressive pub package confirmed beyond all doubt the newfound power and ascendancy of the pubCo sector. This was the Whitbread pub sale in June 2001. Like Allied's sell-out this 3,000 pub package contained the whole of Whitbread's pub portfolio, the pride of which was the 150-strong Hogshead chain, lovingly and expensively developed by Whitbread from the pick of its high street sites over the previous ten or so years. Once again it was the finance houses who dominated the bidding with the new giants Punch and Nomura emerging as front-runners. But it was a new name that secured the £1.625 billion securitised deal, MGPE, the private equity arm of Deutsche Bank. The price of £541,000 per pub raised few eyebrows given the level established by recent deals. The Whitbread pubs also came with their own dedicated management team, based in Luton, making it easier for an outsider to enter the industry. Like the sale of the Allied estate, the properties involved were good quality, well-located, high-turnover pubs.

The strength of demand for pub packages of this size was evident from the thirty buyers who expressed interest in the Whitbread deal. In addition to those already involved as pubCos within the trade, these included many respected and powerful names from the world of commerce and finance. Pubs, despite their fall from grace in the eyes of the brewers, were proving to be an attractive proposition elsewhere.

Meanwhile Enterprise continued its low profile but relentless expansion. After floating on the stock market in 1995 the company acquired 276 pubs from Mayfair Taverns, 500 from Century Inns, a further package from Bass and the entire 300 pubs from the Gibbs Mew estate based in and around Salisbury (for £48 million or £155,000 per pub). This inflated the Enterprise portfolio to 1500 public houses. In May 2000 another package arrived from Whitbread in the form of 183 pubs at a cost of £115 million. These pubs had been taken by Whitbread from Swallow when the combined hotel and pub estate was sold. Having hardly drawn breath, Enterprise, with not a hint of indigestion, swallowed up a further 400 tenancies from S&N and 439 former Whitbread pubs from Laurel. Enterprise profits, and its share rating, continued to rise, whilst the spread of pubs helped to give Enterprise a very comprehensive national coverage.

The critical mass which Enterprise had achieved, and the ongoing over-capacity within the UK brewing industry, gave the pubCo great negotiating strength, meaning that beer supply agreements could be negotiated at very competitive rates, and with a healthy margin on resale. Ted Tuppen, head of Enterprise, summed up the situation as early as 1991 as he completed the purchase of 368 pubs from Bass to launch the company, as he questioned the point of having a brewery when he could buy top products at a significantly cheaper price than he could produce them for.

By the early years of the new millenium this margin, together with rental income on the tenanted and leased pubs, were worth an average of something approaching £50,000 per annum per pub. Naturally, if this could be achieved over a large portfolio it amounted to a huge income.

This buoyant picture contrasted to the continuing story of falling profits and contraction in the brewing sector and huge problems in turnover and viability confronting the high street managed house operators. Suddenly tenanted pubs were desirable and in huge demand. Within a period of a few years the unwanted packages of mediocre, unbranded pubs were the toast of the City and the target of many business tycoons.

Whilst the multi-million pound deals attracted the headlines, rationalisation continued at the other end. The pubCos seemingly thrived on 'churn' as readily as the brewers. As quickly as they purchased they would pick out packages of their pubs which were poor traders, difficult to let or needed major expenditure, and sell them off.

Frequently, these disposals were advertised in chunky brochures containing basic details of a few hundred pubs each, typically allocated half a page together with a photograph.

These selections of pubs, many boarded up and broken down, presented a bleak picture. Pubs with a chequered past and an improbable future. Pubs in the declining areas of northern industrial towns and the unfashionable depths of east and south London. Pubs which were defaced, vandalised, or half-forgotten. Pubs as cheap as £20,000 or £30,000 freehold. They lined up in the sales brochures, prepared on behalf of the pubCos who wanted rid of them, unloved and unlovely, old and faded.

The heart of some of these establishments was still beating whilst the doors opened for trade and a few hard-bitten regulars still turned up. But most were a long way down the perilous path of decline, from which there was no return. Very soon most would close and cease to exist as a pub. They are the casualties of the pub revolution and the greater social revolution which underlies it. These old pubs have a history and no doubt many special and treasured occasions, when their bars once filled with happy customers. However unattractive the building, and inevitable their demise, the loss of these marginal pubs merits more than a touch of regret.

Another unfortunate aspect of the rise of the pubCos is that thousands of pubs have been regularly shunted around from one company to another, with little regard for their long-term prospects, and less for their landlords and customers. The disparity between the detachment of big-city dealers and financiers and the day-to-day grind of caring for a pub and its landlord and staff is inevitable within such huge estates. But, as the size of the estates grew, so did the problem of remoteness and indifference. As Michael Cannon commented when acquiring 282 former Grand Met pubs from S&N in 1994;

"The pubs have been tossed around like a cork in a wild sea and have underperformed for quite a while."[6]

The new pubCos stepped into the vacuum created by the departure of the big six. The brewers' declining influence is summed up by the drop in their pub ownership from 62% of the nation's pubs in 1986, to 53% in 1992 and down to just 22.5% by 1997.[7] The pubCos provided the industry with a new structure and respectability in that collections of even modest pubs came to be regarded as valuable assets in the city. If the enforced pub disposals had taken place without the pubCos, chaos and a collapse of prices would have resulted. But the device of the pubCo had gained its own characteristics and needs. Most of all, an insatiable appetite for more pubs which threatened to dominate and distort the entire industry.

PART THREE

Branded!

The Growth Of Branding

'Brand'
'A distinctive maker's name or trademark, symbol or design, etc used to identify a product or group of products'.
Chambers 21st Century Dictionary.

Filthy McNasty's, The Fringilla and Firkin, Harvey Floorbangers, Boom Boom, Cheeky Tossers, The Orange Kipper, The Slurping Toad, The Pickled Newt. The list of new pub names was endless. They were called contrived, tasteless, banal and irreverent and were all these things and more. But these names, displayed ever more brashly where once the King's Head gazed peacefully down, were more than new pub signs. They signalled a revolution within the licensed trade. The focus may have been on the new names but everything behind that facade was also changing; the new wave of bars were far removed from traditional pubs. Different in appearance of course, but equally significantly in how they were run.

Jimmy Young is someone who used pubs regularly. He was in the *Guinness Book of Records* for having visited the most British pubs, an impressive 24,004 until Bruce Masters of Bedfordshire overtook him in 1994. At the time Jimmy expressed his concern, not about losing his hard-earned record, but about the fate of the old English pub. Alarmed at the trend for renaming pubs Young said;

"I think its awful. If the English pub goes it rather looks like being the downfall of England."[1,2]

Most people would not go that far, but there was plenty of concern from traditionalists, pub landlords and of course CAMRA. The surviving big brewers meanwhile were excited about the new brand-building game they were embarking upon. This provided a welcome break from the pressure of selling pubs, keeping the brewery running and satisfying their shareholders in the face of downward trends in beer consumption and a changing market.

The consumer on the street was possibly more bemused by the sudden growth of new circuits of busy town centre bars and changes to once familiar pubs. Families may have been delighted to discover that there were new restaurants and play-barns to take their children to, women happy that bars were being designed with them in mind, the young because there were new exciting outlets just for them.

In October 1996 Bass responded to objections to the proposed conversion of the Plough at Dulwich to a Goose and Granite, their Wetherspoons copy;

"We want to create a brand name to give customers a consistent standard and formula which they will find in every Goose and Granite they visit." [3]

The comment tells us much about brands and how they operate. With bars designed and run for distinct customer groups, a high degree of standardisation is involved. If one doesn't fit the customer profile then one shouldn't be there and may well not want to be. The place where one may feel more at home is the modest Dog and Duck around the corner. But beware because it was under threat. Firstly it might be 'acquired' for conversion to an Irish bar or a Fuddock and Fishcake fun pub. Secondly, as the brands expanded they not only needed lots of new outlets but they also claimed high turnovers, typically five to ten times an average pub. They were taking trade from the remaining traditional pubs. Some of these were already struggling and therefore whilst the Dog and Duck was being bought out for conversion the Queen's Head was closing down through loss of trade.

The Nineties will be remembered as the decade of the pub brand. A few high street chains had appeared before then but their numbers had been limited. The first brands to emerge were Yates Wine Lodges, Chicago Rock Cafe, Slug and Lettuce and Wetherspoons. It was the independent groups who pioneered these during the Eighties. The big brewers were taking careful note, and when they launched their own brands the availability of pubs for conversion within their large estates allowed them to catch up quickly. But to really establish a national brand required a considerable number of units. Suddenly acquisitions became big business, with the brewers and a range of other operators competing for the best sites in each town and city to convert to licensed use.

Why did branding suddenly take off so comprehensively? Beyond the industry obsession with following the trend and copying everybody else, there were compelling reasons. The big brewers were selling off large packages of pubs and had substantial capital to reinvest. They were losing turnover as a result of their disposals and developing new highly profitable units was a way of recouping this loss. After MMC they were also keen to regain the initiative and restore some prestige by involving themselves in cutting-edge designs in prime locations. Once they became committed to setting up brands, the process became self-perpetuating. The more branded units operators opened, the more they needed; not just because of the attractive turnover levels and profits involved but also to take advantage of economies of scale and reach the number of outlets implied by the branding process.

From the perspective of a large brewer or leisure company these are the main benefits of branding licensed outlets;

1. CREDIBILITY / CRITICAL MASS

The best illustration is within the pub-restaurant market. Early pioneers of brands developed Beefeater, Toby and Chef & Brewer in the 70s and 80s. With varying degrees of success these have stood the test of time and become established and recognisable operations. By contrast when brewers have developed one-off pub-restaurants these have invariably failed, irrespective of the quality of the site or operation. A one-off restaurant within the unsympathetic environment of the brewery was vulnerable. The operation would not receive the attention and protection it needed to maintain standards once the novelty of the opening had worn off and the creator(s) moved on to something else. The manager of the unit would lack the influence needed in a large organisation to ensure that menus would be developed, standards of service and presentation maintained and time and money allowed for this.

Senior management who spent too much time on an individual unit could be accused of 'hobby-farming'. At some stage profitably would be hit and the operation would start on a downward slope, with menu and staff being cut, and the operation losing public and internal credibility. Falling turnover and lower standards would create a vicious circle until the brewer finally gave up and converted the site to something else or sold it off. As a brand, brewery-run restaurants would have an entire team of people dedicated to them to provide specialist back-up support and investment, address ongoing issues, build and maintain trade and adapt to changing circumstances.

2. STANDARDISATION

Before branding, a brewer's area manager controlled a patch of say fifteen or twenty managed houses in and around one or two towns. Some might be tough town centre pubs selling lots of lager to blokes with tattoos and no hair. Others could be dull suburban and estate pubs whilst the balance might be destination eating houses out in the countryside; packed with visitors on sunny weekends but quiet in the week. Assuming that the area manager had the ability to run such a variety of pubs, the poor chap still had a problem. How could he compare staffing costs from one pub to another? Was the dip in trade at the Maypole due to the awful weather or incompetence of the new manager? Where could he find a new couple to run his big catering house when it was the only one in his patch? And was their claim that their inadequate kitchen or awful decor was damaging their trade justified?

Branding signalled an approach which was particularly appreciated by accountants who could ignore the irritating individual characteristics of the pubs concerned. These could then be neatly packaged into homogenous groups. Standardisation became the goal which delivered;

a) Staffing

Throughout companies from brand managers to barmaids, fully trained specialist staff could be appointed to the right type of pub. The square peg in a round hole could be avoided. Companies could develop a personality profile required for their pub staff for particular brands from comparative data with very specific job specifications.

b) Product range

Common sense might suggest that the opportunities to sell wine or sherry in a rowdy young person's venue are limited. What about malt whisky in a real ale pub or stout in a steak-house? If the decision on whether to stock such products, in what volumes and how wide a choice to offer, do not seem immediately obvious they would be if you ran sixty steak houses and were opening number sixty-one.

c) Financial performance

The gross profit which a manager should achieve on his drinks and food sales can be laid down to an accuracy of less than 1%, based on the performance of almost identical pubs elsewhere with similar customers and sales profiles. The number of alleged fiddles in the trade are legion but they are all more difficult when performance ratios are set for a brand. Salaries and running costs can also be tightly budgeted for and controlled. The most difficult but essential item to predict is turnover. However, a sufficient database for a brand and useful measures like sales per square metre or per diner based on past sales history allows confident forecasting. And this became an essential tool on which to base investment decisions and know reasonably accurately in advance what to expect from each outlet in bottom line profit.

d) Design

With an image-conscious market the right appearance for a bar was critical. Before branding, the refurbishment of a pub involved a laborious hit-and-miss approach. Each scheme was considered individually by a large group of brewery men, the licensee, designers and often a few other hangers-on who would study the pub, its competition, the area and other projects. A day would often be set aside by this multi-visionary group to tour the opposition in the area, then return to the subject pub and brain-storm their way to a solution. This would take current fashion, the outlet's existing and potential customer base, what the opposition were planning (often guesswork) and the individual characteristics of the property into account. Then they would brief the designer to come up with an appropriate scheme, usually within a broad budget. If the design was acceptable, and to budget, then this would normally proceed. But sometimes, if the mood took him, the local director might ignore all of this and do something totally different. Compare this with the branded system, where each new outlet for a brand would be developed in line with the 'brand template'. These impose clear guidelines on the type and colour of decorations, layout and size of bars, seating areas, lighting, signage and any other features characteristic of the brand. This painting-by-numbers was a huge advance for the brewers on the amateurish approach which had preceded it.

3. ADVERTISING AND MARKETING

The greatest benefit of branding is the formation of an efficient conduit between the identification of a specific customer group and the commercial exploitation of this market on a consistent, national basis. Or, in non-marketing speak, aiming a lot of pubs at the same type of customers and ensuring that they keep coming back. Young drinkers, or inexperienced restaurant users, are particularly likely to stay with one particular chain if they have established that it suits their needs and they can use it without problems or embarrassment.

Given the critical mass of perhaps 100 outlets within a restaurant brand, major advertising campaigns could be justified to build turnover and increase brand awareness, and thereby the value of the brand. Other ways of building brand loyalty and recognition included the display of the brand logo and more focused, smaller-scale promotions.

4. IMAGE

In the Seventies and Eighties the image of the brewers was poor. The outward face which they presented to the public was via a rag-tag collection of unkempt pubs with many customers to match, indifferent service standards and a mediocre range of products. As the brewers became more self-conscious, they started to appreciate that their pubs were their shop window. Brands became an opportunity to show themselves in a positive light. Not only were the brands developed in prominent locations, but their standardised appearance and operation could be designed to ensure that they consistently gave the right impression. The young, fashionable, and lucrative markets, which the brands targeted, were associations that the brewers were desperately keen to create.

5. GOODWILL

When the Harvester chain was sold by Forte to Bass at the end of 1995, the price was £170 million for 76 pubs. At an average of £2.25 million per property this was regarded as an impressive price, well above the individual value of each outlet. The difference was attributed to goodwill, the value of owning Harvester, a well-established, recognisable brand. Ownership of Harvester also provided the perfect platform for a giant like Bass to expand the operation by converting suitable existing pubs and acquiring new sites, each of which would increase in value as a result of becoming part of a successful brand. In the summer of 1996 Whitbread acquired Cafe Pelican for its Cafe Rouge, the French-style bistro. *Far too expensive* some observers declared as news of the £133 million deal emerged. But Whitbread used Cafe Rouge as an effective springboard into catering on the high street.

The attraction of branded chains was also demonstrated during the Nineties by a dogfight between Regent Inns and Morland, the eventual victors to buy Unicorn, a small managed pub group whose main brand was Newt and Cucumber. And soon after, Marston's, the Regional brewer, paid a substantial sum for the seven Pitcher & Piano bars. The incentives for other operators who could build a successful brand was clear.

ACQUISITIONS AND THE PUB CIRCUIT

The free trade market pioneered branding. The new pub retail groups became established in the most popular town centres, which started to see new circuits of bars grouped closely together. Wetherspoons were often the first, although they were also prepared to develop in isolation. Yates's and Chicago Rock Cafes were the kingpin of the circuit as far as the younger market were concerned, whilst Slug and Lettuce aimed at a slightly older and more discerning customer. All these brands were epitomised by a standard approach to their signage and appearance, their method of operation and their customer base.

The brewers played a passive role during this first assault on the high street at the end of the Eighties and early Nineties. Following the MMC enquiry the big six needed a few years to gather strength, devise a strategy and develop their brand concepts. They were hit further during the economic slump at the start of the Nineties by free trade loans failing. Whitbread alone wrote off debts worth £8m in 1990 and a further £6m the next year.

The intensity of restructuring, downsizing, outsourcing and navel gazing that went on amongst the brewers at the start of the Nineties achieved genuine and fundamental change. They emerged from this cathartic experience fitter and leaner. Their aloofness and conservatism was now infused with a more commercial and pragmatic approach. Bass even appointed a director of corporate change to help create the culture *'for the company to become a more innovative and customer responsive business'*. Large numbers of head office brewery employees were affected by the process, either losing their jobs or having to change roles.

The four survivors from the big six, Whitbread, Bass, Allied and S&N, recovered their poise, and committed to brand building with great enthusiasm in competition with the pub retail groups. They learnt from their previous ineffectual refurbishments. As the brand bandwagon gained momentum it became a driving force. If a rival brand had got a site in Bristol or Bradford then the others also had to be there, as close as possible to the first.

Brewers realised that most of their existing premises were unsuitable for conversion to the new brands. This reinforced the process of churn, and the restructuring of estates continued long after the compulsion from the MMC was gone. Their small tenanted pubs in the backwaters continued to be sold. They were replaced with a lower number of big turnover pubs in the right places. The brewers could afford to sell up to ten small tenanted pubs, whilst developing just one new high-turnover branded outlet and still show a net gain in bottom line profit. This demonstrated the spectacularly higher turnover involved and the advantage of running pubs themselves, in house, so as to retain the management profit of the new unit. And the disposal of ten small pubs more than paid for the development of the new unit.

Wetherspoon's view on the process at the time is revealed in a quote by Tim Martin after opening the massive 8,000-square feet Moon Under Water in Deansgate, Manchester in 1995;

> *"The big pub is a winning formula for us. So much work goes into every application for a licence and permission to open, that the bigger the premises the bigger return for all that effort. And of course, the other element about big pubs is pure ego."*[4]

The operators obtained new branded outlets capable of achieving such egotistic levels of trade by going where the right types of consumer were. Two types of location were targeted; out of town on destination or main road locations, with good parking facilities, or the town centre; but only in prime areas of cities and the bigger towns which were capable of generating substantial turnovers. This meant prominent sites close to main office and employment zones and within, or close to, the core shopping area. The operators were all guided by similar criteria, and so clearly defined circuits of nearby pubs and bars developed through intense competition for any suitable building there. A gaggle of new bars would typically open in these prime strips over a short period. The arrival of one operation could signal the start of a frenzied period of competition for sites, licensing and planning applications and bar development leading to a circuit 'maturing' to bursting point within a year or two.

Another reason why the brand builders wanted new sites was size.

The new 'superpubs' were large. Trading areas were frequently 3,000 to 5,000 square feet as opposed to 500 to 1,000 square feet for a traditional pub. Older pubs were characterised by small rooms and haphazard shapes, awkward posts and beams and a traditional appearance which all prevented the creation of the modern style of large open trading areas. History also mitigated against the possible conversion of many pubs. Whilst landlords could be removed and pub names changed, the local reputation of a pub could not. Heavy boozing locals who regarded a pub as their second home were sometimes loath to depart when the place was converted to a brand, whilst new customers might be reluctant to enter a place which had always been known as a rough house.

Brand operators therefore preferred properties that had never been licensed. The new branded bars were converted from buildings as diverse as banks, shops and churches. Such were the profits to be made that values of sites for conversion soared. Other users of these buildings could normally be outbid in order to secure them for licensed use. The brewers assembled large teams of professionals to scour the right areas in a constant search for such opportunities.

At the peak of the branding process, and the acquisition boom fuelled by it, Whitbread issued swish, glossy brochures. In these they stated their preference for unlicensed property. They suggested the following buildings as having potential for conversion to pubs; waterfront in cities, listed buildings in the suburbs; redundant farm buildings, mills, churches, former court buildings, railway stations, seafront locations, former cinemas and theatres and former banks and school buildings. They added; "*As a company we're interested in developing certain types of market – we call them the three F's – families, females and food.*"

In 1996 the Bass Taverns company magazine signalled the direction that company was heading in;

"*The O'Neill's Irish bar in Sutton is pulling in ten times more business than it did in its old pub guise. The 'bottom line' in the new branded outlets such as Irish bars, All Bar One and Fork and Pitcher (Vintage Inns) is sending a very clear message. So clear, that Bass Taverns is building part of its future strategy on them. From the current 400 branded outlets, the number will grow to half the estate – 1,200 – by the year 2000."*

Tony Hughes, Operations Director, added;

"The opportunities are tremendous. We are in a growth business and staff should realise they are in a company with tremendous resources; one prepared to invest." [5]

As branding gathered momentum it encompassed new ideas and themes. The brewers' extensive teams included people researching and developing new brands. Martin Robinson, theming supremo of S&N, in developing Bar Oz claimed that repackaging a pub;

"Worked on every occasion out of 1,000 over the three years I have been involved. This is what the punters want as long as you're not too crass about it." [6]

Lee Middleburgh, Concept Director for Bass, insisted, like his S&N opposite number, that they were providing what the market wanted;

"Before we do anything, we will look at a set of customer needs, and then at trends in the market, as well as in other leisure markets. We then put those two things together and say, 'how can we meet those needs?', so instead of always following in the wake of a trend, we get in front of it. If we think of something weird and wacky that doesn't meet those needs then we have to dismiss it, but if we think of something weird that meets them, it can be incorporated validly." [7]

A weird, convulted way of describing the design process, one might think. Because, or perhaps in spite of such an approach, the success of brands became self-evident. The throngs of young people who squeezed into these new bars at weekends and the long queues waiting patiently to replace those departing were a barometer of success. The circuits tended to function exactly as the name implies. Young drinkers would circulate from one bar to the next, normally in close proximity throughout the evening rather than remaining loyal to one. One of the biggest changes prompted by branding was the sight of doormen on patrol at most town centre bars. Before the Nineties they could only get work in nightclubs in larger towns, but suddenly they were in demand at bars throughout the country.

By the end of the decade, the acquisition boom peaked. As more operators chased the best sites, prices and rents rose to unsustainable levels. In 1999, Whitbread, so often market leaders, announced that they were reducing their involvement. Soon the others followed. For six or seven years the big brewers and the pub retail chains had been locked in an intensive battle for sites.

Some of the brewers were now distracted by more strategic issues. Like divesting themselves of their breweries, or wrapping up all their pubs in a huge package and flogging them off to the highest bidder.

The change in policy, notably at Allied and Whitbread, was bewildering, as they switched rapidly from devoting huge resources to acquiring individual sites to develop for their brands to disposing of most or all of their pubs. This took place in 1999 for Allied Breweries with their entire estate sell-off and 2001 for Whitbread (who did retain their pub-restaurants). Sites which they had only recently purchased and developed were included.

As a result, the opportunity arose to buy entire packages of licensed outlets at one stroke rather than individually. Bass grabbed the chance enthusiastically when it joined with the Punch bid to gain the right to cherry-pick Allied's best pubs. Many of these were converted to Bass brands whilst some continued in their existing format.

The pub retail groups continued as aggressive purchasers of

individual sites or small pub groups, which were now increasingly available. But only for a couple of years more, before they too would be forced to abandon their brand building.

The circuit-building had finished. But the circuits and brands which had been developed remained, with a significant presence, for both the industry, and society.

The Plague Of Plagiarism

The brewers plagiarised each other unmercifully. The practice of copying competitors' designs and styles of operation was so common in the industry that it was simply taken for granted. Most successful styles of bar were copied, not just in general style, but sometimes in much more detailed and specific ways. The process was assisted by the intimate nature of the licensed trade. The inspirations and influences behind many of the designs came from the same sources; designers and marketing men who worked for many clients throughout the industry.

We had already witnessed the arrival and copying of the cafe bar, the fun pub and the sports bar, as well as many individual concepts. As soon as the Irish bar was discovered, every brewer was unashamedly jumping onto the bandwagon with their own version. They all did this so quickly that it was difficult to judge who was copying whom. The success of Wetherspoons inevitably encouraged some brewers to try and create their own version, obviously after careful study of the original. Whilst they seemed able to reproduce something which looked like a Wetherspoon, they struggled to emulate its success.

The most blatant and extensive example of plagiarism was within the family sector of the pub-restaurant market. The external styles of the 'competing' operations were very similar, whilst internal layout and design evolved into a safe, comfortable but ultimately bland style which was adopted throughout the market. The most obvious expression of the commonality of the pub-restaurant 'formula' was in signage. The market leader, Brewers Fayre, adopted a wrought iron framework in an oval shape with 'Brewers Fayre' inscribed in gold letters on a red background with various indistinct, but presumably hearty, foodstuffs pictured in the centre. Millers Kitchen, the ex-Greenalls family pub, had an oval sign of similar size to Brewers Fayre with the two words 'Millers Kitchen' inscribed in white on a red oval band around a central image of a windmill. The Bass version, used by its Innkeepers Fayre, also featured an oval sign of the approved size with gold lettering on a red background. The two words used, Innkeepers Fayre, with the centre featuring an unclear clutter of produce, meant that the whole arrangement was almost identical to Brewers Fayre but for the one word. The fourth company to follow the convention was S&N with Homespreads. This admittedly displayed some alarming deviations, with only one word on the sign and a large cooking pot in the centre. But otherwise it conformed to the tried and trusted basis of an oval sign with gold lettering on red background.

How could one explain such dogged faithfulness by three of the four operators to copying a sign designed by their competitor? Could they not create something slightly different and less confusing? Why should such a blatant rip-off be perpetrated by companies which were quite capable of designing and promoting their own individual style? The brewers involved were either working together, to jointly teach the world to recognise a family pub-restaurant, or were guilty of copying their competitors out of a fear of failure if they pioneered their own style. But would the radical alternative of a different colour or lettering be so risky?

Presumably the brewers were guided by marketing men who told them that the family market craves familiarity and safety. These consumers were, apparently, not very sophisticated in terms of their experience of restaurants. The theory was that they might therefore be nervous of using premises which they were not familiar with because of the fear that they might make a mistake; they might sit in the wrong place, or order the wrong meal or find that the food was wildly extravagant and not to their taste or end up with a bill beyond their means. And so the brewers had the customers' best interests at heart (and thus their own) when they made their family restaurants so horribly unexciting, predictable and yes, almost identical.

This similarity was underlined by the alleged receipt by Whitbread over the years of letters from customers of the other operations, who understandably, but wrongly, concluded that they had visited a Brewers Fayre. It would be interesting to know what happened to those letters. Such confusion was a price that the brewers seemed happy to accept as part of this strategy.

The plagiarism went one stage further when one compared the remarkably similar menus and pricing at these outlets. Each menu had a range of categories generally incorporating starters, fish, chicken, salads, grills and steaks and overseas favourites (lasagna, chicken tikka, chilli etc.) and then 'light bites'. The choice was reasonably wide, designed to cater for nearly every taste, but all being highly standard, tried and trusted favourites. Pricing back in the mid-Nineties when the four brands concerned were all operating was remarkably consistent between the competitors. Three of the menus provided a combo to share, all at between £5.25 and £5.75. All had Chicken Tikka/Tandoori at between £5.55 and £5.95 whilst the universal eight-ounce Sirloin Steak retailed at between £8.25 and £8.75. And tea to accompany the meal would cost either 75p or 80p. So with little to distinguish between the restaurants in appearance or character, the brewers certainly wasted no effort to entice the customer to their outlets with imaginative cuisine or competitive pricing.

Plagiarism also had its influence on the town centre scene with the proliferation of rats, newts and other small creatures. The S&N Rat and Parrot brand were displeased with the confusion caused by the Magic pub-inspired Rat and Carrot, although the signage was at least different. Magic Pub Company were involved in a similar twist, with their Pickled Newt brand perhaps treading on the toes of the Morland's operated Newt and Cucumber. Eldridge Pope, in developing Slurping

Toad, demonstrated a distinct taste within the trade for the small and slimy which bordered on an obsession.

With the spread of branding the impact of plagiarism was magnified. When one operator imitated the style of another whilst rolling out a brand, it wasn't one or two pubs which emerged in this style, but twenty, fifty or more which appeared as a clone of an existing brand. Once a winning formula was established, it was certainly not confined to the estate of that brewer or operator. Regimentation ruled the industry. Individuality, that quaint old facet of the traditional pub, was being swept away.

Licensing;
Upright Thinking, Vertical Drinking

Control of day-to-day licensing of individual premises was, until 2005, vested in the licensing magistrates, who sat regularly in magistrates' courts up and down the country. Whilst central government set the overall rules, it was the magistrates who implemented and controlled the system.

To obtain a totally new license the applicant had to demonstrate 'need' – a concept which remained fairly subjective. The magistrates had considerable discretion in interpreting 'need'; proving that there was demand from the public, and that the new premises would meet that need. Certain licensing districts become notorious for throwing out new applications, whilst others were noted for taking a balanced view or as being relatively easy to satisfy. In arriving at their decision, magistrates had to consider the comments and possible objections of the police, fire officers, environmental health inspectors and the local authority, and the public. With the possibility of appeals, the whole process could take many months.

Given this background, the attitude of the magistrates was crucial in controlling how quickly, and in what locations and styles, the new wave of brands advanced. The brewers and retail pub groups responsible for expanding the brands employed top licensing solicitors and other specialist consultants, and became very polished in securing new licenses. As a result, until the mid-Nineties, the majority of applications for new licenses for branded circuit pubs were approved. But as the trickle of new applications became a flood, new licences became more challenging to secure.

However, the march of the brands coincided with another process, that of inner city regeneration. It became recognised that one of the key factors in repopulating deserted and threatening town and city centres after shopping hours was the nighttime economy. Bars and restaurants often represented the first wave of regeneration. If they moved into a previously stagnant town centre in sufficient numbers, they brought street activity and vibrancy in their wake, as well as essential facilities like street lighting, CCTV, car parks being kept open and regular late-night buses and trains.

The issues of new licences and regeneration often became intertwined. Some magistrates, influenced by local authorities and their promotion of regeneration, would look favourably on the new wave of bars. Others, concerned at the impact of new licences on town centres and the large number of young drinkers attracted by them, would resist. The impact on and presence in the town of other pubs, in creating the likelihood of 'licensing saturation', was another factor used in arguing against a new grant. Some magistrates became more restrictive after allowing a modest number of new licences. Overall there was a lack of consistency and no standard policy in interpreting the crucial factor of 'need'.

Because the brands all wanted to locate in the same affluent and busy town and city centres, the magistrates in those areas could become alarmed at the rate of new applications. Anxiety, when faced with such a deluge, was understandable, especially if reinforced by public opinion. As the brands first arrived in a town the public were generally enthusiastic that their established range of bars was being livened up. But once the fourth, fifth or even tenth new licence was applied for, concern generally grew as reports of noisy and drunken behaviour increased.

The place that spread out the red carpet most enthusiastically to new licences was Leeds. The city has, with the assistance of its own development corporation, worked hard to shed its old grimy Industrial image, encourage development, particularly of offices, and move forward as a 'European city'. Consistent with the rapid expansion and modernisation of the city centre, Leeds welcomed a wide range of food and drink facilities to cater for its growing workforce. Back in 1994 this policy was attracting headlines such as *'The city that never sleeps'* when a proposal to allow bars to remain open all night was mooted by the city fathers. This was going too far for some, particularly the LVA, the trade group representing tenants and free traders who claimed that they would miss out as they would be unable to keep their bars open as long as the brewers.

"We have tried to encourage people to see the city centre as a playground,"

countered Eamonn McGee, Chairman of Leeds' city-centre committee;

"It's been a slow process to convince licensing magistrates and police of its value, but Leeds is now a place for people to enjoy."[8]

All night drinking did not arrive but the bars kept coming; according to Leeds City Council's Planning and Environment Department, nine new operators arrived in 1992-4. But the conveyor belt really warmed up over the next eight years when sixty, yes sixty, further pubs and bars opened.[9] These created several totally new circuits within the city centre and played their full part in what has been an extensive transformation of the centre of Leeds. But there has been a negative impact for some residents, whilst existing licensees have been affected as the city has long since reached a level of saturation.

The centre of Portsmouth also suffered new bars like a rash. Greene King, Wetherspoons, Allied with a Firkin, and Whitbread's Dome Cafe-Bar all opened within a few hundred yards during the mid-Nineties in the Guildhall Walk area, dubbed Boozers' Boulevard. Portsmouth City

Council welcomed the new outlets, suggesting that they gave the area a more continental flavour and helped promote tourism. Predictably, local licensees took the opposite view, and fought hard and largely successfully to stem the flow of new bars.

Further north one could have witnessed the rarity of nice things being said about Wolverhampton, because of the explosion of pubs and nightclubs in the town. It was claimed that this boom, which saw the number of late licences grow from two to over forty in a few years, was one of the principal factors in the regeneration of the town. Formerly, people just wanted to escape as quickly as possible, but suddenly it was estimated that 20,000 people were drawn into town every Friday and Saturday night.

Some suggested that the link between the return to respectability of the town and the licensing boom was remote whilst the surge of leisure investment was just down to the natural copycat syndrome in the trade. But the local authority pointed out that a CCTV system in the town, intensive policing, a liberal policy and grant aid from the government's urban programme, to assist with the conversion of historic empty buildings in the designated entertainment quarter, all assisted. In addition, amenity and convenience improved with landscaping and pedestrianisation schemes and the provision of good parking and public transport facilities.

Such assistance would have been unthinkable in Canterbury. As in days of yore, the old city was under siege. The twentieth-century version witnessed armies of consultants recruited by the big operators seeking to get their branded bars inside the city walls in order to tempt the good citizens away from their hearths and their traditional hostelries. The city fathers did their noble best to resist by refusing virtually all new licence applications, assisted on occasions by petitions from their worried burghers. Wetherspoons managed to dodge the boiling oil and penetrate the city walls whilst O'Neill's and Hogshead arrived by the devious route of converting existing pubs. The borough planners manning the defences threatened to refuse any new applications for pubs and even restaurants in the city. This policy seemed extreme and regressive in order to protect the historic core of a major tourist city attracting thousands of visitors.

Another tourist venue which attempted to bring down the shutters was Southend. The town has always suffered from a rather raucous image, established during the Sixties, when the mods and rockers used to visit to exchange opinions. The combination of large quantities of youths, seaside and alcohol proved volatile on many occasions, making control of the town a sensitive issue. But Southend was attractive to the brands and so regular applications for new licences were received. Few were granted. During 1997 Brannigan's, Yates, Morland, Greenall's and Wetherspoons all planned new bars but, following police objections, eventually none of them crossed the thin blue line.

In a very different environment, the London borough of Ealing believed that it had a big problem because of the popularity of Ealing town centre. A concentration of lively bars in the commercial area of this West London suburb proved a magnet for people from a wide area who regarded it as a good place to go for a night out. The local authority, concerned by occasional rowdiness, reacted with alarm at such hedonism, deciding to resist the grant of any further planning approvals for pubs. Ken Kettle, a Conservative councillor for Ealing, expressed his concern by claiming, extravagantly;

"The transformation of Central Ealing from Queen of the suburbs to the Las Vegas of drinking is only too apparent."[10]

The dignitaries of Bath in the form of The Bath Society, the Bath Preservation Trust, magistrates and local councillors all expressed their horror as a wave of 'superpubs' sought to open within close proximity in the town centre. The majority of licences were refused by the local magistrates but a number were then granted on appeal at Bath Crown Court. English Heritage, normally expected to be more circumspect, expressed its approval, suggesting that opponents of the new bars were exaggerating their impact. Chris Smith, their historical advisor, commented firmly;

> *"Listed buildings are seriously damaged by the blight of disuse, and we need to get them filled. The whole of Bath is a conservation area and we would not accept plans that would damage it, but we are not in the business of pandering to Nimbys."*[11]

The same arguments ebbed and flowed in towns up and down the land. In Liverpool a liberal approach to licensing was credited with rejuvenating much of the city centre. Similar comments emanated from Glasgow and Birmingham, where a council spokesman suggested that a key factor of the new bars and restaurants was in tempting city workers to stay in the city at 5.30 after work rather than leaving for home in the suburbs, from whence they would not return. From Nottingham, a report from the city centre manager, Jane Ellis, revealed a threefold increase in licensing applications between 1995 and 1996, following a trend for new bars being developed which commenced in 1993.

In Manchester, leisure development was given the credit for revitalisation. Francis Glare, Associate at BDP planning, commented;

> *"For over a decade the city council has promoted cultural activities as a means of regeneration. Castlefield, the Gay Village, the Northern Gateway, and, more recently, the Northern Quarter are all beneficiaries of this vision allied to a relatively benign planning policy and an increasingly tolerant licensing policy."*

But a note of caution followed from Glare regarding the role of the national brands.

> *"The leisure sector is becoming institutionalised. The motley crew of small and local investors behind much of the late 80s and early 90s expansion*

are now having to compete with the national brewers and institutions. The result is less independence, a product that is less identifiably local, bigger in scale and more mainstream. This is blurring the edges of the cultural quarters of the city, reducing the distinctiveness the planners fostered."[12]

York, like most historic centres, remained firmly in the restrictive camp. In 1998 the magistrates, city council and police issued new regulations which included a ban on public entertainment, pool tables, amusement machines, music and vertical drinking, insisting that all drinks should be served to tables. York Police Licensing Officer Arthur Swaine, commenting on these excessive measures which would prevent any sort of genuine pub being developed, claimed;

"The regulations are designed to cut down on violence, maintain the quality of the venue's design and create a more European cafe bar culture in the city."[13]

Presumably the licensed trade and residents of Berlin or Barcelona did not have to contend with such restrictions!

Magistrates at Horseferry Rd, Westminster were quick to jump on the bandwagon soon after, permitting an application at Langleys in Covent Garden on condition that no vertical drinking took place. Horrified publicans were quick to express their concern at such a ludicrous move which, if it became widespread, would destroy pub culture. A CAMRA spokesman commented;

"Banning people from drinking while standing up will be impossible to impose. Not only will the landlord and staff be unable to keep an eye on everybody, but it's a terrible restriction on people's freedom to drink how they like. There are ways of keeping rowdiness to a minimum without resorting to these sorts of measures."[14]

On appeal the restriction was removed and the right of customers at the premises to drink vertically was secured.

Westminster Council was at the centre of further controversy, having devised a series of policies which seemed to suggest an all-out war on the licensed trade. Even though the council administers the West End of London, entertainment capital of the country, with its many prominent clubs and bars, Westminster claimed that their priority was to protect the local resident population from the effects of these activities. In areas that they regarded as 'stress areas', centred on Covent Garden and Soho, there were to be no new bars. Elsewhere in the borough, conversion of larger properties, typically suited to branded bars and themed restaurants, would not be permitted. Smaller premises would only be considered if there was no residential use above, below, adjoining or opposite the proposed site. Another feature of the clamp down was a latest closing time of 1.00am for any new clubs and bars, and a review of the hours of existing operations. A penalty points system for licensees and a licensing task force were also proposed.

Carl Powell, Director of planning, commented;

"We want a balanced community where the large corporates do not swamp the more traditional theatres, shops and pubs. It's a slowing down process so we can take stock. We don't want London to become a 24-hour city like Las Vegas with its monotonous neon lights and compassionless society."[15]

Such sentiments may seem very noble but appeared to be largely unrelated to the intention of the new policies. The leisure companies with the largest stakes in Westminster challenged these and succeeded in having them watered down. The proposals were symptomatic of provincial nimbyism, and totally inappropriate to the West End of London.

A contrasting example, when both planning committees and magistrates adopt an unbridled laissez-faire approach, is the respectable commuting town of Reading. The branding process started in 1995 when Yates, Edwards, Firkin, Newt & Cucumber and a Greene King Ale Cafe all opened within a year or so within the same block at the eastern end of Friar Street, close to the town's main railway station. Further gatecrashers to this extended party arrived at regular intervals in the form of Pitcher & Piano, the Square, Walkabout and O'Neill's. Visually, the result was impressive. On a relatively short frontage to Friar Street, six substantial brands stood virtually shoulder to shoulder, like runners jostling for space at the start of a race. Walkabout, just down a side alley, peered menacingly over their shoulders. Wetherspoons watched in morbid fascination from across the road.

Within shouting distance were four further brands and a safe distance away, other operations like Brannigan's, Ha Ha Canteen and Casa set themselves up. A generous sprinkling of established pubs desperately attempted to stand their ground in the surrounding streets. Thirteen of these bars were totally new licences, granted over a relatively short period. Local young drinkers from miles around regarded this crammed circuit as a major new playground, mobbing the bars at weekends. The large office and retail population kept the bars ticking over contentedly the rest of the time. This concentration could perhaps claim to be the most intensive circuit in the country, although some of these brands have subsequently been converted to take a little heat out of the situation.

The disparity in licensing and planning policies between different towns and cities was extreme. To some extent this is justifiable; towns vary enormously in size, facilities, catchment, functions and character and require policies which are appropriate to their specific needs. But, where authorities that administer a similar area adopted conflicting policies, this raises questions over the motives behind those policies. Contrast Ealing with Sutton, a comparable London suburb where the borough council were pleased that the opening of new pubs had brought vibrancy back to the town;

"Once people travelled to the South Coast or the West End. Now they can stay in Sutton to enjoy an evening out."[16]

For local authorities who wished to promote their area, the trend for new developments of shopping and employment to be concentrated out of town was a major concern. Some town centres were in decline as a result; congested and polluted by day, abandoned and threatening by night. Planning policies were adapted to counter this threat. But, in the short term, the factor which achieved the most dramatic results in many centres was the leisure market, and specifically the pub brands. Much of this vibrancy was simply a result of the streets being busy with people.

In towns as diverse as Sutton and Wolverhampton this rejuvenation had significant benefits. The pub operators profited, but so did many other businesses in the town, particularly retailers, hoteliers, taxi firms and public transport. Towns need a balanced range of amenities and many lacked evening entertainment.

Regeneration was a powerful argument in support of new licences but the trend could go too far. The typical branded blitzkrieg in the most popular centres with a consequent rise in drunken behaviour and noise could push even the most liberal magistrate to caution and negativity. In such a case, the biggest losers were likely to be the established pubs in the town, possibly unfavourably located in relation to the new pub circuit. To protect them and act in the best interests of the entire population, a balanced, objective view was necessary. One suspects that in some of the cases described here this was not achieved.

PART FOUR

Market Mayhem

Worlds Apart

"Every day, somewhere in Britain a country pub closes for good."
CAMRA, Good Beer Guide, 2001.

Twenty-five years ago, a pub was a pub. Refurbishments and alterations to introduce theming only ran skin deep. Underneath this veneer, pubs remained uncomplicated affairs. The character and style of the landlord dominated the premises and this tended to attract a similar or, at least compatible, type of customer.

Landlords came in many moulds but four common stereotypes could be recognised. Firstly the old lag, world-weary and cynical, quick and efficient, but sparing with his conversation. Why use a sentence when two words will do? The natural environment for these old hands were backstreet town pubs, usually tenancies, where they would gaze mournfully out from the safety of their bar, as if waiting for the grim reaper from the brewery. Secondly there was the landlady. She had usually been around the block a few times and was hard as nails. She was well able to efficiently combine running the pub and keeping it in order, whilst tarting herself up a little to inject a welcome touch of glamour. Type three was Jack the Lad, who was streetwise and could look after himself, despite his well-developed paunch. He could be found in the big managed houses and estate pubs, where his brash confidence and physical presence enabled him to remain in control of what could be an aggressive environment. Cigarette in one hand and beer glass in the other were almost as obligatory as the short haircut and tattoos. At home, swapping wisecracks with his cronies at the bar and baiting the barmaid and, on his nights off doing much the same at the pub up the road. The fourth were the sharply-dressed entrepreneurs whose natural habitat were rural pubs or the attractive city pub, either owned or a tenancy. They kept one step ahead of the game with their sharp wit and constant vigilance. As exuberant as type three but with a greater repertoire of stories, some even true, these landlords were real charmers when they wished to be, and usually enjoyed a popular following.

Type one landlords always gave the impression that they had no money, type three spent theirs on fast women and slow racehorses whilst type four used up most of theirs on a flashy car, overseas holidays for the essential tan and maintenance payments from their previous marriages. And the landladies? No-one dared ask.

Enough of the caricatures and stereotyping!

Now pub managers are coached as to how they behave in their pub. And in most branded outlets the first rule is that they are no longer intended to be a hearty presence behind the bar or even be known to customers. Their role is more like the manager of a bank, staying behind the scenes and ensuring that everyone else is doing their job and to represent head office at the coal-face. There are customer care manuals and best-practice regulations and dress codes. There is the ten-second rule during which time the bartender, if he has not been able to actually serve the customer entering his premises, will acknowledge his presence with a cheery; 'serve you in a minute sir'. And of course the One Hundred club for the employee who knows one hundred customers and what each one drinks. Such contrived pleasantries arguably raised standards in the trade, but do little to create a genuine pub atmosphere. Landlords of the new wave of branded bars are inevitably becoming as pre-packaged as the sanitised, comfort-cooled atmosphere in which they work.

Exchanging wisecracks or tales with customers is certainly not part of their role. To discourage such idle banter and free the way for paying customers, many new-wave brands have removed bar stools where customers would sit at the bar, getting in the way and distracting staff. Some brewers started to experiment with dual managers who shared the role for half the week each, to reduce their level of control and authority and render it very easy to rotate and replace them.

The changes also embraced more subtle, but significant modification. Old side-handled pint beer mugs were out as these implied grimy old pubs. Instead, modern elegant glasses were used. Serveries resembled cocktail bars with glass and chrome rather than the old traditional wooden back-fittings. Decorations would tend towards more pastel subtle shades. Lighting, that most critical of features in relation to bar design and atmosphere, had to be more discrete and flexible so that it could be adjusted to control mood.

Accommodation on upper floors for manager and staff was increasingly excluded in order to ditch the friendly innkeeper days, and reinforce an impersonal, 'professional' attitude. This also avoided the many issues that arose when a pub manager was fired for a serious offence, but would remain defiantly in the living quarters upstairs until he could be legally removed.

You can still find some proper old charismatic or eccentric pub landlords. But not in the new wave of branded outlets, where the role of the old-fashioned landlord is a thing of the past.

Another huge contrast between the new branded bars and traditional pubs, is how much turnover they can generate. The average turnover for all pubs and bars in April 2001, according to Key Note[1], was almost £300,000 per annum, £6,000 per week. Curiously few licensed outlets traded at this level. This would be an insufficient figure to justify the level of investment and expectation from a branded operation. At this time these generally started at an absolute minimum of £10,000 per week, and normally commanded weekly turnovers more in the bracket of £15,000 to £25,000. This was especially the case for the really large town centre entertainment houses and destination pub-restaurants. Meanwhile, few traditional pubs, certainly if ran as a tenancy or lease, would be taking more than £4,000 or £5,000 per week, and most a lot less.

The contrast between the two distinct groups had become so fundamental that Key Note did not even classify the two groups together any more. In their survey they distinguished between the 49,500 traditional pubs and the rest of the market which it labelled 'new-style bars'. It is hard to disagree. In effect, the market no longer met in the middle. There were two distinct types of licensed outlet to choose from, with their own particular styles and customer groups. And levels of trade which were poles apart. The customer now had to choose between black and white.

In an opinion expressed in February 1994, Mike Bennett, Assistant Editor of the *Morning Advertiser,* wrote philosophically of the changes he was witnessing;

> *"The common thread that runs through the revolution we have all been subjected to this past five to ten years is this – the consumer wants powerful brands backed by a marketing strategy that he or she can understand. And only the well heeled and well provisioned can oblige. If that sounds like might is right then that inevitably and with more than a touch of sadness is the clear signal that the punters out there are giving. Remember TV commercials for Ford cars that ended with the punchline – everything we do is driven by you. If you don't fancy this brave new world then you can always blame the customer… because they're always right."[2]*

This expressed a deep-rooted concern for many within the trade that the increased competition from the growth of branded pubs, and the change in customer attitudes, would see a serious decline in the traditional pub. Consumer attitudes would be so influenced by the glitzy new world available in branded outlets that they would not want to return to old-fashioned pubs. The customer groups who used the branded bars –

generally the young, fashionable and those with plenty of disposable income – would regard those bars as the modern trendy places to go, whilst the traditional pub as we know it would be increasingly seen as an anachronism, the place where your father used to drink.

The comparison was made with retail, where independent shops had all but disappeared in most town centres to be replaced by corporate-owned multiples. We have all become conditioned over many years of habit, convenience and advertising to think in terms of multiple shops and not see beyond them unless our requirements are rather specialised. Could the traditional pub go the way of the corner shop and die out in huge numbers, to be used now and again for local convenience and as an occasional curiosity? The retailing revolution has led to easy brand recognition, standardised goods and prices, and every high street losing much of its individuality and character. Advertising budgets for high street retail chains can be enormous and have influenced consumer spending and fashions profoundly. Were we about to see the same story with pubs?

Look at the quote from Terry Oates, Secretary of the Local Licensees Federation in January 1994, when Tetley's (the northern arm of Allied Breweries) proposed a 697-person capacity pub in Hallgate, Doncaster;

> *"I have termed this development a 'superpub' – the trade's equivalent of the supermarket. And if it gets the go-ahead then it will have the same effect on our trade as supermarkets did on corner shops. Huge pubs like this could see the end of friendly locals. Many of our members are struggling."*[3]

Meanwhile Peter Jarvis, Chief Executive of Whitbread, seemed delighted in claiming that some of his newest pubs were;

> *"More like Disney World than a boozer."*[4]

The impact of a new superpub could be as devastating as a retail superstore's kiss of death on nearby corner shops. A new Wetherspoons often carries a large threat to marginal pubs because their new outlets are being developed in smaller towns, and in suburbs of larger towns, often the heartland of surviving traditional pubs. A small wave of pub closures can be the consequence of a new Wetherspoons or other 'superpub' hitting town.

In addition to these challenges, the vulnerable pub started to get tossed on the stormy seas of recession. This arrived at the end of the 1980s boom and continued during the early 1990s to further undermine pubs already battling for survival. Another threat came from rising residential values. These had now largely caught up with pub values across much of the country, which rendered struggling pubs vulnerable to the temptation, particularly for freehouse owners, to sell, get their money back and walk away from their problems. With the impact of inner city regeneration, it wasn't just attractive country pubs which were being picked off in this way as large backstreet pubs became attractive to developers for conversion to apartments.

During these difficult years the situation seemed bleak for many individual pub licensees. Pubs were closing at an unprecedented rate, whilst many more struggled. An interview with Pubmaster MD, John Brackenbury in September 1993, demonstrated this pessimism. Pubmaster were in a position to know as they had operated 2,000 'bottom-end' pubs which were described as having received no 'tender loving care' from their former owners, the brewers for many years. Despite Pubmaster's best efforts, which included smart new external signage, many of these pubs remained marginal. Brackenbury estimated that;

"10-20% of the nation's stock of pubs could go to the wall."[5]

The theme of survival featured in *The Times* in April 1994 which commented about pub landlords,

"They know all about beer. They want to know about how to survive." [6]

The newspaper went on to speculate that 10,000 pubs were expected to close down. In January 1993 CAMRA spokesman Roger Protz, considering the effects of the MMC, said:

> *"We are facing a scenario in which 10,000 pubs could close. The situation is absolutely appalling. It is no longer a living for many because the costs are so high. Masses of tenants have gone out of business and there is little sign of any relief."*

Just to round off the pessimism, a NatWest Securities Report issued in September 1993,[7] after 7 months of research, suggested bleakly that the brewers had survived well despite centuries of complacent management, that there were 15,000 too many pubs; that 10-15% of Regional brewery pubs were marginal (and investment would only delay their eventual demise), that one major brewer was likely to drop out of the market, and that some of the Regional brewers were heading for tough times.

The condition and appearance of some tenanted pubCo houses was undermining their performance. Many of the big brewers had deferred repairs on their estates to an irresponsible degree[8] whilst the uncertainty created by the constant market churn did not help in delivering much needed maintenance and tlc. Pub signage was a particularly neglected element. Many pub signs were untidy at best and the worst were suggestive of advanced dilapidation. Not the best way to appeal to passing trade. In contrast to the carefully manicured and landscaped branded pubs being developed, some tenancies looked very neglected. When customers were also thin on the ground, these pubs were running sadly low on charm and warmth – the very qualities that they needed to maintain and build their trade.

Free houses were generally in better order but also found the going tough during the Nineties. This sector had previously prospered, partly due to the mediocrity of the large brewers' own pubs. Individually owned independents had frequently led the way in town centre entertainment and in providing good quality drive-to dining pubs. By the Nineties, the brewers had taken note of the free trade's achievements in this regard and adapted their own brands accordingly. What they also had was the impact of huge investment and superior sites. The free trade struggled to compete with the new, often breathtaking premises which the brewers were developing in prime trading locations.

The free house sector had grown, with a considerable number of ex-brewery pubs having been sold during the turmoil following MMC. Some of the purchasers were people who had retired or resigned from other industries to realise their dream of running a country pub. This 'roses-around-the-door' fantasy would rapidly give way to the tough reality of the trade. Free house owners who invested heavily with their own improvements, to try to recover lost customer spending, added this cost to the existing burden of their mortgage. But the impact of the brands was inevitably drawing customers away creating large holes in free trade owners' business plans and pockets.

Licensees, running their own business, were exhibiting signs of developing a siege mentality. They were being battered from all directions; bureaucracy and new regulations from government; increasing rents and wholesale beer prices; competition from the branded superpubs; a more demanding and less loyal customer base. Despite the pressures, the landlord was expected to be the kingpin of all around them. An employer, beer expert, bookkeeper, licensing expert, caterer, chief bouncer, handyman and gardener, but most of all a sympathetic ear, a figure of respect and chief entertainer. It is hardly surprising that some licensees fail to meet this exacting standard.

Optimism continued to be drawn from the attitude of the smaller, local brewers, most of whom have remained loyal to their tenancies. As John Adnams, Chairman of the small but much admired local brewer in Southwold, Suffolk, said in the early Nineties;

"In this part of the world the village pub provides a focal point for activity that nothing else can. It's a place to meet people and discuss things in a way that would cease to happen if the pub were to go. A village that loses its pub starts to die."[9]

Strategy For Survival

"There is a pub in north-west London... The public bar was a favourite gathering place for pensioners in the area who used to enjoy a couple of drinks and a natter or a game of cribbage or dominoes. In the middle of 1972 the elderly tenant and his wife retired and the pub was immediately closed for extensive alterations...

When it reopened three months later the public bar had been knocked through into the saloon and the whole area covered with wall-to-wall carpeting. The tenant had been replaced by a manager who no longer kept dominoes or a cribbage board – nor even darts, for this board too had been removed. The beer pumps had vanished to make way for a set of keg dispensers and all the prices were several pence up on those charged before the closure.

During the first lunchtime session after the pub reopened the pensioners arrived one by one to renew their old habits. They were told immediately that their custom was no longer wanted, that the pub was aiming for a different trade... Those who can travel to other pubs in the area; those who can't stay at home."

Chris Hutt, *The Death of the English Pub*, 1973.[10]

As you can see, the 'modernisation' of our pubs has been going on for some time now. The process intensified during the Seventies and Eighties, as we witnessed the various stages of theming. During the Nineties, whilst branding was the main focus, the brewers were still, in most cases, addressing their existing estates, and for those pubs which they intended to retain, looking for opportunities to refurbish in a search for additional profit.

The Drewe Arms in the tiny village of Drewesteignton on the northern edge of Dartmoor in Devon became a *cause celebre* in 1994. The Drewe Arms was an institution, run by tenant Mabel Mudge for seventy-five years until her retirement in October of that year. The landlady, known affectionately as Auntie Mabel, presided over a pub which opened in 1646 and was little changed in a hundred years with no bar but a tap-room with beer drawn straight from the barrel. It was not just the internal character of the Drewe Arms which made it so worthy of preservation, but the manner in which it was run; on occasions customers served themselves in a bar whose layout insisted on intimacy.

As Auntie Mabel sadly retired at the age of ninety-nine, enter the big bad brewer, namely Whitbread, who owned the freehold and announced plans to refurbish and run the place themselves. There followed a major outcry from residents and drinkers, orchestrated by the local *Western Morning News* and local TV, the ferocity of which must have shocked even Whitbread. Nevertheless in August 1995 Whitbread regained possession from the villagers who had been allowed to run the place temporarily. As a result of the protests, the refurbishment that followed was reasonably sympathetic and the old photos and plaques on display provide a fitting testimony to Auntie Mabel. But inevitably, a little of that unique flavour, the attentively cared for, lived-in feeling of the Drewe Arms, had been lost.[11]

In the countryside, low barrelage pubs had been closing throughout the last century. The process had become as ingrained as the grubbing out of hedges. For many years there was minimal interest or concern shown by the authorities. Slowly recognition spread that villages were being denuded of services and that the loss of schools, shops and transport could cause the departure of local families. This was often followed by an influx of second-homers and wealthy commuters. Very soon a village could cease to be a living community. Eventually, pubs came to be regarded as one of the essential facilities to prevent such a decline.

Despite this, assistance or protection for threatened pubs was limited. Initially some guidance was provided under planning law that local authorities should normally resist the change of use of pubs where the facility was considered essential to the community. It became common practice for local authorities to refuse planning permission for the conversion of a pub to unlicensed use if it were the last or only pub in the village. Unfortunately the owner of the pub, if refused planning, might resort to boarding up the building and waiting in the knowledge that they couldn't be forced to reopen. Eventually the prospect of the ex-pub becoming an eyesore could force the planners to relent. The measure was therefore only of limited value.

Villagers at Hinchley Wood, near Esher, Surrey, famously tried a different method in 1999 when The Hinchley Wood pub was closed and handed over to McDonald's for conversion to one of their ubiquitous restaurants. They called in the 'e-team' of eco warriors who moved on to the car park and blocked its entrance. After an eighteen-month occupation and planning battle the villagers could claim a victory when McDonald's withdrew, having failed to secure planning consent due to a technical detail. Unfortunately it was a pyrrhic victory as the boarded-up pub was immediately sold for housing development.

As a result of the branding process our national politicians had become concerned at the widespread practice of pub renaming. In 1996 Sir Nicholas Winterton, aroused by the change of name of his local pub, noticed the trend of pub names being changed. He noted that the original name often reflected a local character, event or place, or an historical event when the pub came into being. Sir Nicholas suggested that the change of name should require planning permission. His campaign was followed up three years later by a private members' bill introduced by Ann Winterton, also a Tory MP. These moves may have been motivated by the best intentions but to consider protecting the name of a pub in isolation seemed very naive. The private members' bill, despite cross-party support, failed to become law.

Culture Secretary Chris Smith resisted calls for legislation in the aftermath of this, despite figures which showed that an average of eleven pubs a month had been renamed over the previous five years. Smith called on pub owners to consult before dumping traditional names, saying;

> *"It does appear to me that there is a growing fashion for rebranding pubs with names like the Dog'n'Donut or the Goose and Granite which, I have to say, would appear to have little relevance to the history of any area. We are surely in danger here of losing an important part of local history. While it is up to the owners of a business to choose the name they give it, I hope breweries will bear in mind the unique historic role many of our public houses have and think twice before destroying that link with the past. Consulting with the pub's regulars and the wider local community before renaming it would not seem too much too ask."*[12]

Unfortunately, it was too much to ask for most of the brewers and pub groups, hell bent on rolling out their themes and brands faster than the opposition. But of equal significance was the blinkered behaviour of our politicians in becoming so distracted by one superficial symptom of the malaise without showing any inclination to address the overall health of the ailing patient.

In 2001 John Longden came up with a practical way to assist struggling pubs, and with inspirational encouragement from his Royal Highness, the Prince of Wales, The Pub is the Hub was founded. Within ten years Pub is the Hub could claim 360 successful projects, including forty-two rural pubs, scattered all over the country which are now community owned. There is even a microbrewery at The Farriers Arms, Mersham in Kent which was purchased from Punch in 2011.

Pub is the Hub, in addition to endeavouring to facilitate public funding for projects, provides advice and assistance in two main areas.

Firstly, in advising how a rural pub may incorporate complementary services to run alongside the pub, to assist in its own viability whilst extending the facilities available to the community. The type of activities encompassed is constantly increasing and ranges from the obvious shop or post office to the provision of health and fitness facilities and meals on wheels. Most of these projects are relatively simple to set up, and nearly all have had an ongoing, positive influence on the perception of the pub whilst also benefiting the local community.

The second area, generally relevant when a pub has closed or is in danger of doing so, is advising on community purchase. This area is much more complicated and fraught with issues. John Longden, still running the organisation, and fresh from receiving the OBE in the 2014 New Years Honours (for his voluntary services to rural communities in the UK), kindly made the time from his hectic schedule to discuss with me the problems involved.

Whilst many communities are tempted to save their pub, few realise the hard work and the difficulties involved. Firstly the community, understandably, all wish to be involved in the project but experience shows that success is far more likely if the pub is run professionally, independent of the community owners. Secondly the pub must be viable to survive but to satisfy its community role it must not appear to be blatantly commercial (a potential minefield when setting prices or charging community owners when they have contributed work voluntarily). Finally such pubs work better when operated by an independent local person but there is a real challenge in ensuring that a community-appointed manager is fully up to date with industry best practice, licensing and other legislation.

John cited examples that had worked well and others where insuperable problems had arisen. He mentioned that 50% of community ownership pubs failed after three years, obviously a major concern. As a result he was keen to make potential community purchasers consider what happens if the project does fail. He mentioned that Punch Taverns were very constructive in relation to projects and would often permit the community to run a pub for a six-month experimental period, which must provide invaluable experience.

I visited the Harrow in Little Bedwyn, a delightful spot nestling alongside the Kennet and Avon canal in Wiltshire. This was the subject of one of the early attempts at community ownership, back in 1990. The villagers, lacking the type of advice and support which they would receive now, and concerned at the imminent closure of The Harrow, stepped in to purchase. With a village population of only 200, eighty-five of them became shareholders in the holding company. They appointed a committee of five to make decisions, whilst the pub was actually run day-to-day by full-time paid employees, like any other managed operation.

But after seven years the initial optimism had dwindled away as a series of managers had tried but failed to maintain trade at viable levels, whilst issues had arisen over the role of the committee and their interference in the running of the pub. The property ended up closing down and being put on the market as the villagers' brave venture turned to tears. Two years later, the current owners stepped in and purchased, to operate as a restaurant. They recognised the potential of the Harrow and are still running the business fifteen years later. Initially they created a small area near the bar for locals to be able to get a drink, but this didn't work well and so for many years the Harrow has operated purely as an attractive country restaurant.

Two key failings are evident from this account. Firstly the pub would appear not to have been viable from the outset. For any community that wishes to explore buying their local pub it is essential that they fully investigate and understand all of the commercial aspects of owning and running the premises. This information must be turned into a professional and detailed business plan with projected cash flows to determine whether the operation will be viable. If so, and funding and the legal structure can be achieved and the pub purchased, it must then be run in accordance with the plan, and not with community interference in an enthusiastic, spontaneous but ultimately amateur manner. Which brings us to the second failing. There were clearly issues caused by interference with the pub operation by the committee. These might create a host of problems for a community purchase, and possibly even for the harmony of a village in the future.

Pub is the Hub is not the only organisation to offer assistance in relation to struggling pubs. The Plunkett Foundation was set up by Horace Plunkett, an Irish-born Victorian benefactor. The foundation aims to assist rural communities in the UK. With recognition of the importance of pubs to rural community life, and the high incidence of pub closure in such communities, the foundation has, more recently, adopted pubs as one of its dedicated areas. So far fifteen pubs have been 'rescued' by the foundation and restored to their communities.

A fundamental part of the approach of the foundation is that investors in the pub each receive the same status and voting rights irrespective of the size of their investment. This avoids the situation where one or two wealthy locals purchase a high proportion of the shares in a community pub and then dominate in taking decisions, effectively almost becoming the new owners. With equal voting rights a more democratic arrangement will prevail, which is also likely to encourage community involvement in and use of the pub. Unfortunately this may exacerbate the problem areas involved with community pub ownership.

I spoke with John Longden about an alternative approach, that of part-time trading, and queried whether this had been attempted. The idea behind this is that where it is accepted that a pub is not viable as a full-time proposition, it continues to operate part-time. Logically its trading hours would be at peak times during weekends and perhaps one evening midweek. The owner(s) could combine such hours with their normal occupation, and treat what the pub brings in as a second income, whilst regarding the remainder of the pub building as a pleasant home. John was not aware of any current examples of pubs which operated on this basis but accepted that it might be worth exploring in villages which would otherwise totally lose their pub. What would be required is a sympathetic and flexible approach from the authorities in relation to matters such as rating, licensing and planning. It would also be essential to ensure that this wasn't used as a way to achieve change of use through the back door.

In a very different sphere, a reaction to oppose the march of the brands emerged in the centre of Manchester, where around 300 companies formed the Independents during the late Nineties. These comprised independent retailers, bar operators and restaurateurs who wanted to preserve the individuality of Manchester in the face of the advance of the uniformity of the brands. Independent bar owner Nick Johnson, one of the organisers, claimed the group had the support of Manchester City Council and called for other cities to follow the independents' lead in order that a network could be created across the country. In the summer of 2000 he said;

"Our view is, if cities are going to be successful in the future, then we need to celebrate their individuality. Branding is making city centres very boring and bland."[13]

Some financial assistance arrived for small rural pubs in April 2005 when small business rates relief was introduced. Another means of official protection for local pubs emerged in 2011 in the form of the Planning Register of Assets of Community Value. This was created under the coalition government's 2011 Localism Act. The Conservatives' localism agenda sponsored a radical approach to planning, which encourages community participation. One aspect of this is that properties which are felt, by twenty-one or more local people, to have an important community function, are added to the register. And what could be more important to a local community than the pub? If the property is subsequently put on the market its registration means that the sale is suspended for six months to allow a community group the time to prepare a business plan and negotiate to purchase. CAMRA has issued a guide to its members to assist in the process.

Despite this, government has received considerable criticism that it is not doing more for struggling pubs. A particular grievance relates to the use classes within the planning acts[14] which permit pubs to convert to retail, restaurant, or bank and building society use without the need for planning approval. Local CAMRA branches and other local groups have become well versed in the art of lobbying and protesting to their local authority to object to changes of use of pubs to avoid their loss during the course of a planning application. But in the circumstances when an owner can immediately switch its use, without the need for permission, the pub is already lost, with the community having no opportunity to put their case for its retention. This danger has been illustrated repeatedly, with Tesco and their rivals having converted hundreds of pubs.[15]

A change in the law in this respect, simply to take pubs out of the use class system and classify them independently (as *sui generis*) would be very simple to achieve and would be instantly effective. The onus would then be on the campaigners to demonstrate that the pub can be viable.

The message underlying much of this account is that government regulations, or very worthy schemes like Pub is the Hub, can go some way to assist in saving pubs when they are in trouble. Community ownership of pubs is a wonderful concept. But it is not an instant fix and can create its own problems. To some degree it remains a work in progress until the model can provide an effective structure more consistently.

There is nothing in the gift of politicians or anyone else which can make an uneconomic pub viable. Pubs do not work as a museum piece. They need to attract a regular flow of customers to maintain their authenticity and ambience as a pub, and without this any amount of government or voluntary support is meaningless. The number of pubs which have been victims should make us all understand this. And as individuals we should also appreciate the most critical element in keeping a pub alive; if we the public do not use it, our local pub will die.

CAMRA

Consumer action to protect the traditional pub is largely the affair of CAMRA. The Campaign for Real Ale has entered the national consciousness, such has been their influence. Formed in 1971, CAMRA were recognised as a consumer body by the MMC, and at the time of the inquiry had their own hearing. Their proposals may have had some effect as they spoke out against free trade loans and demanded guest beers. They also sensibly spoke of the need to protect the tied-house system to protect the traditional pub. However, the effect of some of their more radical proposals, like banning any future takeovers in the industry and banning all national advertising of alcohol, were ignored and may have had unfortunate consequences.

CAMRA clearly feel that their 'guardianship' of our beers extends to the places in which those beers are consumed. Over the years CAMRA have frequently passed judgement on tasteless refurbishments or pub developments carried out by the brewers. They have rarely failed to condemn such 'outrages' in strong language. For example in 1996 whilst praising Wetherspoons for their sympathetic conversion of Bristol's Commercial Rooms, an old gentleman's club at a cost of £1.3m, they commented;

"In the 1990s pubs are gutted, shorn of an identity that has been built up over decades, if not centuries, just to conform to a blinkered view which uses next month's sales as its fundamental yardstick. During 1996 the

most cherished concept was the 'Genuine Irish Craic House', a Hibernian Brigadoon where plastic shamrocks and chilled nitrofizz help to create an atmosphere for cardboard Celts. The very elements that attract customers back to a pub – a warm welcome, a comfortable interior that has evolved with time – are sacrificed."[16]

CAMRA long ago recognised the threat to the small country pub. Their then-national spokesman Mike Benner, talking on the subject in the early Nineties spoke of the threat to small free houses or old-style tenancies, that the breweries were unwilling to put money into. He mentioned the concern within villages at the prospect of losing their pub, which was often their only meeting place, and how such a loss undermined the community.

The future of pubs is a constant theme in their annual *Good Beer Guide*. The 1997 edition focused on the need for protection for pubs to preserve their interiors. It suggested that unspoilt bars were being gutted and refitted, suffering the equivalent of ethnic cleansing. Disappointingly, CAMRA research from 1991 hoping to find 500 interiors worthy of preservation yielded under 200. These were mainly in three categories; plain rural beer houses – 'time-warp' establishments which survived modernisation because of their very isolation and limited commercial potential; gin palaces (mainly in larger cities) – veritable cathedrals amongst historic pubs – and suburban road-houses – surviving 20s and 30s interiors which epitomise their eras. CAMRA demanded that if these were not protected as a listed building under the planning acts that these establishments were given some other form of protection.

CAMRA condemned the marketing power of the brewers but they now possess more than a little of their own. They proudly claim to have been influential in saving the British guest beer law from the interference of the European Parliament; 'showing that CAMRA is a powerful, effective and credible champion of the British beer drinker'. One of many highly professional leaflets which they have produced is 'Support your local pub'. This states;

'The British pub is a cornerstone of our way of life, more popular than restaurants, clubs, cinemas or other entertainment. Whether you drink real ale or not, people care about their pubs.'

CAMRA membership has increased rapidly as the organisation has achieved a higher profile, and as real ale becomes more popular, and beer festivals more frequent and better attended. The impressive figure of 100,000 was achieved in 2009 and, in the short period since, has grown to 156,000.

CAMRA's campaigning has become more thorough and sophisticated over the years and, with the growing membership and its increasing experience, very influential. Understandably, the pub has, given its vulnerable state, become CAMRA's prime concern, seeming to occupy far more of its political attention than matters relating directly to beer. Its website contains many pages advising its members how they can campaign to help the pub.

CAMRA can claim many achievements over the years, none greater than its initial triumph of demanding cask-conditioned beer from the brewers. As a result of this clash and the big brewers' behaviour they remained CAMRA's natural enemy. This rivalry was fundamental to much of what the organisation said and did, to the degree that taking on the brewers almost become the *raison d'etre* of the organisation, an institutionalised and permanent Punch and Judy show for the pub trade. Just occasionally CAMRA's view of the brewers would mellow when their brewing heritage or production of an approved real ale came to the fore or as a result of a sympathetic pub restoration.

As the big six withdrew from the industry with indecent haste, in the aftermath of MMC, they were replaced by the pubCos. CAMRA's attitude to and hatred of this new enemy appears to be unbridled. Not only did the pubCos have no history, but they were created as a financial speculation. It was very easy for CAMRA to portray the pubCos as the cartoon villain, ugly corporate goliaths bullying their way to huge and undeserved profit at their tenants' expense.

CAMRA, with their incessant criticism of the brewers and their submission to the MMC Enquiry, will have contributed in some degree to the break-up of the beerage, and the rise of the pubCos to fill the void. This could serve as a lesson to CAMRA to beware what they campaign and wish for because they may end up getting it!

The maintenance by CAMRA of a virtual 'war footing' as they battle against the evils perpetrated by the brewers or the pubCos is perhaps a happy convenience; the ever-present menace of a demonised opponent to provide a constant call to arms for those who wish to banish the enemies of the venerated real ale. Real ale can indeed be almost a religion to those with a passion for it. The perpetual need to analyse the brewing process and compare ingredients and flavours. The continual tub-thumping by CAMRA has whipped up a very strong belief in the cause amongst many card-carrying members of the organisation. This has enabled them to continue their campaigning with as much fervour and enthusiasm now, forty years on as they had when they set out, which is quite an achievement.

Unfortunately the lack of objectivity that this campaigning sometimes entails can reduce the credibility of their message. To the outsider, CAMRA and its members can seem a little one-dimensional, not because of their commitment to beer but because of the narrow perspective that they often hold on the subject.

CAMRA have elevated beer, and by association pubs, from being a fringe subculture to the mainstream. This has been achieved not just at headquarters in St Albans but through the extensive and dedicated structure and membership of their regional and branch organisations all around the country. The continued activities and promotion of real ale has fostered what is now an intrinsic British appreciation of the importance of cask beer to our culture. It is easy to take this for granted now, but back in the dark days of the Seventies, such a suggestion would have been ridiculed. The existence of such an environment is now an essential element in the survival of the pub.

PART FIVE
Ripples From The Revolution

Brewers Droop;
The Non-Brewing Brewers

The rise of the pubCos was matched by a trend of equal significance. Brewers no longer felt like brewing. For the brewers to contemplate such a move should have been alien to all of their instincts and traditions. But, in order to overcome the grave economic realities assailing their breweries, many brewers were indeed considering whether it was time to cut the umbilical cord and stand on their own feet as pure retailers.

Grand Met were the most publicised example, handing over their breweries to Courage with never a backward glance, having made far-reaching decisions on its pub estate in the form of Inntrepreneur. But they were not the first brewer to abandon their heritage. That dubious distinction in the post-war period belonged to Beards, a small Sussex company, based in Herstmonceux, which opted out of production way back in 1959. Its beer requirements for its forty-six-pub traditional estate was supplied by local brewer Harveys, and then Arundel Brewery. Having operated in this manner for nearly forty years, independence was ended in 1998 with the sale of its surviving forty-three pubs to Greene King. It hardly seemed to be the prelude to the decline of a major industry either when Heavitree of Exeter closed its brewery in 1970 to concentrate on running its pubs, or four years later when Grays of Essex, a similar-sized company which had run its Springfield Brewery in Chelmsford since 1828, did the same, procuring its supplies from Greene King.

A little earlier, in 1969, when faced with a hostile takeover bid from Allied Breweries, Boddingtons had mounted a firm defence of the company's independence. Charles Boddington, the aging chairman of the company and grandson of the man who established Boddingtons as a force in Victorian brewing, spoke earnestly to his shareholders;

> *"You will be only too aware that present-day pressures bear heavily towards the elimination of individuality and character in many consumer goods. There is an inexorable progression towards the mass-produced nationwide product of standardised quality. You, however, are still, at this moment in time, a shareholder in one of the remaining independent brewery companies whose traditional draught beers have a reputation for quality and individual character beyond the immediate area of the north of England in which we operate... The takeover of Boddingtons and its consequent elimination can achieve very little. It will do nothing for the national economy, add nothing to the nations exports, and contribute nothing at all to the quality of life that we are all used to enjoy."*[1]

Boddingtons duly survived. This was the first time that a regional brewer had seen off one of the nationals, although its survival probably owed more to Whitbread's intervention, raising its shareholding stake in the company from 13 to 22% than Charles Boddington's impassioned speech. The chairman of Whitbread at the time, Colonel Whitbread, is reputed to have said;

> *"You are a very old firm. You have a very good name. You mustn't go out."* [2, 3]

Throughout the Seventies and Eighties Boddingtons dedicated themselves to avoiding any repeat of this. They strongly promoted their prize-winning Boddingtons bitter, achieving national distribution. To increase their stature, and make themselves more difficult to pick off by predators, they purchased both Oldham Brewery and Higsons, the

Liverpool brewer, increasing their tied estate to over 500 pubs. But, despite this, and some serious rationalisation including the closure of the Oldham brewery, they didn't achieve the national sales which they were able to secure in their Lancashire homeland. As a result their revamped Strangeways brewery continued to run at well below capacity.

And so sadly, in 1989, Charles' son Ewart waved the white flag and sold the brewing business to the former white knight Whitbread in a negotiated deal. Whitbread were interested in acquiring the eponymous beer brand because of their lack of a flagship bitter brand, whilst the Boddington board appeared to have concluded that they could take the brand no further. Symbolically Charles Boddington had died seven years earlier. At least he was saved the ignominy of ceasing to brew, or worse still in 1995 when Boddington gave up completely and sold its pubs to Greenalls.

In previous decades, Greenall's had stormed through the Midlands, buying brewers for their pubs and closing down breweries to the severe indignation of the conservation and real ale lobby.[4] In 1991 and under no particular financial pressure at the time Greenall's closed its Warrington plant.

At that stage Greenall's were a dark horse in the industry, rapidly growing, and the most powerful of the Regionals. The controversial and surprising decision appears to have been carefully considered and was seemingly based on the economics of beer production, a focus on brands and a desire, with expansion in mind, not to be caught by the Beer Orders. Their two major purchases afterwards, Devenish in 1993 and Boddingtons in 1995, had both already sold or closed their breweries, perhaps making them ideal bedfellows for Greenall's.

Initially the move away from brewing earned the approval of their shareholders, but by 1997 the company had issued a profits warning; its share price had fallen from 600 pence to little more than half this in under a year and takeover speculation was growing. Lord Daresbury, formerly Peter Greenall and Chief Executive of the Group, admitted that the company had 'taken its eye off the ball' after buying Boddingtons pubs by not investing sufficiently in its brands to counter the activity of its rivals.

There followed a frenetic period of brand-building as the company committed to opening fifty new licences per annum for its range of brands, including Square and Henrys Café Bar in town and the destination restaurants Quinceys, Millers Kitchen and Henrys Table. It transferred large numbers of its weaker managed houses to its leasehold estate and sold off many lower-end tenancies. Greenall's endeavour to convince the markets that it had turned things around extended to heavy investment in its three strong hotel brands, namely De Vere, Premier Lodge and Village Inns.[5] It was also busy developing Greens, the standalone health and fitness operation. One would have expected their financial performance to materially improve, but the share price continued to decline and, only two years later, in 1999 having already sold their tenanted pubs to Nomura S&N came knocking to end Greenalls' long association with the licensed trade.

Yet another example of brewers abandoning their ancestry came from the diminutive Eldridge Pope which announced in April 1997 that it was selling its Dorchester brewery, established 160 years earlier in order that it could focus on retailing. The brewery did not immediately close and remained operational as Thomas Hardy brewery. But this was only a stay of execution as it struggled to achieve sufficient sales and closed in 2003. The outrageous decision by Eldridge Pope to stock national brands in its pubs rather than its own beer clearly did not assist in Thomas Hardy's survival battle, or impress many of Eldridge Pope's tenants. Meanwhile, the company's feverish activity included expanding to 200 pubs, over half of which were eventually managed, whilst huge effort and investment was devoted to its brands. But having tried to emulate its bigger competitors, losses grew in the tough trading conditions, and in 2004 Michael Cannon stepped in to take control. After under three years in his hands Eldridge Pope went the same way as Greenall's when, in 2007, the aggressive Marstons (W&D) gobbled it up.

It appeared to brewers, large and small, that they could achieve better returns by running pubs than brewing beer. Throughout the industry, brewing profits were yielding a falling proportion of profits. Constantly reducing national beer consumption ensured that, as fast as breweries closed, capacity always remained well above demand. The breweries could all have ramped up production substantially if there was anyone to buy it. The laws of supply and demand determined that this was therefore a buyers' market. The substantial discounts which the large pubCos could negotiate showed the disparity in negotiating position which existed.

As a result brewing for third party contracts as opposed to one's own tied estate was yielding minimal profit. And as the large brewers quit brewing there were no longer big tied brewers estates. Therefore, nearly all beer production was for third-party contracts and therefore for thin margins. Brewing profits were further eroded by the rising proportion of take-home sales which were low margin, and the need in such a competitive market to spend substantial sums on marketing and promotion.

The MMC had disturbed the equilibrium of an industry where the brewers' huge tied estates had acted as a reservoir of demand to soak up sufficient orders from its brewer and guarantee production into the future at a viable price.

As a result, after less than ten years' involvement in the UK brewing market, Elders were happy to sell Courage to S&N in 1995 and beat a rapid retreat back to Australia. Their main concern was that the Inntrepreneur supply agreements were coming to an end, and with the loss of this substantial captive market, the Courage market share was in danger of dipping drastically. Without its own estate, and with an average product portfolio, Courage would have been unlikely to survive.

But why did S&N, who already had a 12% share of the UK market, spend £425 million to buy surplus brewing capacity? The purchase made S&N, or Scottish Courage as the brewery arm was labelled, the largest brewer in the country with a 30% market share. Given the oversupply situation which had long prevailed, the fewer players involved in the market, the more control they would have over levels of production and pricing. Rationalisation became a fact of life, with further changes inevitable. The purchase ensured that S&N would have a large say in those changes.

The new order amongst the brewers was acknowledged in 1994 when the long established and somewhat exclusive Brewers Society became the Brewers and Licensed Retailers Association. Because brewers were abandoning their roots and thus invalidating their membership, a desire amongst the giants of the trade to stick together meant that changes had to be made. Qualification for membership to the new body, in order to maintain some exclusivity, became either a minimum volume of brewing sufficient to exclude the microbrewery minnows, or ownership of at least 100 pubs.

In the early months of 1997, all eyes were again directed towards the Monopolies and Mergers Commission to discover their reaction to the sale of Allied Domecq's 50% share of Carlsberg-Tetley to Bass for £200 million. Allied had been floundering for some time, with the quality of its beer brands and pub estate rarely reflected in its performance. Its problems, and apparent lack of a clear strategy, were deep-rooted. Back in 1978 Allied Breweries had purchased J Lyons, the catering company which manufactured a wide range of products and ran the famous corner-houses. Allied showed its commitment to this new subsidiary by renaming the whole company Allied Lyons in 1981. But many of the Lyons products and activities were in decline, Allied was rarely able to integrate the new company and Lyons became increasingly marginalised.

In the Eighties, Allied had some successes with its pub developments, and fully committed itself to branding in the Nineties, but was relatively ineffective. The company seemed far more enthusiastic about expanding its wines and spirits division, and this was reflected in the sale of a 50% share in its brewing interests to Carlsberg in 1993. The joint venture was not a success, and given Allied's apparent discomfort with its situation, the sale of its share was not unexpected.

Imprudently, the transaction was not conditional upon approval from the competition authorities. Bass, as well as wishing to recover top spot from S&N by achieving a massive 35% market share, seemed to harbour similar long-term ambitions to S&N. But given the effort which had gone into the MMC inquiry, official approval would have been illogical, to sanction a brewing monopoly far more concentrated than the situation which existed at the end of the Eighties.

The four-strong MMC panel decided that the merger would be against the public interest. Despite this, and no doubt pressurised by the threats of inevitable redundancies if the purchase wasn't sanctioned, they recommended to allow it, provided Bass sold 1,900 pubs, almost half of its estate at the time. Margaret Beckett, Trade Secretary in the new Labour government, had a different view and in June 1997 totally blocked the deal entirely, even with the pub sale, ruling that it would be anti-competitive. She took the unusual step of justifying her ruling, basing this on the significant concentration of brewing which this would create.

Unfortunately, the then-independent Carlsberg-Tetley was very exposed. In anticipation of a merger with Bass, investment had stopped and brewery closures and some redundancies were inevitable. Worst of all, there would be no tied estate to underpin sales once the supply agreements to the Allied estate expired at the end of that year.

There remained the unfortunate business of reversing the deal, by which the 50% Bass share of Carlsberg-Tetley returned to the Danish parent company, Carlsberg. Bass and Allied had to accept the cost of unravelling the process. This left market share between the big brewers at 78%, a similar level to the 1989 MMC report figure, but now concentrated in the hands of only four companies. Individual shares of this were; Scottish & Newcastle 30%, Bass 24%, Whitbread 14%, Carlsberg-Tetley 10%. In addition to the bloody nose given to Carlsberg the judgement must have caused headaches elsewhere. On the MMCs own figures, the wholesale price of beer had fallen by 8% in real terms over the previous 4 years. Over the same period retail prices had risen by 10%. And so the beer market continued its slow and painful contraction.

The real damage to Bass was not the £30 million or so in reversing out of the deal but in losing the ability to rationalise. A formal statement was issued that the company would continue to look to reduce the cost base at its eight UK breweries, and to build high-margin drink brands such as Caffreys and Carling. This lacked conviction and, after almost three more years of continuing profit erosion, a sale by Bass of its entire brewing interests was announced to the Belgian brewer Interbrew. But typically, Bass had been beaten to the post by Whitbread, who in May 2000 had sold out their brewing arm, also to Interbrew. The order of sale proved to be critical, because if the parties felt that the combining of brewing power overseas was a way around the UK competition laws they were in for a nasty surprise. The matter was referred to the renamed 'Competition Commission' after advice from the Office of Fair Trading.

Reaction to the two disposals to Interbrew, and realisation that the bulk of Britain's most popular beers were to be produced under the control of foreign companies, was scathing. Peter Haydon, General Secretary of The Society of Independent Brewers, felt the erosion of British ownership regrettable;

> "It is clear that Bass are more interested in running hotels in Indonesia than they are brewing in Burton or anywhere else in Britain. They clearly have lost any respect for the brands they once championed. They have no emotional attachment any more to beers like draught Bass, which used to be one of the best in Britain and had the first registered symbol… We've got a beer culture that is envied by educated people in other countries. It is just sad that we as a nation are not particularly aware of it. The brewers are to an extent to blame for this. The national brands that are being promoted are undistinguished and undistinguishable. The result is mass market, characterless products."[6]

The brewery disposals were also a bitter pill for CAMRA to swallow. They were equally disparaging of the attitude and performance of Bass and Whitbread but viewed the involvement of Interbrew with some hope as they maintained a variety of beer brands.

Interbrew seemed confident that the £2.3 billion Bass deal would be approved and promised full co-operation. The deal was not conditional on official approval. Why Interbrew should have been so complacent after the Carlsberg decision only three years before is surprising. New Trade and Industry Secretary Stephen Byers used much the same comments as his predecessor in ordering Interbrew to sell Bass at the start of 2001. The decision caused a slump in the Interbrew share price, threats from the Belgian government to intervene, and drew considerable complaint from Interbrew, the latest in the long line of brewers to have cause to regret their involvement in the industry. Speculation involving how Interbrew would comply included a break-up of the various breweries, and interest from Heineken, and, probably most ironically, Carlsberg.

The decision of Byers was challenged by Interbrew. As the case headed slowly towards the courts, an international slanging match developed, with the Belgian government stepping in to show its support of Interbrew by criticising the decision. Our own government was accused of being protectionist and reactionary and was threatened with an unprecedented challenge in the European Court of Justice over its competition laws. Eventually this wasn't needed as the British High Court, whilst stopping short of overturning the decision, told the two parties to go away and sort things out whilst giving the government a rap over the knuckles by making it pay most of Interbrew's costs. Finally after more political wrangling, a compromise was agreed that Interbrew could simply sell Carling, Britain's biggest-selling lager. And so off went Carling for £1.2 billion to the American brewer Coors, whilst the rest of the deal went ahead. Bass had finally reached their end game, and had abandoned their famous red triangle logo into the bargain.

Having quit brewing in May 2000, perhaps it was logical to Whitbread that it should dispose of its pub estate within the next twelve months. This was a shock to those who had come to respect Whitbread as the most focused of the former big six. It also suggested that strategic planning in our top companies was lacking, when only eighteen months previously in the summer of 1999 Whitbread had led the bidding in the hard-fought battle to acquire the 3,500 strong Allied Domecq pub estate. Was such a somersault in attitude indicative of the Whitbread hierarchy acting like a group of spoilt kids? If they couldn't have the Allied Domecq estate then they would throw their other pubs out of the pram.

The official explanation was of course rather different; Whitbread had decided to move away from the slow-growing pub market and concentrate on the more dynamic world of leisure. Despite all the spin, and the impressive £1.625 billion raised in the sale, scepticism remained. The share price dipped slightly whilst the *Daily Telegraph*'s barbed comment was;

> *"Whitbread… promises to be a sad shrunken thing whose management can concentrate on the excitements of Beefeater, Pizza Hut and David Lloyd Leisure. Enjoy! as the company's own teeth-grinding slogan insists".*[7]

To give some credit to Whitbread, it seemed to have started to hedge its bets as early as the 1970's recession when it suffered serious financial problems. From then onwards it commenced a major programme of diversification, purchasing interests in hotels, restaurants and entertainment, and continued to develop these. Thus when MMC arrived Whitbread was less reliant on brewing and pubs, had experience in other sectors, and was better placed to transfer its focus elsewhere, which it has done effectively with Premier Inns and Costa Coffee. The only distraction in its determined withdrawal from the drinks industry was the attempt to buy Allied Domecq's pub estate. When this failed Whitbread moved rapidly in the other direction, with a disposal of all of its own pubs. Was it sentiment that persuaded it to draw the line at its famous pub-restaurants like Beefeater and Brewers Fayre? It now operates these, and other members of its pub-restaurant stable, with the accent very much on food, seemingly distancing itself from its former affiliation to the drinks industry as much as it can.

In hindsight therefore Whitbread was not following the path of Sam Whitbread, its 18th century founder who had committed suicide. But the experience of the other ex-brewers during this phase of rapid withdrawal was less fortunate. Greenalls, whose focus on their retail estate after closing their breweries had failed to overcome a tumbling share price and poor results had, like Whitbread, stated they would concentrate on leisure. In their case this was running their De Vere Hotel chain and Greens fitness clubs. Having renamed the shrunken rump of the group De Vere, speculation grew that it would be taken over completely.

Meanwhile Allied Domecq continued to meander through what seemed destined to become its twilight years. The omens were not good back in 1994 when the group, then Allied Lyons acquired Domecq, a Spanish-Mexican spirits business. The purchase coincided with the assassination of the Mexican prime minister and a disastrous devaluation of the *peso,* which hammered profits. In the light of this, Allied's decision to adopt the quixotic Domecq, in its new name of Allied Domecq, suggested a strong disenchantment with brewing. And so, its remaining share in its breweries was sold to Bass (and subsequently blocked by the MMC).

Tony Hales, Chief Executive of Allied Domecq, described the deal as;

"The culmination of a two-year disposal programme of non-core businesses which will enable us to concentrate fully on the development of our spirits and retailing businesses."[8]

Another bold statement defying the reality of a spiral into mediocrity. Allied Domecq then went in search of a merger with another drinks group. Instead the retail business that the company had claimed it was concentrating on was sold only three years later, after a particularly poor set of results. This represented the sale of the family silver as Allied now only had its wines and spirits business to focus on. The shareholders continued to wait expectantly. *The Times* commented after the pub sale that investors would be looking for some change after ten years of spectacular bad luck and under-performance.

For the big brewers, the large disposals to comply with MMC had disrupted their business model. With a reduced estate to drive demand for brewing production, and constantly haunted by over-capacity, the brewery came under increasing scrutiny. The writing was on the wall when brewing activity had become relatively peripheral in terms of profit contribution. This had fallen to only 22% of total profit at Bass and 15% at Whitbread by the late Nineties. The comments made by the retiring brewers suggested that the presence of the brewery was increasingly regarded as a constraint to more effective pub retailing. However convincing one finds this argument, it lost credibility when the pub retailing was terminated in the case of Allied and Whitbread so soon after.

The huge amounts bankrolled by the brewers, from the sales of their pub estates and breweries, had to be re-invested somewhere. One suspects, given the pressures to diversify, that the supposedly enticing financial prospects of some of their purchases were illusory. It is notable that many of the brewers who abandoned brewing, supposedly in favour of an alternative strategy, lost their way very quickly. Although they appear to have concluded that their brewery was something of an impediment, without it they appeared to be bereft of direction or resolve. These were difficult times for the industry, but the sorry retreat by so many ex-brewers into mediocrity and relative anonymity was particularly unimpressive.

For lovers of tradition, the Nineties was an unmitigated disaster. Traditional pubs were closing, being branded and receiving outlandish names. Brewers were routinely signalling the end to proud and historic brewing dynasties. Breweries were closing almost as fast as the Tory government was losing MPs. In addition to the personal trauma for their employees and the impact on local economies, each brewery closure represented a little more of the nation's working heritage being dismantled.

Some of the old breweries survive as a museum piece, but their closure will have eroded part of their town's tradition and character. The old ex-brewery towns can now only live on their memories rather than retaining the vitality and pungent charm conferred by the presence of its brewery. The loss of an active and productive industry with its own animated cast of workers and associated pubs and drinkers.

As more brewers abandoned their traditional undertaking, the surviving brewery sector moved forward in uncertainty. When Whitbread and Bass sold out to Interbrew in close succession they were not just selling a collection of breweries. They were finalising the sale of one of the nation's industries. The UK market was now irrevocably part of the international brewing market.

But the transformation in the industry was not yet complete. The turmoil was set to continue for the large pub estates and their owners.

Dancing With Wolves;
The Regionals Go To War

Whilst the big brewers were absorbed in their particular version of Russian roulette, the surviving Regional brewers were engaged in their own conflict. Around the turn of the millenium several acrimonious and extended takeover battles raged with Wolverhampton & Dudley Brewery (W&D), the wicked witch of the west at the centre of them. Looking on with more than a passing interest was the equally ambitious other major regional brewer, Greene King, who held sway to the east.

Those who had hoped to see some stability in this sector, to compensate for the turbulence elsewhere, were to be deeply disappointed. This battle for survival degenerated, in the prevailing climate, into a predatory free-for-all. Justification for this distasteful rough and tumble focused once more on brewing capacity and profitability.

The changing beer market was squeezing the Regionals, tightly. The big brewers were fighting hard for market share and were offering very keen discounts on beer supply agreements. For the larger pubCos and retail chains these were at a level which the Regionals couldn't match. Following MMC, the opportunity for selling guest beers into the larger brewers' tenanted estates had been exploited but most of these pubs had now been sold and their new owners the pubCos were not brewers and were therefore not subject to the guest beer regulations. These pubCos had formed their own advantageous supply agreements, largely with the breweries formerly owned by the big six. With such sales opportunities removed and brewery margins eroded, the Regionals looked for more pubs over which the high unit costs of running their own brewery could be defrayed.

The campaigning season commenced at the end of 1998 with W&D squaring up to Marston's, a similar sized outfit based in the great Midlands brewing town of Burton-on-Trent. Marston's, which had already rung the changes by talking to Nomura about a securitisation deal involving its tenanted estate, reacted to W&D's opening offer by calling it woeful and suggested that it had already told W&D earlier in the year that it was not interested in a merger. As the W&D bid increased, Marston's reacted by launching a counter-offer for its assailant, the so-called 'Pac-Man' defence. The acrimonious war of words raged until a shareholder election in February 1999, when W&D secured 73% of Marston's shares. The game was up and another bastion of the trade, established two centuries before, was suddenly no more. Marston's had gone for a Burton!

W&D had succeeded in taking over a larger competitor with its bold approach, adding 900 pubs to its estate, which was now serviced by three breweries. It immediately announced that 165 pubs, mainly in the south and east, would be sold to Greene King for about £433,000 per pub, a fair price for a mix of tenancies and managed houses.

In the summer of 1999 Greene King made its first move with a £145 million bid for the Thames Valley brewer Morland, which it had bid for in 1992, an exercise which had been stoutly rebutted at that time. Since then Morland had made a few modest acquisitions of its own and had dabbled unconvincingly with a little brand building. The company had failed to reconcile itself to its new size or the changing market. In particular it had been struggling with Ruddles, the beer brand it had acquired in 1997, and had announced half-year profits down 38%, dragging the share price down with it. Instead of battling for its independence a second time the Abingdon brewer waved the white flag almost immediately, indicating that it would accept the offer, representing £355,000 per pub. But W&D were not going to watch passively from the sidelines and offered £173 million. This merely pushed the stakes up and Greene King responded with £182 million, 25% above the original. W&D were seen off and the deal was done.

The chairman of the 288-year-old Morland, Britain's second oldest independent, Martin Mays-Smith, advised of his sadness but suggested that the pressure for consolidation amongst the Regionals was too great. No less sad were the 100 employees at the 138-year-old Speckled Hen brewery at Abingdon who would lose their jobs at the inevitable closure, or the members of CAMRA who once again expressed their anguish as another brewery was about to be converted to 'quality residential apartments'.

Almost immediately Wolves (as W&D are often known) were on the prowl again. Having digested one regional and missed out on a second they now had Mansfield Brewery in their sights. Despite a 'Save Mansfield Brewery Campaign', the 523 pub-strong brewer proved to be an easy target. The £253 million offer was accepted by Mansfield, accompanied by the promise that the brewery in the town would be kept open for at least two years. Perhaps that period of time represented a modicum of security in the vulnerable world of big brewing. W&D had now reached the significant mark of 2,000 pubs. The four breweries gathered in the process remained a potential millstone in any accountant's eyes, the solution to which seemed all too obvious. W&D's aggression had secured a very strong position in the Midlands, and a large estate almost within the national brewers' league, if that competition hadn't been disbanded for lack of competitors. W&D confidently claimed, in familiar terms, that consolidation in the regional brewing sector was necessary and acquisitions achieved increased scale and competitive advantages.

Only months later, in May 2000, that claim was sounding rather hollow. Retail profit margin at the much-expanded company's 941 managed outlets had fallen 1%. This was blamed on the impact of high street competition putting pressure on drinks pricing and promotions. The share price dropped 11% at the news and the vultures immediately started to gather. Wolverhampton & Dudley, which had so recently been the school bully, was now in the sick bay, subject to regular takeover speculation, and with its performance subjected to intimate scrutiny by the city and potential predators. Judgement on W&D became harsher with the announcement of results by Greene King in October 2000. Six month profits there had risen dramatically whilst even beer volume had increased by 15%.

So while the men at Greene King's historic home in Bury St Edmonds congratulated themselves on their traditional pubs and values fighting back against the new generation of superpubs, financial worries afflicted David Thomson and his board 120 miles to the west. A strategic review was announced which effectively signalled that the company was up for grabs. The Wolves, heavily in debt from their spending spree, had lost their bite. And of course, one of the main areas of consideration in the review was the closure of up to three of the company's four breweries.

In the speculation on possible purchasers, the finance men originally featured heavily. Then a management buyout from former chief executive Thomson was speculated upon. Not only had W&D to suffer the humiliation of being forced by its own shareholders to put itself up for sale, but at the April 2001 deadline there were no proper bids. Even by the second deadline of 1st June, the two serious contenders who had emerged, Pubmaster and Robert Breare's Noble House Group, were in no rush to put offers forward. Instead of competing with each other the two potential predators appeared to be working together, with Noble House apparently ready to take a package from the spoils.

Pubmaster's bid appeared to be rather insulting at 480 pence a share, well below the expected level, submitted just before the deadline. Following intense lobbying and great speculation the pubCo secured agreement from only 47% of the W&D shareholders. In a really tense situation, David Thomson had just managed to desperately cling on to the family heirloom. W&D rapidly consolidated after this narrow escape, closing the Mansfield brewery and selling Camerons brewery in Hartlepool. And by March 2004 W&D were hunting again, buying up Wizard Inns from Nomura, the pub estate of Burtonwood of Cheshire and in 2005, most sadly for real ale enthusiasts, Jennings, the Lake District brewer. These took W&D to 2,200 pubs and a position of third in the brewers' league.

Symbolically, after all of the aggression was over in 2006 and exactly 120 years after the company was formed, W&D ceased to exist, renaming itself Marston's. This was a shrewd move as Marston's had enjoyed a solid image as an old Burton brewery, and, unlike W&D, was untarnished with the blood of so many other brewers on its hands. In line with this image the new Marston's has, since then, dedicated itself to promoting an excellent range of beers and operating breweries in Burton, Wolverhampton, Cockermouth, Ringwood and Witney.

Greene King had been relatively quiet on its patch in the east, apart from a brief foray to purchase the 136-strong Old English Inns, an estate of charming old country pubs and inns in 2001 and in 2002 it renewed acquaintance with Michael Cannon to buy the rump of the Morrells Oxford pub estate. It started warming up for serious battle with the purchase of 432 former Whitbread neighbourhood pubs from the pub group Laurel in 2004. And then in 2005 it burst into action again, buying Ridley's, the Essex brewer and its seventy-four pubs, whilst immediately announcing the closure of Ridleys delightful little rural brewery. Belhaven, Scotland's largest independent, based on the coast east of Edinburgh, was added in the same year with its 300 pubs, and just a year later Hardy and Hanson, the Nottinghamshire brewer, was the final flurry in the spending spree in a £271m purchase of its 268 pubs. The brewery was again an early victim. This took Greene King to around 2,200 pubs and thus on a par with Marston's.

CAMRA and other traditional beer lovers had been observing this process from the sidelines with increasing alarm as more breweries disappeared, along with popular and well-loved beer brands. When, following the purchase of Morland, Greene King announced not only the closure of the brewery but the transfer of production of the popular Old Speckled Hen from Oxfordshire to its main brewery at Bury St Edmunds, there was a huge outcry.

CAMRA complained that the quality of the beer and the original flavour would be impossible to replicate by using water drawn from Suffolk, far removed from its traditional source. It highlighted its disapproval by banning what they saw as a false product from its major beer festivals.

But, important as water is to the flavour of the beer made from it, brewers can go some way to doctor the water available to them to improve its qualities for brewing or to replicate a flavour more accurately. 'Burtonisation' is familiar within the trade as the treatment of softer water with minerals to simulate the flavour of the excellent brewing water obtained from the ground in Burton-on-Trent. In the brewing process there are only limited sources of barley and hops, and the most popular of these tend to be employed by many brewers and often come from the same sources. If the use of similar barley and hops are common to many standard bitters, and water can be replicated, the fourth of the basic brewing ingredients must be especially critical in providing our hundreds of different beers each with their unique flavour. And this magic little item is yeast.

In recognition of the critical role which yeast has to perform, most established brewers have their own individual and lovingly nurtured culture of yeast which is carefully preserved within the brewery, to ensure that its flavour and contribution to the brewing process remains consistent and unique to that brewer and its beers. There is even a National Collection of Yeast Cultures, the NCYC, which is based within the University of East Anglia in Norwich. Most brewers safely store a sample of their own treasured yeast there, kept at suitably low temperatures, to freeze the fungus for posterity and in case anything goes wrong at the brewery, like an infection of their working supply.

As the various predatory brewers would take control of their former rivals, not only did they ensure that they acquired all of their pubs and other operational land and sites, they would also secure comprehensive legal rights over the beer and pub brands of their victim. Equally importantly they would also ensure that they acquired a supply of the secret ingredient, the nectar of life, the brewer's yeast, without which they could not reproduce their beers. As Jack Hibberd, General Manager of the new Trumans brewery, happily reborn in East London in 2012 put it;

> *"A brewery's yeast is what makes its beers unique. If hops provide the flavour and malt is the body, then yeast is a beers soul."*

And perhaps by extension, the soul of each departed brewery?[9, 10]

Greene King and Marston's thus swaggered around the country, using their cheque book-powered expansion to capture the pubs and the yeast of a host of old brewers. It was almost as if they had put a line roughly down the middle of the country and parcelled up all available breweries between them, so that they emerged with equivalent estates. And in this dog-eat-dog world they had replicated the behaviour of the big six in the 1950s and 60s. But with S&N having gone the same way as its big six rivals in April 2008, the two former Regionals had now become the big two British brewers.

With these two leaving a trail of closed breweries in their wake they lost all semblance of their former 'cuddly' status to real ale enthusiasts. The main consolation for concerned drinkers, as they looked anxiously on, was that the mayhem which had devoured the Regional brewers had only nibbled at the local brewers.

Despite the tumult and apocalyptic headlines regarding unprofitable pubs and redundant breweries most of the local brewers carried on quietly about their business. Many took advantage of the churn within the industry to modestly expand their own tied estates. Some were also increasing their retail activity by building their managed estate and developing one or two interesting brands in the process. London brewer Fuller's were very active, in both respects in and around their London home. Shepherd Neame meanwhile continued its determined search for purchases away from its Kent base, whilst Hall and Woodhouse bought out Sussex operator King and Barnes and its fifty-seven pubs, closing its Horsham brewery in the process. At the other end of the country Cockermouth-based Jennings had grown significantly to 186 operations, with the purchase of Lancashire-based Cafe Inns. At the time few would have sensed that Jennings was to be a victim itself soon after.

The main reason for this calm whilst all around was battered by the winds of change was the structure of these companies. Most were family-owned businesses. Others that were quoted had complex voting structures which deterred potential predators. If profits did suffer for a year or two, management were able to take a calm, rational view of the situation and wait for an upturn. A critical aspect of the demise of many brewers post-MMC was their failure to handle the pressures of being a plc and retain the trust and loyalty of their shareholders during this volatile period.

The Wonder Of Wetherspoons

Wetherspoons is the most recognisable high street licensed operation. It is the only pub brand which can bear comparison with McDonalds, WH Smiths or Boots. Surprisingly, the pubs themselves don't have a standard brand name, although in the early days the Moon Under Water or some other lunar reference was often favoured. Now, each operation receives an individual name, usually based on a local character, industry or incident. These are invariably thoroughly researched by the company with the results displayed around the newly opened premises. For brand recognition, the name is academic as signage and styling makes the affiliation to Wetherspoons obvious for any drinker.

Despite all of the other changes in the industry, Wetherspoons are the single most remarkable phenomenon in the licensed trade over the last three decades. The chain's emergence and the challenge posed to the brewers' cartel during the Eighties provided the first hint of fundamental change. Wetherspoons' founder Tim Martin has become a notable figure, not only for his stature at six foot five, but also for his talismanic presence, insistent pragmatism and, more recently, his forthright views.

In the early days, Martin was Wetherspoons, operating as a virtual one-man band. Now he heads a major public company, employing the equivalent of a small town, 30,000 between its Watford head office and its 900 plus pubs around the country. Martin is relatively unchanged; he is still a dominant figure, leading from the front, applying for and obtaining new licences in person, regularly touring his extensive estate and involving himself in all facets of the organisation.

He first entered the trade by purchasing brewery disposals in the North London area. His first pub opened in Muswell Hill in 1979. His early pubs were the sort of unloved, secondary outlets that the brewers had tried and failed to salvage, and sold off as the easy way out. Tim Martin and his friend and sparring partner Andrew Marler were enthusiastic purchasers of these. They realised that they could refit the pubs cheaply in a workmanlike but attractive style. Because their formula was so simple and the refurbished pubs contrasted with the generally tatty brewers' pubs around them, trade improved immediately. They also realised that such pubs, once restored, were of great value, particularly when Marler sold a pair of pubs to Vaux the north-east brewer for over a million pounds. At the time there were plenty of Regional brewers[11] who were trying to gain a foothold in London and prepared to pay big money to do so.

Martin admitted that at this stage he did not have any grand strategy or knowledge of the industry.

> *"Essentially, I didn't have a clue. What sustained the business in the early years was the fact that we were invading a monopoly. What happens in any monopoly is high prices, poor service and a lack of investment."*[12]

Marler went for the spectacular in his buying and selling and acquired The World's End at Camden, a landmark pub. Tim Martin kept a lower profile and after a slow start steadily built up his estate with modest pubs. The major brewers within London had by now got wise to Martin. It became embarrassing to them that he could revitalise pubs that they had given up on so they stopped selling to him. Denied further brewery disposals, Martin focused on empty shop units in secondary shopping parades. He rang the changes in suburban north-west London, where he targeted modest neighbourhoods in the underpubbed area. He used his growing knowledge of running basic pubs to convince magistrates that he could provide a clean well-run bar.

As the numbers grew so did the ambition. Martin had by then gathered a team of specialists to find and develop the sites and then run them. He recruited some experienced ex-brewery men, including his brother Jerry, previously with Taylor Walker, part of Allied Breweries, and John Hutson, who has stayed with Wetherspoons since and been rewarded by rising to the position of Chief Executive. Jerry soon branched off on his own with the Old Monk company, looking to emulate big brother by developing his own pub chain.

The quantities of beer being sold by Wetherspoons enabled them to purchase cheaply. If they didn't get the terms they wanted then the oversupply in the brewery market meant he could easily go elsewhere for the right deal. If he could buy it cheap, Martin realised that he could also sell it cheap and still maintain decent margins. At this time the brewers were being criticised by the MMC for operating a cartel to maintain high prices. Martin was able to step in and claim the moral high ground by offering remarkably cheap beer. Tartan remained at under £1 in his outlets for years whilst numerous other special offers were available. This enabled him to be seen as the man of the people, selling beer cheaply and taking on the big bullying brewers in the process.

Wetherspoons were now sufficiently large that they could proceed to the next phase. Landlords of good quality property are always reluctant to lease buildings to small and unknown companies because of the supposed weakness of small tenants and the impact of this upon investment value. Martin's fast-growing pub estate was now large enough in landlords' eyes to enable him to take on leased properties to convert in high streets and better quality areas. Martin had gained enough confidence to take on the brewers and compete with them for sites, even in areas with a strong circuit of pubs. And the result was quite staggering. Wetherspoons' quiet little community pubs with no music and no fruit machines were perceived as such a breath of fresh air that they were instantly trendy. Young circuit drinkers adopted them enthusiastically.

After ten years of growth, Wetherspoons was sufficiently established to float on the stock exchange. This occurred in October 1992 at a time when the chain had forty-four outlets. The initial share price moved rapidly upwards and is currently steady at around the 700 pence mark, representing an enormous profit for the early investors and making Martin a multimillionaire, listed in the *Sunday Times* rich list. With capital from the flotation the expansion accelerated, with the property deals growing as relentlessly as the company's share price. The inevitable step of expanding nationwide came in 1993, with The Bell, Norwich being the first opening outside London. Prime sites were now considered as targets, with the company being prepared to pay substantial rents to gain the best trading locations.

Wetherspoons has demonstrated its versatility as a brand by being developed in high streets, city locations, leisure parks and in a number of airports. Notable sites along the way have included Leicester Square, Hamilton Hall, the vast and ornate old ballroom of the Great Eastern Hotel on Bishopsgate, London, the opening of the first pub in frightfully middle-class Frinton, Essex and some spectacular conversions of closed-down cinemas including Colchester, Gloucester, Swindon, Stafford, Holloway Rd and Manchester.

CAMRA seemed to be impressed after the opening in Manchester;

"The JD Wetherspoon organisation's arrival in Manchester was greeted with awestruck enthusiasm by local CAMRA branches. With its 8,000 square feet of floor, its gallery bar and its huge floor-to-ceiling stained-glass window, the £2 million Moon Under Water in Deansgate, a former cinema, gasted the flabber of all who beheld it." [13]

The company have broken many new frontiers. The Commercial Rooms in Bristol were converted to great acclaim, at a cost of £1.3

million, winning awards from English Heritage and CAMRA in the process. Some surprises along the way were the opening of the old Marquee Club on Charing Cross road, London, in December '96 and the purchase of Lloyds Number 1 bars, from Wolverhampton & Dudley brewery, at an opportunist moment. The company stated that they intended to continue the operation in its existing style, very distinct from the standard Wetherspoons, and have maintained this policy.

The success has been achieved by exploiting a distinct gap in the market. Wetherspoons' strength is Wetherspoons the brand. Despite constant trade objections, magistrates and licensing authorities have been regularly convinced that a Wetherspoons will provide the market with something different. As a result of this a very healthy proportion of applications for new licences have been approved. The food offer has evolved enormously to claim a substantial share of overall turnover with sensible dishes and very reasonable prices, supported by a generous range of wines. Coffee and breakfasts have followed along with other innovations like the popular curry night with irresistible prices for a curry with all the trimmings washed down by a pint.

Martin has retained the approval of the real ale brigade by constantly stocking a good range of cask ale, by his pricing policies, and by providing the type of environment that they are comfortable in, all of this supported by regular beer festivals.

Wetherspoons is open and public, more airport waiting lounge than intimate pub. Most Wetherspoons are large and although they can be atmospheric when busy are designed to be more impersonal so that customers can claim their own private space if they so choose. Their size, and zoning into areas of different ambience, is a hidden strength of the brand. Wetherspoons' size means customers are not pressurised as they arrive. Instead they can proceed at their own pace, decide on what they want and where they want to sit or stand. That allows customers who wish to remain in a discrete corner to do so, whilst those who are more inclined to be gregarious to participate and contribute to the pub atmosphere in a more prominent area.

There is of course a danger in all this, for the wider pub market. A generation bought up on the convenience of Wetherspoons may fail to understand, or be able to appreciate, the atmosphere of a genuine traditional pub.

Wetherspoons are prepared to develop in isolation away from other pubs but they will also sit within a circuit. They were often the first of the new wave of bars to arrive on drinking circuits, with young drinkers readily adopting them. After Yates's and other young persons-orientated pubs arrived on these circuits, in most cases Wetherspoons has been left to its usual eclectic mix of pensioners, families, real ale buffs, students, the unemployed and lunchtime workers and shoppers. Company spokesman Eddie Gershon, discussing their customer base as long ago as January 1996, said;

> *"We are part of a new breed… We ban all music – we feel people would prefer not to have music imposed on them – and we don't have pool tables. Young customers are not at all put off by this. They like our atmosphere. We serve food all day, so there's no question of someone coming in at 2.30pm and being told that he can't have a meal. Many of our pubs are in the high street and we have a lot of women customers coming in after shopping. They enter an atmosphere in which they don't feel threatened, as they do in some grotty pubs. We are open-plan. We inspect the toilets every hour. In our pubs you won't find an indifferent landlord with a fag in his mouth. Our people are well trained. Forgive us if we sound pleased with ourselves. We have reason to be."*[14]

The cause of such smugness attracted the attention of the brewers, who monitored Wetherspoons' expansion with a combination of resentment and intrigue. The bubble didn't burst as they might have hoped and neither did Wetherspoons sell out to a brewer, as had happened with pub groups in the past. So instead, the brewers carefully analysed the success of Wetherspoons and, in the time-honoured fashion of the trade, copied them. S&N developed a chain of converted community pubs by the name of John Barras which mimicked Wetherspoons in internal style, whilst Bass went even further with their Goose and Granite chain. Others looked carefully for inspiration. If imitation is the most sincere form of flattery, then Martin can consider himself thoroughly flattered.

Milestones have regularly been reached during the last three and a half hectic decades. There is now virtually complete coverage throughout England, with Scotland and Wales catching up fast and a start being made in Ireland. 900 pubs was reached in December 2013, and with openings running at around forty to fifty per year (demonstrating what a juggernaut the company now is to handle expansion by individual sites at that rate) a final target of around 1,500 is coming steadily into sight. This sort of figure implies a comprehensive coverage, and, in line with this, the company has returned to many towns to develop a second and even third site.

The downside of the march of Wetherspoons is the effect of this on existing pubs. By developing such a dense network, not only within high streets but in the suburbs and in small market towns, they are taking trade from nearby local pubs. At worst the impact of a Wetherspoons opening in a small town can be the early closure of several local pubs. Wetherspoons command such a high turnover, generally £25,000 plus per week, that even if half of this is 'new business' the balance will be achieved by taking this from other pubs, with inevitable consequences. There may also be an impact on the economy of the town because the money earned by local pubs will tend to remain in the local economy, given their use of local suppliers and tradesmen.

Wetherspoons is keen to break into new territory. Like airports where its outlets are ubiquitous and, most recently, motorway service stations where the government has surprisingly decided to allow alcohol licenses. Having been granted the first such license, Wetherspoons is operating on the M40 at Beaconsfield, Bucks. Martin has suggested that this will be the first of many.

Despite the many years of intense, dedicated effort Martin is still brimming with enthusiasm. His rugged appearance and informal, homespun manner belie an immense capacity and energy, and, when things don't go according to plan, a defiant determination. In the process of developing the brand, Martin has regularly demonstrated this, peppered with a touch of humour along the way. Like the edge of town centre Reading site named 'The Back of Beyond' in response to an adverse comment, and the 'Lord Moon of the Mall' at Whitehall, London bearing a face on a swing sign, which is somewhat Martinesque.

Tim Martin has developed from precocious first-former to school prefect. He is often referred to as the most influential man in the pub industry. He clearly takes this role seriously, dishing out regular advice to fellow senior pupils like the brewers and pubCos. His chain of ubiquitous bars are so well established that they will almost certainly be a permanent feature on our high streets. He still has plenty of time and energy to do more. His unique achievement is to create a retail pub chain which has not only survived in the volatile and demanding UK market but is positively thriving in it. Whatever he manages in the rest of his career he can reflect proudly that he has firmly stamped his original mark on the industry, and one which will be lasting.

Secure As Houses;
The New Order

The driving force behind the next wave of changes was an unexpectedly new influence. Money. Corporate money. The City had hijacked the pub industry agenda and was now running matters for its own ends. Or so it seemed.

Few people in the trade were familiar with securitisation in the mid-Nineties. A few years later it was difficult to avoid the term. The first securitised deal surprisingly was on behalf of Wellington pubCo, which tends to maintain a low profile. Their leases, almost uniquely, are entirely non-tied and are more akin to an arms-length property deal with the landlord standing back from the pub business. Perhaps this made Wellington suitable territory to lead the charge. The securitisation financed Wellington's purchase of 845 free-of-tie pubs from Nomura's Phoenix Inns in 1997. Punch followed with their securitisation soon after, and within five years, 25% of the nation's pubs were subject to the invisible manacles of securitisation.

Securitisation has been adopted in many sectors. Financial experts have commented that the pub market is ideally suited to the process because of its freehold property basis, diversified geographically into lots of small components. Put simply, securitisation is the conversion of future income streams into an immediate lump sum. Effectively the subject company is loaned the capital sum and then services this loan with annual payments over a number of years. The structure of a securitisation is quite restrictive to an operator. A legal charge is placed on all of its properties. Operating profit must be at least 1.25 times the cost of servicing the debt, or it could be placed in administration. Any income from property disposals has to either be re-invested in other pubs, or repaid to investors. A certain reserve fund must be retained, and only capital in excess of this can be paid as dividends. Another defined percentage normally has to be spent on maintenance.

Despite all this, securitisation was favoured because it 'leveraged' a much higher proportion of the value of the estate into the pubCos' hands than other forms of financing. There were other constraints. A securitisation was a big undertaking, requiring the involvement of a lot of specialist advisers, and was both expensive and could take up to a year to set up. But they were the current rage, and seemed to hold a hypnotic attraction for any pub company that required substantial capital.

As a result of the breathtaking deals involving the former big six up to the start of the millenium, the influence of brewing had become largely divorced from that of pub ownership. The pub industry had gained a new profile. The industry top ten in terms of pub ownership in 1990 were all brewers. The new giants, ten years later, were a mixture of the old guard, repackaged, the pubCos and the largest Regionals, promoted to the top rank by growth and the disappearance of other players.

But such was the pace of change, the amount of churn, the thirst for deals, that this elite held their positions for little longer than football teams in the early season league tables. Below is the line-up of the new giants of the industry, presented by number of licensed outlets, in the middle of 2001, after the dust had settled on the Whitbread pubs estate disposal;

1	NOMURA	6,000
2.	PUNCH	5,100
3	ENTERPRISE	3,400
4	BASS(6 CONTINENTS)	2,600
5	MORGAN GRENFELL (LAUREL)	2,550
6	SCOTTISH & NEWCASTLE	2,500
7	PUBMASTER	2,000
8	WOLVERHAMPTON & DUDLEY	1,800
9	GREENE KING	1,700
10	ALCHEMY PARTNERS	1,000

Below this leading pack came further pubCos like the Pub Estate Company and Avebury Taverns, both with around 700 pubs, and Inn Business with approximately 500. At a similar level came the largest of the retail pub groups, Wetherspoons. Even though it had been established and expanding for longer than all the new pubCos it had grown slowly and organically, almost entirely by individual acquisitions, as opposed to buying substantial packages.

A report on the pubCos by investment banker Commerzbank Securities in May 2001, entitled *Securitising the UK Pub Sector*[15] suggested that financial markets still had massive funds available to invest in pub packages. According to the report, 12,750 pubs had already been securitised and a further 7,000 were predicted to join them over the following two years. The prospects of the companies in our league table confirmed this was the case, as big city financiers continued to dictate the destiny of vast numbers of pubs.

At the top of our league briefly was Nomura, a massive group, Japanese based, but with tentacles spreading around the world. Its interests encompassed activities as diverse as cars, new technology, trains and hotels. Whilst the pub holding made them number one in Britain, these pubs were relatively small fry for Nomura as a whole. The pubs were spread across four different companies: Unique, Voyager, Inn Partnership and Wizard Inns. The first three were leasing pubCos, whilst Wizard was a managed operation. The Unique pubCo, which contained the bulk of their holdings, had been securitised and set up by the highly-regarded Guy Hands for a stock market flotation at the right time. The remaining chunks of their estate were relatively modest tenancies and leases, some of which were the bookends of Inntrapreneur, some free of the tie and others with a group of discontented and litigious licensees. The attraction of the whole unwieldy package to other pubCos was the enormous critical mass it would confer. Rumours abounded of imminent change.

Punch, although another newcomer, appeared to have a longer vision as an operating entity. Its founder, Hugh Osmond, showed, both in developing Pizza Express and at Punch, ability as an operator and a cold commitment to pull off big deals. He had the benefit of experienced support staff inherited from both Bass LeaseCo and Allied. Punch started life as a tenanted group, but with the Allied purchase it gained a significant managed estate and some strong brands. Spirit came into existence to get the best from these, and this company was to demerge from Punch, then merge again, before finally demerging in 2011.

Bass appeared to have lost all appetite for its pubs, preferring the more prestigious distraction of their Inter-Continental hotel chain. The company wasn't even Bass any longer, having adopted the much derided name 'Six Continents'. Clearly the new outfit saw its future away from the grimy backstreets of Birmingham. Of its massive 'war chest', amassed from the various pub and brewery sales, a large chunk went on picking up the PostHouse chain of hotels from Compass (formerly Granada). It was ironic that the hotels that Bass was committing its future to were showing a weaker financial performance than its remaining pub portfolio. But, having shed its brewing tag with the convoluted sale to Interbrew, the next question was when rather than if it would follow Whitbread and rid itself of its pubs.

The answer came, after abortive discussions to merge with S&N, in April 2003 when a demerger was announced, in the usual official jargon, 'to create shareholder value'. Mitchells and Butlers, the original force in Birmingham brewing, which had merged with Bass back in the 1960s, was brought back from the grave. But this was no attempt to win hearts and minds and return the pub operation to its roots, as the tiller, once it was in the hands of M&B, remained firmly in the direction set by Bass with a commitment to brands and food.

Morgan Grenfell, part of Deutsche Bank, had just completed the purchase of the Whitbread pub estate. Having done this, they withdrew. The pub estate was named Laurel. It inherited Whitbread's Luton offices and dedicated management team, and Ian Payne, an experienced brewery man, was placed in charge. He quickly geared the estate to a managed basis by selling 2,300 tenanted pubs, most of which went to Enterprise. Investment was thrown at the remaining 600 or so managed pubs whilst the group appeared to commit to further expansion, but was never able to deliver on this.

The market recognised how vulnerable this managed house rump could be, with only Hogshead as a recognisable brand. It soon lost its independence in the tough trading period at the start of the millenium. Firstly Greene King purchased the 432 neighbourhood pubs in July 2004. It was announced that this would allow Laurel to concentrate on the high street. In November 2004 R20, the investment vehicle of Robert Tchenguiz, stepped in to buy the remaining 160 branded pubs. For the management displaced as a result of this sale, their only concentration on the high street would be for Christmas shopping!

The pubs acquired by R20 went on to experience a turbulent ride, being combined with Yates, part of Surrey Free Inns, after SFI's entry into administration in 2005, and then La Tasca restaurants. This property portfolio experienced a pre-pack administration in 2008, demerged into the Town & City Pub Company which then, owing to the funding crisis and financial chaos of that period, came into the ownership of Kaupthong, the Icelandic bank, then Commerzbank, the German bank, before finally finding their feet as a pub estate, in the ownership of Stonegate in 2011. And, for most of this breathless journey, they remained under the control of Ian Payne, who then became chairman of Stonegate.

Scottish & Newcastle have always been a little different amongst the big six. They were considered a provincial outsider and not part of the London-Burton beerage. They were also a latecomer, still prowling around for takeover victims such as the Blackburn-based Matthew Brown in 1987. Another contrast was their concentration on free trade accounts, supplying beer to many clubs, restaurants and free-houses, especially in their backyard of the north and Scotland. In 1989, whilst the MMC was involved in its colossal survey of the beer industry, it was distracted by Elders, the then-owners of Courage who had secured the hostile take-over of S&N. The MMC stepped in to block the takeover, citing a reduction of consumer choice and competition between beer brands. Following this salvation, S&N went on the hunt themselves, buying most notably the 1,654-strong Chef & Brewer estate from Grand Met for £830 million in November 1993.

Perhaps as a result of a different underlying philosophy, they stood back from the Nineties frenzy apparent in the other big brewers. They kept their pubs, whilst looking for more and, surprisingly, purchased more brewing capacity. In 1995 they acquired Courage, renamed themselves Scottish Courage and, at the turn of the millenium, remained as the only former big six member still brewing. At the time this was supported by an extensive network of breweries and depots. The acquisition of Kronenbourg made S&N the second largest European brewer, and the eighth largest in the world, with almost a third of the domestic market. Its status as an international drinks company alongside its extensive pub estate would surely provide stability and profitability. And so it seemed in the company's financial performance at the time. They also sold off Pontins and Center Parcs which had, on occasions, given them a minor nosebleed, thus helping to balance the books and remove any distraction.

Unfortunately such stability and commitment seemed impossible to maintain amidst the turmoil of the drinks industry. Two years after our league table and only a few months after acquiring Bulmers cider in October 2003, S&N had sold all of its 1,400 managed pubs and the former Greenall's-owned Premier Lodge hotels to Spirit Group. Partially that was attributable to the performance of those bars in the tough trading conditions then prevailing. Retailing and developing brands was never S&N's particular strength, despite a lot of effort and investment. Putting Chef & Brewer to one side, a list of their in-town brands tells its own story; Rat and Parrot, Bar 38, De Alto, Bar Oz, Finnegans Wake, TJ Bernards, Norwegian Blue, Pit and Pendulum, and Via Fossa. They sound more like a holiday tour itinerary or a list of B-movies. The sheer number of alternatives suggests a lack of focus and an inability to commit to or identify one or two real winners.

But S&N had more fundamental problems than wayward brands and, in 2004, some radical cost-cutting measures commenced on the brewing side with Fountains Brewery in Edinburgh and Tyne Brewery in Newcastle both closing. When it appeared that this had steadied the ship in 2008, Heineken and Carlsberg came forward with a joint offer to purchase. The S&N board endeavoured to fight this off but when the offer had climbed from 730 pence per share to 800, S&N's shareholders forgot all sentiment or loyalty, grabbed the loot and voted to accept. S&N had become part of Heineken.

Although some of the former Bass pubs remain in the name of Mitchells and Butlers, and Whitbread still operate their restaurants, April 2008 marked the final demise of the last of the big six brewers. Considering the size and strength of these six companies in 1990, their rapid decline and withdrawal from the pub trade, with the qualified exception of M&B, was remarkable. Their disappearance will not have been mourned everywhere, but their era covers a fascinating and essential period in the evolution of the pub.

Next, and shortly to leap to the top of the league, were Enterprise Inns. The company had battled to this stage by regularly swallowing other pubCos to establish itself as a giant. Most of its then 3,400 pubs had come secondhand from other pubCos like Discovery, Mayfair Taverns and Century Inns, which it had consumed in its quest for supremacy. Life for Enterprise was a balancing act of collecting rents from its tenants and supplying beer to them from third-party brewers at a profit, and using this to pay off the finance cost of acquiring these pubs whilst continually looking for the next deal. The canny and determined Ted Tuppen, who had first launched the company back in 1991, appeared to have the key to this formula as he guided Enterprise ever upward.

The expansion of Enterprise to hit the top of the league was achieved very quickly, albeit at huge cost. In 2002 it purchased 1,864 former Whitbread pubs from Laurel. The price of £875m represented £470,000 per pub on average which was, perhaps, a full price to pay for a large package of tenanted pubs. The mechanics of the subsequent purchase of the Unique pub company properties were anything but simple as Enterprise worked with private equity groups and financial experts to gain control of the company. The figures involved, with 4,054 pubs changing hands for a couple of billion pounds, were truly eye-watering. And as Ted Tuppen gazed down triumphantly on the rest of the pubCo league from his lofty perch, sitting on an empire of 9,000 pubs, he was to find the rarified atmosphere at this altitude not entirely comfortable.

Pubmaster had the oldest heritage of the new breed, stemming from Jack Walker's pub empire, assembled during the eighties. Its backbone came from the Camerons and Tolly Cobbold estates in the north-east and East Anglia respectively. Over the years small packages from other brewers were added to reach around 2,000. The Pubmaster estate was modest, mainly backstreet and village pubs, at levels of trade which could only ever be tenanted material. But the company showed a commitment to these and their licensees. Some pride was restored by addressing maintenance which had long been neglected by the brewers and installing simple but distinctive signage. December 2000 witnessed a takeover by German Bank LB West, financier Rotch and property group St Modwen. The estate was 'securitised' by floating the pubs to raise money to repay the original finance costs.

After this, and with new capital available, the company became more aggressive. A £485 million hostile bid was made for Wolverhampton & Dudley which narrowly failed. Pubmaster continued to expand with smaller purchases to raise the estate to around 3,100 pubs. This proved to be fattening themselves up for the table as Punch stepped in with a £1.2 billion bid which was quickly pocketed by Pubmaster's management and new investors, many of whom did very well from the deal. The price represented £385,000 per pub overall which, like most of the post-millenium deals, was not cheap in relation to the modest nature of the majority of the houses involved. With this purchase, Punch had the pleasure of hitting the top of the league, with 7,400 pubs. But only for a few months until Enterprise completed hauling in the Unique catch.

Wolverhampton & Dudley and Greene King have already been described very comprehensively in the previous part.

Alchemy Partners, the venture capitalist, is probably better known than its pub company, Innspired group. Its story is a microcosm of the entire pub market of this time, a sad little tale. Ushers was an historic old brewer, based in Trowbridge, Wiltshire, until 1960 when it agreed to merge with Watneys. In 1990, at the time of MMC, Grand Met was happy to agree to a management buyout by a holding company Innspired, whereby Ushers reappeared with its brewery and about a thousand low-trading local pubs. Nine years later, the initial optimism and enthusiasm had drained away as the brewery, struggling for viability and with a small limited estate to service, was forced to close. And the clock was ticking loudly for the rump estate. Sure enough, in September 2004 Punch stepped in to purchase and relieve Ushers once more of its brief independence.

The systematic transfer of huge pub estates taking place at this time was handled with a mercenary nonchalance as vendors walked off with millions in profit and the purchasers increased their empires to ever more incredible and unmanageable proportions. During 2003 £4bn worth of pubs changed hands in several deals. They involved 10,000 properties, over one in six of the nation's stock of pubs. The mechanics of these transactions were totally and grotesquely divorced from the character and philosophy of the backstreet and village pubs, which were the subject matter of the deals. Chris Hutt, then Managing Director of Wizard Inns, but a man who knew the industry inside out from the many positions and perspectives which he has held, succinctly summed up the general concern at the time;

"These pub companies are property companies, not retailers."[16]

The City and members of its financial markets were of course transfixed. The potentially huge rewards and the regularity of the mega-deals were attracting the most affluent and ambitious speculators and investors. They could see the rising pub values, the steady income streams, and the cash-raising potential of securitisation. They could see the number of huge portfolios that were coming forward and they wanted a share of the action. The income was impressive, something like £50,000 per pub per annum, if rent and the margin from the Beer Tie were combined. But as more money chased the packages, acquisition costs were rising, to an average of around £500,000 per pub for typical packages. This was around three times the prevailing price per pub when the pubCos were merging and buying each other out only six to ten years before. Some of the later packages of pubs, which were of a higher quality, were selling for significantly more. Prices appeared to be nearing the tipping point where the cost of the finance to buy these pubs was exceeding the income they would generate.

The individual pub had become totally insignificant within the process. It wasn't the Rose and Crown or the Mitre; it was simply one of several thousand pubs being evaluated by accountants and passed around in legal transfers and conveyances by big-city solicitors. The securitisation and manipulation, the wheeling and the dealing, reduced each pub to a tiny fraction of an overall income flow in a calculation. A tiny insignificant dot in a huge equation.

The pubCos were an integral part of this process when they routinely inherited another package of three or four thousand pubs. And, with limited staff resources, the challenge of establishing a satisfactory relationship with the tenants of each one of those pubs was never going to be met. Many of these pubs' tenants were new to the trade, and were looking for the sort of partnership with their landlord that they had originally been promised when they signed up to their tenancy or lease agreement. As their property passed dizzyingly from one landlord to another, how could their new business development managers start to understand the individual foibles and characteristics of them, their pub, its location and its customer base, to properly advise about building trade or addressing other issues?

Punch and Enterprise started to learn the lesson that it is tough at the top. They may not have dwelt long on such matters but their colossal size had made them a target. They are now paying a price for their expensive trophy acquisitions in the discomfort of carrying debt measured in billions of pounds. They are having to dispose of huge numbers of pubs to keep their heads above the icy waters of debt. And they are finding that the very size they wanted to exercise their egos and negotiating muscle is making them remote from their licensees, and a target for widespread resentment and disaffection.

The media popularity of leading individuals within the industry is a useful barometer as to the real movers and shakers. In the pre-MMC days, brewery figures were dominant. By 1996 we were reading about the success of Michael Cannon. He made an estimated £170 million from the industry, primarily in three deals: the sale of Devenish to Greenalls, the sale of Magic Pub Co to Greene King and turning Eldridge Pope around within a couple of years and selling to Marston's. Cannon's record is impossible to compare with that of Tim Martin whose achievement at Wetherspoons is more enduring.

But their period of pre-eminence was usurped by the relentless march of the money men. The spotlight was now glaring on people like Guy Hands at Nomura, Hugh Osmond and then Giles Thorley at

Punch and Ted Tuppen at Enterprise. As the trade advanced hesitantly into the new millennium, it was these men who seemed to hold the future of the industry in their grasp.

PART SIX

Sober October

T he new millenium has presented the licensed trade with many challenges and pressures, some inevitable and others more capricious. The era of the themed pub and brands, the drama as vast brewing dynasties imploded and the rise of entrepreneurs creating private empires, was ending.

Instead the initiative has been taken away from the trade. The last decade or so is notable not for what pub owners have done. They were no longer in the driving seat. The game was how or if they, and the individual licensees of our pubs, could cope with what was being thrown at them; by the politicians, society and the economy.

The millenium signalled a new atmosphere of sobriety within the licensed trade. Gone was the spontaneity and eccentricity of the 1990's age of brands when new concepts were launched and new drinking circuits arrived with the reckless abandon of the era of alcopops, Hoopers Hooch, Caffreys and the manufactured craic of the Irish bars. The Nineties party was over.

The century started badly and got worse. 2001 witnessed Foot and Mouth disease, with calamitous results for the countryside and agriculture, and to a degree pubs serving these areas. Then came the tragedy of 9/11 in New York and its uncertain legacy.

In the period leading up to 2003 the industry was diverted, and divided, by debate on the Licensing Bill. Opinions became impassioned between those who saw benefits and others, notably Wetherspoons and the small brewers, who anticipated problems, especially with local authority control and the increased cost of fees and extra bureaucracy. In 2003 the Licensing Act became law, to come into effect in 2005. Almost from the moment it was approved there was a reaction against twenty-four-hour licensing. To be followed at regular intervals by the threat of further regulation.

A bigger hangover for many was created by the Smoking Ban, which after much debate finally arrived in July 2007. Some pubs died from the shock almost instantly, whilst others are still struggling to come to terms with it.

To accompany this, somewhat viciously, recession arrived at the end of that year and remained, like a dark cloud, for the following five or six years. Most would agree that it has been the most serious economic downturn since the 1930s. Its effect on the licensed trade has been extremely damaging in a number of ways. The Labour government of the time showed little sympathy by continuing to impose its unfair, unwise and hugely unpopular beer duty escalator.

The industry commenced its axethebeertax campaign in December 2008. Every year witnessed the ritual build-up to the budget in which the huge inequalities of duty compared to the rest of Europe were highlighted. And every year the government would ignore all of the appeals and logic and increase the duty at inflation plus the duty escalator of an additional 2%. When VAT was temporarily reduced, additional duty was imposed to ensure that pubs were the only sector to get no help from this measure. Any benefit which might have filtered through to beer prices was vindictively cancelled out. And when VAT eventually went back up no reciprocal reduction in duty was passed back.

In 2009 the British Beer and Pub Association pointed out that British drinkers paid nine times the level of duty of German drinkers. Beer consumption had fallen by 6.1% over five years, leaving Britain sinking to 13th place in Europe. A calculation on behalf of the BBPA showed that the government took five times the amount (in duty, VAT and employment and other taxes) per pub than either the tenant or the pubCo.

The Labour government of Gordon Brown was particularly savage. It ignored endless pleas for assistance made because of the ravages of the recession. The indignation within the industry, as the garrotte was tightened around its neck every budget day, was heightened by the indifference shown to the alarmingly low take-home price of alcohol from off-licences and supermarkets. Consequently the off-trade was snatching huge amounts of business from pubs.

In July 2009 the BBPA had confirmed that the rate of pub closures had risen to fifty per week and that 5,000 pubs had been lost since the 2003 Licensing Act, 10% of the nation's total stock. This brutal rate of attrition underlined how great a toll was being taken on the nation's pubs by the unsympathetic tax regime and harsh circumstances then prevailing.

After another hefty increase in the 2010 budget the 'Wilson Drinks Report'[1] showed that in the previous ten years inflation had totalled 29% whilst beer duty had increased by 43%. By 2011, as the alarming rate of pub closures continued to prove how the industry was suffering, 100 MPs signed a motion calling on the government to scrap the duty escalator. Again, this was to no avail as pub prices were hit by 7% extra duty over the year, the VAT increase to 20% and brewers' price increases of 3-7%.

An unfortunate consequence of the spiralling drinks prices was the widening gap between on-trade beer prices and those available for the same product in the off-trade. Supermarkets were increasingly selling cases of beer at reduced prices as a loss-leader to build overall trade. Organisations representing the on-trade were quick to complain about this unfair competition, and the harm which was arising from it.

In November 2010, Home Secretary Theresa May announced a crack-down on binge drinking to,

"Reclaim the high street for sensible law-abiding drinkers."

She added that twenty-four-hour licences had failed to produce the benefits of a cafe culture and tougher action was needed.[2]

And if that catalogue of woe was not enough, the industry started to tear itself apart with the intense and very protracted battle over the Beer Tie and the relationship between the pubCos and their licensees.

The new head of the British Institute of Innkeepers, Neil Robertson, reacted to the malaise by saying that the industry must be careful not to paint itself as being in terminal decline as to do so may tempt government into treating it as a 'sunset industry' and as such undeserving of help. Instead the industry should convey a message of positive realism and stop punching below its weight.[3]

Governments in England, Scotland and Wales had all been making a great deal of noise about imposing a minimum price per unit of alcohol to restrict the cheapness of the supermarket booze but continually backed off before progressing legislation, perhaps because of a lack of conviction that it would do any good, but primarily as it was felt that this could be held illegal under EC law.

With the threat of draconian new licensing laws to combat binge drinking and alcohol-fuelled disorder, representatives of the trade continued to point out that those who purchased alcohol from the off-trade could be consuming it unsupervised wherever they chose, whilst drinking within licensed premises was closely supervised. By now it was widely recognised that much of the alcohol-fuelled disorder was generated by 'pre-loading', the tag given to consuming large amounts of alcohol at home or elsewhere before going out on the town. The iniquity of threatening pubs, bars and nightclubs with punitive controls for something they had little control over finally started to hit home with the politicians. Attention was focused on the pricing of alcohol by supermarkets and off-licences.

Calls for Minimum Unit Pricing increased during 2012 as a result. Following positive statements issued by David Cameron and his new coalition government, it appeared that introduction would only be a matter of time. This was despite vehement protests in some quarters, and criticism of the Sheffield University research upon which the effectiveness of the measure had been based. And then, bizarrely, Bulgaria objected because of the potential impact on its wine producers. Before long the Scotch Whisky association threatened a legal challenge and, by October the government was forced to admit that due to challenges under EC law it would be at least 2014 before the matter could progress.

Meanwhile the anti-duty campaign continued to gain support in Parliament with a series of motions by the growing pro-pub lobby in the house. Further ammunition was provided in July 2012 with BBPA/CAMRA figures showing that the average pub paid £66,500 pa in beer tax, a rise of 38% since the escalator was imposed in 2008.[4] In September 2012 a petition calling for the government to drop the beer duty escalator reached 100,000 signatures, the level which was required to trigger a Parliamentary debate. This took place on 1st November and, although no vote was taken, the tone of the debate was very supportive of the pub trade and sympathetic to the financial problems which landlords faced.

This prepared a lot of the ground for what was to follow in the March 2013 budget when government finally responded and the hated escalator was scrapped. For good measure, 1p was taken off duty. The action only had a small immediate effect but it provided a huge psychological boost for the industry; that someone was listening at last.

The Political Dimension

"I take the view that our licensing laws are among the most complicated, archaic, uncivilised and restrictive parts of our legal system. I realise that there are those who have come to accept our restrictive licensing laws, and these laws are becoming almost an adopted and accepted part of our way of life. There are also those who firmly believe that the laws do social good and are an advantage possessed by this country which other countries do not have.

I believe that both assumptions can be challenged. I certainly have serious doubts whether the licensing laws achieve any useful purpose. We tend to have them because we have always had them. They are taken for granted and nobody has seriously questioned their supposed social purpose."

The words of a young Kenneth Clarke, Conservative MP for Rushcliffe, during the debate of a Licensing Amendment Bill in 1976.[5] Despite such insightful eloquence and the liberalising recommendations of the very comprehensive Errol Committee four years earlier, in 1972, Parliament decided to reject this Bill and retain our 'archaic' licensing system for a further twelve years.

Those licensing hours were increasingly regarded as ridiculous by many of our visitors from the more enlightened continent. Whether the restrictive hours actually damaged our tourist trade is open to debate. What is easier to substantiate is that they did have an ongoing influence on the national psyche in relation to alcohol consumption;

the creation of a milder six-o'clock-swill[6] mentality of 'down it and get another in quick' because the shutter would be coming down soon. But successive governments failed for over seventy years to restore the hours which had been taken away from us as an emergency war-time measure in 1916.

Politicians, acting as a group, seem to have an unerring instinct for getting it wrong in deciding when and how to intervene in the licensed trade. Here are other notable examples:

During the 1950s and 60s the large brewers were running rampant around the country, buying up their weaker competitors. The politicians of the period apparently showed little concern or inclination to get involved. This permitted the creation of the large and fearsome corporate combines which became the big six. The growing giants' next act was to close down many of the breweries which they had recently acquired. The Monopolies Commission was created as early as 1949, so it was in existence during the whole of this period. A period that witnessed the purchase of long-established and substantial local employers and the blatant and total asset stripping of these soon after. But it would appear that there was never a politician who was sufficiently concerned to demand some protection for our heritage or the many people whose livelihoods were affected.

This non-intervention was all the more difficult to understand when in 1986 the director general of Fair Trade, Sir Gordon Borrie, a highly-qualified Labour politician, during the Thatcher premiership, referred the drinks industry to the MMC for investigation. We are still experiencing the effects of the judgement which finally emerged from Lord Young. The depth of the MMC analysis meant they understood the likely impact on the big brewers, but such was the MMC contempt for them, that they ignored the potential damage to the industry. The pubCos can be viewed as the illicit love child which resulted from the government's unseemly tangle with the industry.

In 1997, New Labour were swept to power. Blair and his babes had finally arrived. After the death of the mining industry, the decline of long-established working-class communities, and Labour's poor showing at successive elections, the party had moved to the centre. When they won their landslide victory in 1997, the parliamentary Labour party was composed of a new breed of young, ambitious career politicians, many inexperienced in life and business, and peppered with champagne socialists and political opportunists, all guided by the spin doctors who we became so familiar with. Few of these politicians would appear to have cared a jot about pubs, brewing or the pub trade. To them these probably seemed to be constituent parts of another of those declining working-class industries, which they were tactfully distancing themselves from. The playground of this upwardly-mobile and aspiring group was in trendy restaurants, theatres and the like. And of course the heavily subsidised House of Commons bars.

The huge Labour majority and the inexperience of many of its back-benchers was critical in not imposing any restraint on our foreign policy of the time. But that is another story.

New Labour did not get too involved with the drinks industry. It appeared to have better things to do with its time. But it introduced the Smoking Ban. Its one major intervention was the 2005 Licensing Act, designed to streamline and modernise the system and sanction flexible licensing, to take the heat out of closing time and make us all that little bit more sophisticated and grown up. And so, twenty-four-hour licensing, the ugly monster, the all-consuming beast of society's safety and security, was born. Rarely has a measure been so well-intentioned and, in retrospect, so ill-conceived. But once it was out of the bottle it spread its curse far and wide, with the price still being paid in the form of a whole raft of restrictions and regulations on our pubs, created to combat the misplaced fear of anarchy on our streets.

Gordon Brown was equally disinterested in the pub. Except as a means of fund-raising. He and chancellor Alistair Darling squeezed the industry mercilessly and cynically at a time of recession when the pub business was desperate for some assistance. These policies, inflating pub beer prices whilst ignoring the growing use by the supermarkets of discount beer sales as a loss-leader, were damaging in a number of ways and greatly encouraged the phemonenon of pre-loading. Pubs not only lost a lot of trade, but they also received the blame for any misbehaviour which resulted from young drinkers who were heavily intoxicated before they left home.

The arrival of the coalition in 2010 contained the promise of some relief for the trade. The new Parliament seems to be brimming, on all sides of the house, with MPs who have declared their sympathies for the plight of the pub, and their desire to assist it and reduce the horrendous attrition which it is suffering. They have demonstrated this in numerous long and impassioned debates on the subject. By 2014 the Parliamentary Beer Group could claim a phenomenal 300 MPs and 100 further members in the Lords.

So surely this must be good news for the trade? Well very much so, when Chancellor George Osborne, following receipt of a 100,000 – plus petition on the subject, removed the hated beer duty escalator at the 2013 budget. Also possibly, in respect of the coalition's determined, but apparently even-handed, intervention in licensing policy. Although the regular introduction of new measures and restrictions represent both a challenge and a cost to the industry, the government's strong stance has at least quelled the media paranoia which had existed.

Meanwhile, the longer term impact of David Cameron's Big Society and its localism agenda raises concern. Many observers are still perplexed as to what is actually implied by this slogan, beyond the obvious attempt to engage local communities. The small positive aspect for pubs is the Register of Community Assets and the encouragement given to communities to take over their local pub. On the other hand, localism creates concern at the rights given to local people to intervene during planning and licensing. This creates the spectre of nimbyism by giving official sanction to local vendettas by intolerant neighbours of long-established, well-run pubs.

The single issue that has occupied an inordinate amount of time, both in Parliament and within the trade, has been the Beer Tie and the relationship between the pubCos and their licensees. This is discussed in detail later in the book. The dispute has been magnified by the involvement of a number of politicians and may well have been resolved by now without them. And those politicians, who clearly believe in impassioned terms that they are acting in the best interests of the pub should, given their elevated role in society, have been capable of acting somewhat more objectively than they have.

The dispute, having been stirred up to its current intensity, is unlikely to be resolved quickly or satisfactorily for anyone involved. A widespread anticipation of statutory intervention to save pub tenants from unfair oppression has been created. Even the suggestion that this intervention would prevent further pub closures and save the entire industry. Life is never that simple. And the government, having been dragged into the dispute by the intense campaigning, has been placed in a difficult situation.

We return finally to where we started this analysis: on the thorny subject of licensing. Although the licensing agenda for pubs, over the last 100 years, has been decided entirely by the politicians, with only occasional regard for what the public may want or need, they have always been extremely adept at taking absolutely no blame or responsibility for the outcome. When things go wrong then it is the fault of the licensed trade, or irresponsible sections of society. The trade is entitled to wonder whether it may have been better served over the years if politicians were properly accountable for their actions and decisions.

Hard Times On The High Street

Overshadowed by the huge pubCo securitisations and flotations, the start of the millennium saw a constant flurry of lesser deals as pubCos spat out odds and ends from their acquisitions. The retail pub groups awaited to cherry-pick houses from these, which were suitable for their brands. SFI (formerly Surrey Free Inns) were very active, firstly buying the thirty-two prime location Slug and Lettuce bars for £31.6m in 2000, to be followed very shortly by the chain of Parisa Bars. Its competitor Barracuda trumped this, spending £120m in acquiring three packages, from W&D, Enterprise and Ambishus. The relentless thirst for growth evident in the Nineties brand scramble remained amongst these companies, and other players like Yates's and Luminar. The hungry operators stalked each other, with a view to the opportunity for hostile takeovers, whilst picking off any smaller targets they encountered.

In 2001 Barry Gillham of specialist trade agents Fleurets reported that the number of high street superpubs due to open was just seventeen, down from around eighty in each of the previous three years. He also advised that rents on these showpiece bars were double or treble those for traditional pubs and that profitability would fall if their substantial turnovers weren't maintained. He not only called the end of the branding boom but also the start of the subsequent downturn, the 'morning-after' for the High street retail groups.[7] The rentals that Fleurets reported that the superpub operators were paying were indeed unnervingly high, with an average figure approaching £100,000 per annum.

Over the next year, the sector's virility totally withered as the operators were hit by the double blow of a downturn in trade and a stockmarket slide. An EU directive on working hours and an increasing minimum hourly wage had also imposed additional operating costs. More critical was the impact of ten years of relentless brand-building and expansion in town and city centres. Saturation had been reached, and probably passed in some centres. Not only were there too many bars but some observers wondered whether customers were also sated and were drifting away, in need of a new experience.

The high street operators who had been most actively acquiring, and thus heavily burdened by interest payments, along with expensive rents on their leasehold outlets, derailed alarmingly quickly. During 2002 SFI's shares were suspended whilst a £20m accounting black hole appeared. SFI subsequently went into administration and the pub estate was broken up. Old Monk, a chain of city bars created by Jerry Martin, brother of Tim, also entered administration, and was sold off. Luminar Leisure issued profit warnings. Barracuda was pulled into a long decline from which it never recovered. Mustard Entertainment which ran Brannigan's went into receivership and Po Na Na, the nightclub operator saw its profits slashed.

S&N also felt the pressure and sold its managed house estate soon after. In January 2003 the unthinkable happened and the darling of the stockmarket, Wetherspoons, issued a profits warning. The impact on shares in the sector was immediate and brutal, increasing the nervousness of a stockmarket that was already falling. The reaction of the operators was to discount their prices in an effort to build trade. But with many on the high street following suit, the only winner was the customer and turnover simply dropped further. In such cutthroat circumstances, survival proved to be a real challenge.

Yates, who ran the oldest brand in the country, albeit unrecognisable from the original, had expanded steadily over the previous decade. They seemed determined to secure an imposing outlet on every circuit to demonstrate and exploit their dominant position. They had already issued a profit warning in September 2000, and their knee-jerk reaction of redesigning units and shuffling their management team didn't seem to help. As the cracks started to appear, the share price slumped and Yates's reputation as the kingpin of the circuit was shredded. Yates's started selling pubs but none of this could avoid the final humiliation, the departure of Peter Dickson, great-grandson of the founder after a management buyout in 2004. Worse was to come and in May 2005 the company lost its long and proud independence, being taken over by R20's Laurel.

The carnage was not confined to the high street. During this period a number of breweries closed, Bass suffered a 24% drop in pre-tax profits whilst Youngs were under takeover pressure and McMullens, the Hertford family brewer, was reviewing whether to sell-up. Meanwhile, Bulmers the cider magnate experienced a share collapse and found itself absorbed soon after by S&N. Sadly the company appeared to have lost its way with growing international ambitions, distractions like beer distribution and a host of new products whilst neglecting what it did best. Making cider.

As the giant pubCos, Enterprise and Punch, were applauded for their financial wizardry in pulling off their breathtaking purchases, the tenanted sector appeared as a haven of stability. Whilst the pubCos basked in their new stature, the crisis amongst the brand operators prompted an overreaction in relation to both high street brands and managed houses. This was evident in a massive wave of conversion of managed houses to lease. Many of these were, arguably, unsuited to the medium, whilst a lack of suitable lessees did not help the exercise. The extent of the reaction can be gauged by the 4,000 managed pubs which were transferred to tenancy during 2001-3.

Further reaction to the crisis on the high street was a sudden belief that suburbia was sexy. Bass, soon to change its name to Six Continents, had contributed to the licensed high street malaise by taking many sites for a host of high street brands, often at very steamy rents. They now decided that this market was declining, and diverted huge resources and investment into Ember Inns, and to a lesser extent Arena, its community brand. Ember Inns, mainly developed in prominent suburban locations, was marketed as a cosy home from home, designed to be convenient for wealthy suburbanites.

The insecurity in managed pubs even spread to the more reticent family brewers. Whilst Fullers were selling their small Broadwalk chain aimed at young persons, Jennings Brothers at the other end of the country announced it was quitting managed houses, with plans to sell half of its forty-four-pub estate and convert the other half to tenancy. Meanwhile, such was the confidence of the pubCo sector that in March 2003 Hugh Osmond came close to launching a £5.6 billion Punch hostile bid for Six Continents pubs, hotels and all.

And then, as most operators appeared to be gradually emerging from the crisis, the UK was hit by the 2007 credit crunch and started sinking deeply into recession. It was scant consolation that the demise of the shop and the death of the high street was replacing the tedious media headlines on the theme of the death of the pub.

And prospects for the retail trade were truly grim. Many retailers with household names entered administration and disappeared, whilst other solid companies, like Mothercare and Thorntons chocolates, trading in sound retail sectors, were forced to issue profit warnings and consider restructuring. On the streets the damage was clear for all to see through the growing number of empty town centre shops. By February 2012, a survey by Local Data Company suggested that the retail vacancy rate had reached its highest ever recorded level, at 14.6%.[8] One in seven of our shops was empty. Subsequent analysis claimed that twenty shops per day were closing during the course of 2012.

The reasons were generally accepted as being threefold; changing spending patterns, particularly due to internet shopping; competition from out-of-town retail and the large supermarkets, and of course the unforgiving and damaging recession. Additionally, fundamental structural changes were undermining some sectors, like photography and home entertainment as a result of new technology.

The obsolescence of some types of shop was one thing, but given the startling rate of shop closures, did this herald a terminal decline in high street retail? Had society turned its back on old-fashioned shops with all the rigmarole of congested roads, expensive parking and dirty streets in favour of pressing a button on a computer or one-stop shopping in a convenient out-of-town superstore? If high streets were on the critical list, and our town centres soon to resemble some of the abandoned and desperate downtowns of America, then pubs located in those centres would probably also decline and die.

In fact, there is considerable evidence that the pub and the nighttime economy gives greater succour to the rest of the high street than vice versa. Currently, few retail schemes are developed without a substantial element of restaurants and leisure included. A number of local authorities, who encouraged new investment and supported the grant of new licences during the 1990s, acknowledged that the nighttime economy kick-started the regeneration of their town and city centres.

It is easy to forget that before the Nineties many town centres had few residents, and when the shops closed at 6.00pm the streets would be deserted and not particularly welcoming. Town-centre regeneration, which took place all over the country, was a social trend which made city-centre living fashionable and it was happening only twenty to twenty-five years ago. It was delivered through the development of new apartments in town centres, the conversion of old buildings like warehouses and redundant offices to residential use and the re-use of vacant space above shops. But it was the flowering of the nighttime economy; not just pubs but cafes, restaurants, theatres, cinemas and nightclubs, which put people on the streets and made these a safe and inviting environment for the new residents to enjoy. Leeds and Wolverhampton provide contrasting examples of the benefits derived from the masses of people drawn in to use the pubs and bars which mushroomed there.

A more recent example is provided by Shoreditch, an area on the northern edge of the city of London which twenty-five years ago was little more than a deserted and slightly menacing ghetto of empty warehouses. It is now one of the most happening districts in the country, full of creativity and new independent restaurants and bars. A visit there will leave one in no doubt that this rousing regeneration is attributable to the nighttime economy.

Seasonal cheer in the industry was rather limited during December 2009. Whilst the row over the Beer-Tie raged on, several companies had significant problems. At the Punch AGM trading profit was revealed to be 11% down for the second year running and, possibly as a result, the directors' remuneration package was voted down. At Mitchells and Butlers a long-standing board battle came to a head, with four directors being removed, the board writing to shareholders to explain its position and the whole affair sounding as professional as a schoolgirl spat.

Meanwhile at Luminar, profits were sliding and the share value was following suit. The company advised that it needed its customers to party hard over the coming holiday season. But with dire trading, rough weather and the threat of further brutal increases in excise duty few in the industry appeared to be in the mood for such frivolity. Luminar limped along until the company was sold in October 2011, and now trades as Luminar Group. Barracuda had also hung on throughout the difficult years but, having been restructured into Bramwell Pub Company in 2012, entered administration a year later.

The increasing share of overall alcohol sales by supermarkets and off-licenses drew further comparison with the retail trade. Greater use of the internet to make purchases also represented a preference by consumers to remain conveniently at home, and buy more cheaply. Retailers pointed out that they were not competing on a level playing field because of the expense of operating from high street premises and the imposition of high levels of commercial rates.

In October 2010 the BBPA chief executive Brigid Simmons had called for pubs to be recognised in the high street regeneration plans.

She pursued this with the newly-appointed minister for the high street, Brandon Lewis, stressing the importance of the nighttime economy for the vitality of the high street. Finally, in December 2013, the drinks industry was invited to join the Future High Streets Forum, represented by Simmons herself and Spirit Chief Executive Mike Tye. Meanwhile, both shops and pubs continued to close. By May 2013 the bleak forecast was that up to 20% of shops could close over the next five years due to the internet. It was suggested that this would double its share of the retail market to 22%.[9]

Putting aside concerns for the pub, the survival of town centres is a critical issue in preserving our way of life. So much of what we do and need is within town centres. Unless we wish to accept that we can function simply by the use of the internet and an occasional trip to the one-stop suburban mall, American style, we need to understand the essential vitality of the high street and rally to support it. The factors which are undermining town centre shops are similar to those which have affected traditional pubs; cheaper prices elsewhere, the erosion of community life, the convenience of sitting at home, the impact of marketing and changing lifestyles.

There are clear synergies linking high street shops and pubs. Both have suffered badly during the recent recession. The longer-term threat from the changing market place is obvious for both. Politicians and representatives of both the retail and pub sectors must explore and find new and positive strategies to change attitudes and reverse current trends. The closer integration of the town centre and the nighttime economy should be an obvious element of this.

The Smoking Ban

As Sober October progressed, the issue of a Smoking Ban became ever more topical. An increasing number of restaurants went smoke-free. Some pubs did the same, generally to their cost. The Hare and Hounds in Todmorden, West Yorkshire, reported that it lost 95% of its business having banned smoking, back in 1995.[10] But attitudes changed substantially in the ten years that followed, and most people recognised that a ban of some sort was inevitable.

The impending ban impacted on the strategy adopted by a number of larger pub groups which hastened to dispose of smaller wet-led pubs, with limited food potential, which were regarded as the places which would suffer most when the smoking ban arrived. Wetherspoons experimented with non-smoking pubs and found that this resulted in an increase in food sales but a drop in liquor sales.[11]

The formalities commenced in November 2004, with a Public Health White Paper, which outlined the steps until 2008 for phasing in what was originally intended as a partial ban. In October 2005, after external challenges and internal parliamentary consideration, the government agreed to implement a ban within pubs, bars, restaurants and public buildings by summer 2007. Considerable discussion was to follow on the exact details of the ban. Proposals were put forward that it would be partial, not applying to private members' clubs and only within pubs serving food. Many MPs demanded a total ban, whilst another large group insisted that the ban be more selective.

The importance of the issue within the licensed and restaurant sectors created huge debate and diverse views. The trade was initially fairly solid in opposing the ban but, influenced by the distinct possibility of a partial ban, self-interest intervened. Those running food-led businesses determined that they did not want to lose out to other outlets where people could still light up. So they campaigned for a total ban. This undermined those defending the interests of the pub by arguing for a partial ban because the drinks industry no longer spoke with one voice. In the meantime, individual operations like Wetherspoons and Pizza Express took the initiative and introduced their own bans ahead of the official one.

On 14th February 2006 the House of Commons held a free vote, which decided, by a substantial majority, to introduce a total ban. The two amendments that would have allowed smoking in just private members' clubs, or both these and non-food pubs, were also voted out convincingly.

In July 2012, five years after the introduction of the ban, a survey of *Morning Advertiser* readers showed that seven out of ten wanted to see legislation to allow separate smoking rooms.[12] Given five years to have adapted to the new situation this did not suggest, as government spokesmen claim whenever the subject is raised, that the ban has had little impact on the trade.

The Smoking Ban has done for community and local pubs what myxomatosis did for rabbits. Like rabbits, the survivors have learned to adapt. It must be hoped that the strong ones will survive.

Licensing Lament

Victorian attitudes towards temperance influenced the policy of our licensing magistrates until well into the last century. The impact of this was particularly evident in the formulaic 1930's 'improved' architectural style and layout of public houses from that period. The other feature, which shaped not only the appearance but the running of our public houses for over seventy years, was the First World War.

The two enduring legacies of the Great War were restricted trading hours with compulsory afternoon closure, and in response to shortages of Barley, reduced-strength beer. Since then beer strength has rarely reverted to the levels which were common in 1914.

The 1980s and 1990s witnessed a slow liberalisation of the licensing system. In 1988, following successful changes in Scotland, extended hours were introduced to the rest of the UK, allowing pubs to trade all afternoon and until 11.00 pm, Monday to Saturday. With few problems arising, in 1993 the government rolled back the boundaries a little further by allowing children into bars, with the grant of a children's certificate, and a month or two later, by extending all-day drinking to Sundays. These long-overdue changes gave the licensed trade a significant boost, perhaps lifting overall trade volumes by 5-10%.

Licensing policy was dominated for many years, by the urge to restrict. Magistrates and politicians decided that they knew best and what might have been good for the trade, or desired by the customer, was rarely considered. Many of us grew up in that long stagnant era when pubs had to close after lunch and again sharp at 11.00pm. The licensed trade may not have enjoyed working to hours which were introduced as an emergency measure, but it stuck stoically to its task of making the best of them for seventy-odd years, until the politicians finally decided that they could trust us with slightly more grown up hours.

Having been granted these hours, the trade and its long-suffering customers settled down to enjoy their new freedom when suddenly further reform was in the air. Given the long wait for the Eighties and Nineties reforms, further changes seemed to be premature, and weren't widely anticipated. The government statement promising further change was issued in 1998. The chairman of the Working Party, Christopher Haskins, stated;

> *"It is time for regulators to refocus on the reasons for regulating the sales of alcohol – to prevent nuisance and disorder and to protect young and vulnerable members of society. Frequently pub hours are out of tune with modern social life. There is ample evidence that a single closing time creates rather than controls nuisance and disorder. We therefore propose the introduction of more flexible hours based on the circumstances of the local community."*[13]

This set the scene for The March 2000 White Paper, 'Time for reform; proposals for the modernisation of our licensing laws', which proposed flexible hours, a personal ten-year licence and separate premises licence, and tougher powers to control rowdy pubs. Included was the radical proposition of twenty-four-hour opening. Otherwise, the Act was largely concerned with restructuring and rationalising the administration of the system and addressing concern that the planning and licensing systems didn't properly integrate.

The White Paper and subsequent Licensing Bill sparked huge debate within the industry and a great deal of reticence over the transfer of the system to the control of local authorities. Whilst the arguments continued, and the demands for alterations and reassurances grew, the Act went through, to take effect two years later in 2005.

At the time a mood of expectation and a spirit of liberty and progress was emerging. The *Evening Standard* typified this with an article entitled 'twenty-four-hour pubs to end yob culture' adding that the move towards twenty-four-hour licensing was backed by police chiefs.[14]

Few pubs applied for, or obtained twenty-four-hour licensing or anything close to this. Bizarrely a high proportion which were granted these hours were in rural areas of Norfolk and Dorset, where the new licensing authorities encouraged all bars to apply for twenty-four hours to cover all eventualities. In November 2007 the Department for Media Culture and Sport reported that of 176,400 licensed premises of any type in the UK only 5,100 had twenty-four-hour licences and most were hotels. Only 460 were pubs bars or nightclubs.[15]

Yet the fact that twenty-four-hour licensing exists, with the suggestion that people might be drinking all day and night, was seized upon by those with any gripe against the licensed trade to condemn the new Act, the audacity of pubs to take advantage of it, and everything else associated with it. The fact that hardly any outlets traded in that manner and that actual licensing hours were only extended modestly were conveniently forgotten. The media were soon unable to run any story about pubs without prefixing it with a banner headline along the lines of 'twenty-four-hour licensing mayhem'. The phrase 'twenty-four-hour licensing' appeared to be so emotive that a certain type of journalist couldn't handle the concept with any objectivity or accuracy.

As a result, the Act has turned out to be a Trojan horse for the industry taken as a gift from a Labour government that knew what it was trying to achieve, but not how to make it work, or make the public understand the long-term philosophy underlying it. Its strategy of flexibility to achieve the twin dreams of orderly streets and a wine-supping sophistication was fine, but not the forlorn hope that such a virtuous world was going to instantly and effortlessly appear simply by staggering closing times. Licensing requires a long-term approach. Just witness how long the 1916 regulations remained in force. Yet the new Act was expected to function perfectly from day one. To quote again from the Haskins Task Force;

> *"There is no evidence that longer opening hours increases hooliganism –*
> *by reverse it reduces it. People drinking up very rapidly in the last half*
> *hour before closing time is a much greater problem than if they make*
> *their own decisions."*[16]

A recent report by The University of Cambridge Institute of Criminology based on data provided by Greater Manchester Police before and after introduction of the Act[17] shows that there has been little change in street crime figures throughout the period. These undermine Labour's short-term expectations for the legislation, but more importantly, the media frenzy which sensationalised binge drinking. The report also advised that additional licensed hours in the Manchester area were extended much less than expected, at forty-three minutes on average in the week, and one hour twenty minutes at weekends. On the fifth anniversary of the introduction of the Act BBPA[18] released figures which showed that, nationally, pubs stayed open for an average of an additional twenty-seven minutes per day after the Act was introduced.

Therefore, remarkably little appears to have changed on the streets, or in our pubs, as a result of the Act. Binge drinking was taking place and getting headlines well before 2005. But the media latched onto trends like more women drinking and the presence of some raunchy pub promotions, and perpetuated and exaggerated the urban myths of laddettes, happy hours and all sorts of other horrors, stirring up an element of paranoia in the process. In 2008 the government reacted by introducing Alcohol Disorder Zones. Not one was actually declared despite the widespread reports of anarchy. The Home

Secretary Jacqui Smith clarified that these were only to be used in the last resort, and has since stopped them.

Whilst Home Office statistics, released in September 2009,[19] showed that arrests for drunkenness in public places were down by three-quarters over the previous thirty years; even the humble beer glass was under pressure as over-zealous campaigners demanded that pubs find a less dangerous product to be permitted in the powder-keg environment that was apparently our high street pub.

Agitation following further 'over-reporting' of binge-drinking incidents created a serious reaction. In 2010, a two-stage mandatory code was introduced. In April the first stage banned all-you-can-drink promotions, or women-drink-for-free, made speed drinking competitions and 'dentists chairs' (pouring of drinks down a victim's throat) illegal, and made it obligatory to provide free water to customers. The October code added the obligation for bars to check and demand ID for anyone who appeared to be under 18 and to provide and offer smaller drinks measures. The code was backed by the not-inconsiderable threat of loss of licences, fines of up to £20,000 and six months imprisonment. Few within the trade struggled with these regulations, or wept at the passing of the OTT promotions. A greater impact was felt by tabloid headline writers, who had to find a new subject to frighten us all with on their sordid front pages.

Fortunately, the architects of the code were not tempted to include one of the more fanciful measures speculated upon at the time; a ban on pub staff asking customers if they wanted 'the same again' as this might be construed as an incitement to customers to drink excessively. Such was the atmosphere of over-indulgent repression on the one hand and siege-mentality defensiveness on the other.

By this time, the coalition were keen to milk whatever kudos they could from their tough stance. Cynically, they seemed to see licensing as an undoubted vote-winner from the trembling citizens of middle England, rather than an issue to calmly deal with. The Lib-Dems, through their then-home affairs spokesman, Chris Huhne, extravagantly blamed;

"Labour's lax approach for creating a booze Britain in which an epidemic of drink-fuelled crime and illness is ruining lives and costing the country billions."[20]

The politicians had conveniently forgotten that the streets of 1990s Conservative Britain had been plagued by another media invention, the 'lager lout' and the same stories were being run then under that strapline as now, with a different name for the anti-social menace concerned.

The statistics on law and order showed that alcohol-fuelled misbehaviour is less common now, whilst contemporary accounts of the anarchy and violence of the 'skinhead-infested' streets of the 1970s or 1980s would suggest that we have come a long way since then. The liberalisation of licensing has much less impact on such matters than wider social trends and patterns of behaviour.

The local authorities had gained a central role in the licensing system. And contrary to fears from within the trade, most have proved to administer this in an objective and efficient manner. But a few councils with a significant nighttime economy have been quick to pursue their own agendas. Most notorious are Westminster, already discussed at the end of part three for their reaction during the Nineties pub expansion. Westminster is responsible for over 3,000 licensed premises. Parts of the borough effectively operate as the nation's entertainment capital. The councils' intention to restrict the licensed trade, in order to 'protect' its privileged local residents, became so unbalanced that a planning inspector intervened to insist that the council must amend its local plan, saying;

"… Policies are not only draconian but would be difficult to apply, justify and defend."[21]

In the meantime the courts have also stepped in with sensible appeal decisions on licensing matters in Westminster. This provides some reassurance that the system contains an effective range of checks and balances. But licensees should not have to undergo such a battle in the first place if policies are drawn up and applied sensibly and fairly.

On a national level, the coalition has continued with its very comprehensive alcohol strategy by publishing a series of carefully constructed documents, setting out options and justifying decisions, interspersed by regular consultations with all interested parties. And whilst it demonstrates that it has created the means to take an iron grip on the industry if disorder continues, this is matched by a reassurance that it only intends to adopt such measures judiciously.

Owing to the paranoia created by twenty-four-hour licensing, perhaps a firm intervention was required to demonstrate that the situation was under control and that any alcohol-fuelled disorder in the streets could be dealt with. The government has certainly made available to police and licensing authorities a range of measures. These include late night levies, Early Morning Restriction Orders (EMROs), Cumulative Impact Policies (CIPs), Special Policy Areas (SPAs), and a range of specific local area initiatives and community responsibility schemes such as Best Bar None.

Unfortunately the progressive mood of 1998 is no longer with us. The growing list of local authorities who have declared that they are considering the adoption of EMROs and imposing late night levies casts the spectre of intense regulation over the trade. This conflicts with all of the reassurances provided when the 2005 Act was being introduced that it would be applied with a 'light touch'.

Such a 'light touch' is certainly not in evidence in Hackney, east London, where the local authority have introduced a 'Special Policy Area' (SPA) in Dalston. This was justified because of a fear that the nighttime economy was having a detrimental effect on residents. The residents clearly did not agree because in a public consultation carried out during 2013, 84% of the 2,800 who gave their opinion on the issue were opposed to the restriction. Despite this the council introduced the SPA in January 2014, meaning that new licences will only be approved in exceptional circumstances.[22]

The new licensing act has now bedded in and, despite fears and protests, appears to work reasonably well, on a day-to-day level. The media-fuelled paranoia has finally quelled. One can only hope that the excesses on the part of the authorities endeavouring for example to ban 'vertical drinking' are not going to be repeated and that the 'emergency measures' like EMROs and late night levies will only be adopted in extreme circumstances, where they are fully justified.

The industry and the public accepted restricted and 'archaic' licensing hours for generations. Now that the politicians have finally agreed that we can progress to a more enlightened regime, licensing policy should cease to become a matter of politics, controversy, and repression. The system should be permitted to quietly operate in an impartial and fair manner in order that the laudable aims of the 1998 Working Party will be given time to blossom.

PART SEVEN

Starting A New Life[1]

I n the years up to the 1930s, land was cheap and relatively plentiful.
Public houses built in those days were often allocated generous
plots and plenty of space for expansion. In rural settings there
might be a field for horses, subsequently becoming car parking.
Alongside the pub there might be a cottage or two retained by the
brewery for possible future expansion, and use by pub staff. To the rear
there was normally a yard, possibly with a function room and extensive
outbuildings, whilst on upper floors, particularly in the case of town
pubs, one or two floors of ancillary living space.

When pubs were controlled by the beerage, this ancillary space and
land was relatively unexploited and normally retained with the pub. In
the continual process of churn since MMC, when pubs have parted
company from their brewery owner, some pubs have been sold as part
of packages, two or three times and then possibly again, individually.
The new owners have tended to exploit any extra value they could find,
selling off such areas before disposing of the trading pub. Or companies
with a longer-term commitment to the pub have, in their
determination to 'make their assets sweat', explored every opportunity
to identify and isolate unlicensed and non-trading parts of their pubs
and sell them. A lot of pubs have therefore been raked over repeatedly
in the search for any additional asset value which can be squeezed out.

In recent years, developers cherry-picked through the lists of
available pubs owned by the pubCos for large Victorian pubs in
desirable and bohemian suburbs of London and elsewhere. When
acquired, upper floors were sold off to become apartments and the
ground floor trading space was then leased out. The lock-up, ground-
floor space of an old traditional pub, reborn as a restaurant or gastro
pub, could command a turnover twice the level previously generated
by the entire premises. The developer thus received a substantial rent,

in addition to recouping his purchase cost from the sale of the upper floors.

A good example of this process is the Duke of Clarence on Old Brompton Rd in South Kensington. In September 2001, planning approval was applied for with the Royal Borough of Kensington and Chelsea by a developer who had acquired a package of pubs from S&N. At the time this pub traded as the Bram Stoker, one of S&N's somewhat esoteric 'eerie bars', complete with a waxwork model of Dracula, shelves of fake books, a scattering of scientific equipment and a fine mural of Dracula on an external wall. As planning approval was granted for conversion of the upper floors to four expensive apartments, nearby residents were probably relieved to be rid of their blood-sucking neighbour and his gothic followers.

The ground-floor lock-up was leased to Geronimo, a fast-expanding gastropub operator. The chain was steadily built up, by concentrating on leasing, in fashionable areas of London. The trading area of these pubs was adapted within the available space, concentrating on providing cool simple décor. The refurbished Duke of Clarence matches this perfectly. Food is at the heart of its operation, with alluring drinking corners to encourage a relaxed element of wet trade. The pub provides a bright, pleasant environment, far removed from its dark past. The downside of this type of conversion is of course the loss of old genuine, traditional drinking environments, or in this case, an intriguing and eccentric one-off. Geronimo operated over thirty London gastro pubs, when they were purchased by Young's, the London brewer for £60m in 2010.

Abington Piggots is a tiny settlement in Cambridgeshire that feels sleepy and remote, as far removed from Chelsea as is possible within fifty miles. To reach it involves a few miles of winding lanes with road signs tempting one to divert off to places like Shingay Wendy and Guilden Morden. On arrival the single street houses a community of about 150 in thatched and tiled cottages around the solid three-storey Pig and Abbot. It dominates almost like a castle in a French medieval village. The village is certainly not a place where one would open a new pub. And yet a pub has survived there since 1701, being renamed the Derby and Joan in the nineteenth century and the Pig and Abbot towards the end of the last century.

In the early Nineties when the 'Pig' was threatened with closure, a Save Our Pub Campaign transformed into a company to purchase the property. Forty shareholders from twenty-nine households in a total population of just 120 raised £130,000 to buy the property. They decided to treat it as an investment and let the house to a series of tenants. Unfortunately, this arrangement did little to address the poor underlying trade, and none of the tenants achieved great success. The community owners, having experienced this frustration and disappointment, gave up on the place and sold to a small investor from London. Fortunately he knew the current landlords, who stepped in to take the place on about twelve years ago.

From the moment one enters the 'Pig', the rich ambience of the pub dominates. The layout, with a long wrap-around central servery overlooking what were formerly three or four small rooms, now all connected, unifies the whole and brings those serving into intimate contact with customers. The menu specialises in a range of enticing pies whilst four real ales are maintained. The pub manages to achieve that rare balance a 50:50 trade of wet and dry, which allows it to maintain a proper bar trade and a quality food offer.

As a result the pub's reputation has spread around the district and customers will apparently travel from a twenty-mile radius, although regulars tend to live somewhat closer. Its obvious success, over an extended period, with few chimney pots in the village and no passing trade, suggests that even in the current market, if a pub has the right characteristics and the management are sufficiently focused, it can succeed almost anywhere.

Michael Cannon purchased Eldridge Pope in 2005. He sold the estate for an impressive profit to Marstons only two years later. A property which illustrates this period is a fine, four-storey Regency building in the centre of the elegant town of Cheltenham. The building, a former bank, had been acquired by Eldridge Pope during its frantic brand-building period as a 'Toad' young persons' pub. Reflecting the life cycle of many other similar concepts, the Toads were initially highly successful, providing daytime food in pleasant surroundings and then turning the lights down and the music up to pull in the circuit drinkers by night. Unfortunately, pressure on Eldridge Pope saw changes in management at head office, control of the operations slackened and, as standards dropped, turnover and reputation quickly followed suit.

By the time Michael Cannon had taken control of Eldridge Pope it was time for Toad at the Olde Bank to step aside. The shrewd Cannon immediately replaced this and other Toad sites with his own town centre brand Que Pasa. The look, with garish latin décor, salsa music and tapas menu was very different, but the loud boisterous entertainment continued where Toad had left off. With a new image and focused management the site threw itself into a further two years of music-driven hedonism. Marston's then stepped in to spoil the party, completing the purchase from Cannon in February 2007. Marston's were never very keen on the high street and they soon closed the pub, selling it to Wetherspoons. Now it trades as JDW's second site in the town, whilst the youth market go elsewhere for their fun and games.

Tucked away in an obscure but beautiful area of Georgian terraces and squares between King's Cross and Islington one could find the notorious Filthy McNasty's. At least it sounds as if it should be notorious. It did achieve notoriety of some sort during the Nineties furore over renaming pubs when Filthy's was nominated as the daftest new pub name in London by the *Evening Standard*.

But to those who moved in the right circles 'Filthy's' was on the map, because it was often frequented by luminary figures from the music world like Shane McGowan and Pete Doherty, who would participate in acoustic and open-mic sessions. Celebrity poetry readings were also a feature. Given the relatively small size of the two bars those sessions must have been an intimate and privileged occasion for the watching locals.

Although Filthy McNastys conjures up images of a very rough and ready Irish bar, the pub is hidden away at the heart of a gentrified residential community. Now that the wild spontaneous days are long finished, the pub has returned to its community. This has been achieved by evolution rather than any dramatic or symbolic refurbishment. New management appear to have contented themselves with minor redecorations and an interesting approach to catering. The pub name has not actually been changed although there is little external signage apart from 'Whisky Café' which is a reference to the pub's speciality in the spirit. Rumours circulate that the pub's original name of The Fountain will be restored, but the owners currently prefer to keep people guessing.

In the meantime the pub is certainly not filthy or nasty. The plain décor and low lighting, enhanced with candles, creates a comfortable ambience for local customers to enjoy.

Although only a couple of miles away from Filthy's, nothing could be further removed from it than Kanaloa. This establishment, occupying part of the ground floor of a mid-town office complex called Hill House, is more club than pub and certainly more Honolulu than Holborn with its thatched roofing and imitation palm trees. Which is all rather sad as, prior to redevelopment, presumably in the 1960s or 70s, the site of Hill House was The Crown and Anchor Tavern. This venerable establishment had a long history with records indicating that it was used as a Masonic meeting place as far back as 1771 and that the suspect in a grand larceny trial of October 1800 was resident at 'Mrs Sabine's Crown and Anchor'. The tavern featured heavily in the trial as the suspect was followed back there and the loot was allegedly found in his room.

The architects or developers should be ashamed of the replacement space allocated for The Crown and Anchor within the new office block as it comprises a huge chunk of space in the bowels of the property with little frontage at the rear of the building. The long list of failed operations since would suggest that the area is more suited to blanket storage than a bar operation. In addition to the new Crown and Anchor the space has masqueraded as a long list of failed bars; Alibi, Spatz, Fleets and Old Cobblers as well as housing a Walkabout for a time.

If running this space as a tropical fantasy is the only way to make it work then good luck to the current management. Kanaloa is an unfortunate footnote in the history of a noted old pub.

If Filthy's celebrity associations are impressive they are beaten by Dovedale Towers in Liverpool. This extraordinary building combines a landmark tower which seems almost art deco at the front of what appears to be a large and elegant Regency villa. Its impact is all the greater as it sits opposite rows of standard brick-terraced housing. For many years the property was Grove House and, having started its life as the home of a wealthy Victorian family, it then saw service as variously an orphanage, a church hall and a dance hall.

It commenced as The Dovedale Tavern as recently as the 1960s, when its prominent location on the iconic Penny Lane earned it some notable connections. Freddy Mercury, in the early days of his career, apparently lived upstairs for a time, whilst John Lennon and the Quarry Men played there more than once. Many other household names were raised in the near vicinity. Unfortunately its pub career was almost as mixed as its previous life, with a succession of highs and lows as it meandered from boozer to food pub to the quirky Alma de Santiago and back in 2008 to The Dovedale Tavern. In 2010 this ran out of steam and the building was closed for two sorry years.

It reopened as Dovey, part of the select chain operated by Urban Gastro Pubs, a local group. The pub uses all of its generous floor space in providing an innovative range of food and a solid selection of ales and other drinks. Sports screens are also prominent whilst live music is featured. Given this range of facilities and the pub's charisma and surroundings, one would hope that the operation will have a long and rewarding future.

The ancient and attractive city of Worcester witnessed a few significant battles during the English Civil War. More recently, it has been subject to a battle for the survival of its many old pubs. One victim was the Paul Pry, named after a popular Victorian play. It was built in 1901 just as the Victorian era ended in the back streets of the city centre. The pub occupies the prow of a building, which narrows to a point. It has many historic features and an interior listed under the Planning Acts.

The pub closed in 2007, more because of management issues than poor trade. Because of its listed status and layout, and its lack of potential for retail use, away from main streets, redevelopment did not happen and in 2010 it became a Polish restaurant, complete with Polish beers and spirits. The venture was not a failure but the management lost their way and the building once again closed. Briefly, it again reopened as a pre-club venue geared to two busy nightclubs around the corner. When it closed again, soon after, hope started to fade. Until early 2013 when it was reopened by local licensee Catherine Ottaway, with the genial Marco installed as manager. A visit demonstrates a timelessness to the pub which belies the fact that it was ever closed. The imposing carved mahogany back fitting dominates the bar area. The bar's unusual, almost triangular, shape creates an area suggestive of a temple to the golden nectar. With its friendly and attentive management, chatty locals, a good selection of real ales and the other period fittings, that is indeed what the Paul Pry is.

Compare this to the former Fountain in Peterborough, which has shared a similar, chequered history. The pub, an undistinguished brick 1930's building in a dull residential street just outside the city centre, had a bad reputation and was noisy. So, its neighbour Roger Payn, instead of complaining about it, simply bought the property! From 2006, for about four years it was run as The Glass Onion, establishing itself as a serious venue for local live music and arts exhibitions. Mr Payn's son Luke, who named the venue after The Beatles song, was heavily involved. But then this project lost momentum and reverted to its former occupation as The Rose with a new licensee in charge. The same management has now evolved The Rose into Embe, which is a lively Afro-Carribean restaurant.

Although this latest change in its meandering career makes the building count as a further lost pub, one anticipates that there is a limited sense of loss to local drinkers, certainly compared to the reaction when The Glass Onion closed. By contrast the Paul Pry is every inch a pub and, it would seem, cannot function as anything else.

The Jack of Both Sides is an unusual pub name but there were two of them in adjoining towns in the Thames Valley. Both have experienced dizzying changes of name and character in recent times. Although Jack of Both Sides is an old-fashioned term for being able to view things objectively, strangely both pubs sit at a road junction between two roads so perhaps there was some subtle double meaning at work when these names emerged.

The Jack of Both Sides in Maidenhead was a Whitbread pub which had the misfortune to be refurbished as a Tut n Shive, one of the craziest pub brands devised. The site was then sold in one of Whitbreads' package sales and next turned up as Bar Metro, a wine bar with go-faster yellow bands. This only lasted for a short period before the building endured its third change of identity, reappearing as the Honeypot Bar, an interesting concept, aimed at a specialist market.

Nearby, in Reading, the other Jack of Both Sides traded for years in a large 'roadhouse' situated near Cemetery Junction[2] in the centre of a major one-way road system. The pub had a mixed reputation, perhaps accounting for the name change to the equally cryptic Upin Arms. There were few changes until Bass stepped in to purchase and convert to one of their Scream student bars, endeavouring to exploit trade from the nearby Reading University. Having sold the Scream brand, and 330 pubs in 2010, this pub was excluded from the sale – a vote of confidence in its potential. It now trades as the refurbished Abbot Cook, and provides an interesting mix of food, decent ales and entertainment in appealing bohemian surroundings.

Bass are also involved in the next story. Princess Beatrice, fifth daughter of Queen Victoria and Prince Albert, outlived all of her royal generation, surviving until 1944 to see the dawn of a few new ages. Her name was given to a Victorian pub on Camden High Street, north London, possibly constructed soon after her birth in 1857. The pub was an old Charrington house, known as being a haunt of the local Irish community. The name remained for almost 140 years and is cut into the stucco parapet above the second floor. Then, in 1996, Bass decided to convert a real Irish bar into a branded pub. O'Neill's had arrived. Given the history of the pub, and the nature of this part of Camden, which is geared towards the local community as opposed to the visitor orientated bazaar, north of the underground station, this was a questionable move. And it appears to have been one of the first O'Neill's to be abandoned as the brand scaled down. The building was acquired by Enterprise Inns, and reappeared, still retaining its Irish accent, as Tommy O'Flynns, part of a small pub chain, providing food and entertainment.

In March 2011 the pub was sold by Enterprise at auction, for the very respectable figure of £1.57m as an investment. Especially as the old Princess appeared to have reached its nadir. It was now signed, and traded as the Wheelbarrow. This was apparently a music bar complete with a stage and plenty of support from the local community, but images of the exterior present a very undignified and run-down impression.

Happily the old lady has nearly gone full circle and is now back as the Beatrice, scrubbed up, reborn, and with a new image. There is even a mural on the side of the building, presumably with someone's impression of Beatrice. The pub is still geared to music and a young local following, which does seem entirely appropriate for this proper old boozer and, like the actual Princess, determined survivor.

The Globe in Swindon is another survivor, but only just. In 2008 it was closed and boarded up, whilst owners Enterprise Inns submitted plans for conversion to seven flats. The Globe is a street-corner community pub on the edge of the Old Town and neighbours came forward to object to the closure and redevelopment plans. The council took notice and threw out the planning application. When two of the residents then approached Enterprise to purchase, the pubCo had little alternative but to accept.

And so in 2010 the Globe reopened, to the delight of its surrounding neighbourhood. It remains very much a community pub, with darts, pool, sports screens and a king-size smoking shelter facing the large external garden.

Nearby, within Swindon Old Town, another pub known for many years as The Fountain and an imposing listed Victorian building, has experienced many recent changes. The local online CAMRA guide advises that the property was erected in 1847 as a beer house called The Brittania. It became a pub soon after, ceasing brewing on the premises, and in 1870 was purchased by the local North Wilts Brewery and renamed The Fountain. It remained, happily plying its trade, for almost 130 years, until acquired by Wychwood Brewery as a Hobgoblin during the Nineties. The ale apparently flowed for quite a few years but changes in ownership of the brand following Marston's acquisition resulted in the pub closing, and then briefly reopening as The Pipers, a gay venue, leased by freeholders Enterprise Inns.

This only lasted a few months, the operation closing in 2009 after a dispute over the lease. Hopefully the building's total refurbishment as the Pig on the Hill a year later as a food-based pub will provide some stability in this twisting tale. The pub certainly seems to be resilient in its ability to remain in operation. Its status as a listed building may of course have assisted in this, by making it difficult to redevelop for other purposes.

The former Moscow Arms, in London's Bayswater, would seem to have experienced the most dramatic changes in identity of the pubs featured here. For many years it was simply a large, rough and ready boozer, a refuge from the busy cosmopolitan thoroughfare of Queensway just around the corner. Then slowly and organically, in the days before pub owners endeavoured to manage these things themselves, it became a counter-cultural haunt. The clientele was mixed, but a strong punk following developed, whilst loud music and a happening vibe predominated.

S&N, perhaps feeling that a change of image would be beneficial, identified the pub as the ideal spot for its latest branding brainchild, Bar Oz. Their theming did not adopt half-measures, with boxing kangaroos on the walls, Australian road signs, surfboards and diving suits. The ladies became Sheilas, the predictable and uninspiring food selection was labelled Tucker and even the ceiling was covered in Australian flags. Clocks gave the time Down Under whilst the featured beer was of course chilled lager. It appears that this excessive tribute did not enjoy a particular following from the large Antipodean population in London and the pub was largely viewed as a bizarre novelty.

Now, with S&N only a memory, and the Oz era more of a bad dream, matters have returned to normal for the old pub, which has been renamed The Phoenix. It has become a standard pubCo lease with all the conventional trappings of gaming machines, pool, and a safe food menu. The only hint of its wild and eccentric younger days are the incongruous display of world flags covering much of the ceiling. The pub, with its high ceilings and extensive floor area, requires a bit of a crowd to create some atmosphere and otherwise appears to be treading water and living on its past.

A more uplifting 'afterlife' is currently being enjoyed by The Rose of England in central Nottingham. The Rose, as depicted on its unusual late-Victorian elevations, was built as the Brewery Tap for the Nottingham Brewery. It was renamed for the first time as long ago as 1967 when then-owners Whitbread hoped to achieve a change of image as the pub was known as a prostitute's hangout. Whether the strategy succeeded is not recorded but the renamed Yorker survived until 1993, when it became the City Alehouse. This entity does not appear to have been a success, as the pub was acquired by Allied Breweries soon after for conversion to its fast expanding Firkin brand. The Rose became the Filly and Firkin, but unfortunately, by this time, the original spontaneity and ethos of the Firkins had been lost in the remorseless grind of brand-building.

In 1999 Allied sold their entire pub estate and the property reverted to Punch. The Rose was restored, and as a Punch tenancy it has slowly blossomed, under two long-serving tenants. Unfortunately, the changes and regular makeovers it has experienced do appear to have taken their toll internally, where little of the eccentric Victorian charm still evident in its exterior remains.

From Hawaii to Bondi Beach, pigs, punks and royalty, the Masons to Mercury, and delving into three former Fountains, this journey around the recent histories of just fifteen of the nation's pubs embraces a remarkable variety of culture and life. These illustrate the typical changes taking place and the resilience of the pub to endure such change. Meanwhile, there are hundreds of other similar stories out there which are still unfolding.

One can judge little from such a small sample but a common thread is that where a building is listed or has historic features it is much more likely to remain a pub, if it closes or its survival is threatened. The character of a building, and its effectiveness as a pub is clearly important. Generally, where these pubs have closed, this has taken place because of changes in ownership or the decision to brand or transform the business. Which provides a note of optimism that, with focused management and stable ownership, those pubs that have reverted to trade traditionally, based on their original character, can flourish.

PART EIGHT

The Beer Tie Untied

A s landlords to large numbers of pub tenants, the image of the pubCos differed in two ways from their predecessors, the big brewers. Having evolved as part of a financial venture the new landlords seemed more impersonal and hard-nosed than the brewers. Secondly, the brewers brewed and it therefore seemed to be a natural part of any arrangement with them that they would expect their tenants to stock and sell their products. That was certainly not the case with the pubCos, who had no liquor to sell other than that which was delivered by a totally unrelated third party under supply agreements. This appears to have created a significant psychological hurdle.

It is now over twenty years since the brewers started their massive disposal programmes. The ongoing churn and disruption, almost constantly since, has sustained a mood of instability. Feelings of insecurity for licensees have taken their toll in the form of high turnover rates amongst tenants. As a result, many are relatively inexperienced. After the high street crisis at the start of the millenium thousands of managed houses were acquired as packages by the pubCos for conversion to tenancy. New tenancies or leases on these were offered to their former managers which created a further group of new tenants.

Whilst the parties have changed, so has the relationship. Most tenancies in the estates of the larger pubCos have been replaced by leases, often modelled on Grand Met's Inntrepreneur. The new leases allow pub landlords to assign their lease; a sale of their business. This is a massive incentive, over the non-assignable tenancy, to build up trade and create value, which can then be pocketed by the leaseholder upon sale to a purchaser, the ingoing lessee. PubCos require, in return, higher rents and normally that the tenant is responsible for repairs. This is a significant difference from the old-style brewery tenancy as the onus is on the lessee to maintain and develop his premises with the incentive of recouping the cost of his improvements and goodwill from the enhanced trade upon a sale.

From the pubCo landlord perspective, the intention was that they would receive a clean rent, free from deductions for maintenance, as is the case with commercial property leases. This avoided the need for small armies of employees continually visiting leased pubs to carry out repairs. Given this greater freedom and responsibility, a new type of licensee was required who had capital behind him and the experience and acumen to operate and steer his business in the right direction. Entrepreneurs rather than old-fashioned publicans. Some of the new generation of lessees fitted this role. PubCos signed up many multiple tenants; small businessmen who knew the trade and built up a chain of several leased pubs and installed their own managers in each. A few were also taken by the larger pub retail groups, who leased town centre or destination premises suitable for conversion to their own brands.

Unfortunately for the pubCos, taken as a whole, such businesslike lessees were the exception. The majority of their licensees were inexperienced and expected their landlord to hold their hand and get them on their feet, guide them through any problems or help when the money ran low. A feature of leases which restricted the amount of new talent available was the requirement that ingoing lessees had sufficient capital to purchase the trade inventory, pay a deposit to the landlord, purchase stock and have sufficient working capital to operate, until the business became established. If they were also buying a lease from an outgoing lessee then this ingoing capital could be £50,000 or more. If improvements or alterations were planned, then it could be substantially more than this. This reduced the talent pool available and forced compromises to be made.

An interesting perspective on the relationship was provided by a report published in Spring 2001 and carried out by Leeds Metropolitan University, commissioned by the British Institute of Innkeeping.[1] They interviewed 100 pub tenants and lessees. The big surprise was that only one in twelve stated that their priority was to make money. Other more common reasons for running a pub were the lifestyle that being a licensee provided, and the independence of being their own boss. Most of the licensees suggested that they would welcome more advice and supervision over how they ran their premises, but received very little. These were clearly not experienced entrepreneurs, and as the report concluded seemed unsuited to the philosophy of the pubCos.

The pubCos themselves started off as small, efficient operations, contracting out many functions. As the empires of the more enduring companies grew alarmingly their staffing did not always keep pace. Their business development managers (the main day-to-day link between landlord and tenant) were often stretched, especially with the challenge of constantly dealing with more and different pubs, and a regular turnover of tenants.[2] As a result, the relationship between the pubCos and their licensees were often remote and sometimes strained. Initially tenants felt, or complained, that communication was poor and support given to them insufficient. If issues arose the pubCos' ability to address and resolve these was, by all accounts, inadequate. And it was only one step beyond this that relationships started to break down, with the pubCos accused of treating their tenants unfairly and not honouring agreements.

The Beer Tie is entirely neutral in terms of its impact on the financial standing of those licensees who sign up to it. This is because rents are calculated on a 'profits method', which automatically builds into the rent calculation the amount paid for the products which contribute to the gross turnover figure. If the tenant is paying more for his stock then his gross and net profit will be proportionally lower, reflecting the additional cost of buying tied products through their landlord. The result will be a lower net profit or divisible balance upon which the 'tenant's bid' or annual rental is based.

Unfortunately, especially in the case of leased rents, there are many other factors which would be taken into account when agreeing an initial rent, like rent-free periods for disrepair or some other concession. It became common for landlords to offer to carry out, or pay for, agreed improvements, or to take on responsibility for repairs if the tenant agreed to a higher rent. What commenced as a modest tied rent could increase substantially as a result of such non-market based adjustments, meaning that trade at the premises would not necessarily support the adjusted rent.

In a rising market, rents are rarely a problem. Trade is normally sufficient to cover the rent and provide the pub landlord with a decent return and everyone is happy. In the last recession this was clearly not the case, and rent and its affordability became a big issue. This didn't mean that the Beer Tie was inherently unfair; simply that rents that had been agreed, possibly inflated to cover agreed improvements or repair liability, were not affordable in the tough conditions which prevailed. But, given the pressure felt by tenants and the influence and advice from external parties, it was convenient to pick upon the Tie as being an emotive area in respect of which pubCo landlords were pocketing huge sums. The Beer Tie was attacked and scandalised, on the basis of the alleged pubCo profiteering. As a result, the wide range of issues that exist were frequently distilled down to a simplistic focus on the Tie.

The Tie obliges pub tenants and lessees to purchase beer, and other 'nominated' products, from their landlord under supply agreements. The pubCo landlords clearly make a huge profit margin on the difference between what they pay buying these products in bulk and the amounts which the tenants are obliged to purchase them for under the supply agreements.

The device has been examined for its fairness by trade and industry groups on behalf of the government and the EC on no less than an astonishing seventeen times. A wide array of politicians and others, across the UK and Europe, have instinctively felt that there was something unwholesome within this peculiar anachronism from the Victorian age. The latest probe was an inquiry in 2004, by a House of Commons Trade and Industry Select Committee. Like all its predecessors, this committee concluded that the Beer Tie was not perfect but that it served a purpose and was better retained than not.

Four years later more MPs, this time as the Business and Enterprise Committee (BEC), examined the relationship between pubCos and their tenants, following a recommendation from the previous enquiry. The BEC reported its conclusions to Parliament on 13/5/2009 in the depths of recession. Beforehand, representatives of the most antagonised lessees had been lobbying furiously whilst the pubCos must have been relatively complacent in view of the previous investigation. It was therefore a shock to the pubCos when the BEC recommended, in very strong and critical terms, that the Tie should be referred to the Competition Commission (successor to the MMC).

The pubCos had clearly made a very poor impression on the BEC which, in its report, spoke of the dominance of the pubCos causing serious problems, of abuse and of downright bullying. Specific issues identified were agreements not being honoured, the lack of a dispute resolution system, the imbalance of power between the pubCos and their lessees and the low income enjoyed by many lessees (the alarmingly low figure of £15,000 pa was quoted). The BEC wished to see the Tie severely limited as a result and lessees given the choice of a free of tie alternative.

Over the next four years a long and divisive slanging match developed, with lessees' representatives and linked campaigning organisations, backed by supportive MPs, hurling criticism at the pubCos. Their case was backed by a number of trade bodies. Whilst the antagonism and vitriol flowed a mediation process was attempted, initiated by ALMR, the Association of Licensed Multiple Retailers. Voluntary reforms were suggested, promises made and forgotten. The process of negotiation combined with accusations and demands. With the involvement of a host of interested parties and external organisations, the bad-tempered and unwieldy debate rumbled on ineffectively. Throughout this, the pubCos were heavily criticised.

Enterprise Inns, in particular, was accused of being uncaring and a bully. In July 2009 CAMRA entered the fray to insist on a referral of the Tie as a 'supercomplainant', (which it was entitled to do as an interested consumer body).

In October 2010 the OFT (Office of Fair Trading) decided that the Tie would not be referred to the Competition Commission. After further challenges and confrontation CAMRA announced in February 2011 that it would withdraw its legal action against the OFT (because of its non-referral of the Tie) and would focus on the June 2011 deadline for the voluntary self-regulation reforms that had been promised. The campaigners on behalf of the licensees, with CAMRA prominent amongst them, had adopted 'Fairpint' as their campaigning name. The pubCo faction, supported by BBPA, and most of the brewers, claimed that many more pubs would close if the Tie was scrapped, and traditional breweries and their tied pubs could be rendered uneconomic. Despite such warnings, it was clear by this time that the Fairpint campaigners would settle at nothing less than the release of the Beer Tie.

Both of the warring parties were experiencing financial pressures. Many tenants complained about low overall income within their leased pubs and their financial loss as a result of the Tie. The figure of £15,000 income for many tenants was regularly argued on their behalf. This low figure was questioned by the pubCos. What was indisputable was that tenants were going out of business due to financial pressure.

On the other side of the equation, Enterprise and Punch had been vigorously selling pubs. Small, high-value packages from the top end of their portfolios were sold within the trade whilst bottom-end and problem houses were sold to anyone who would take them. Both pubCos were battling to service interest on their huge piles of debt, still quantifiable in billions of pounds, despite the ongoing disposals. Punch, which had appeared to be in a more comfortable position then hit problems with their bond-holders. In June 2013 the dispute became public and was likened to a bar-room brawl. It appeared that both giant pubCos had little room for manoeuvre, and if statutory intervention restricted their income flow, problems could quickly surface.

An examination of Enterprise's yearly accounts to September 2013 are illuminating.[3] (Of their net profit of £373 million, £190 million came from their profit margin on the supply agreements whilst only £171 million, less than half, came from tenants' rent. This gives the impression that Enterprise are forcing their tenants to pay over the odds for their Tied products. The pubCo case is that the tenants were paying list price for their beer, and only a little more than what it would cost a free house, which could always negotiate a small discount. The pubCo margin reflected the lower price which they could negotiate because they were buying in such bulk. As such, the margin is Enterprise's reward for having a large estate, enabling it to obtain very favourable terms. Provided tenants were not worse off then there was no reason why the pubCos should not be better off.

What the Enterprise yearly accounts do suggest is that if Enterprise were to lose the profit margin on the Tie, then with over half of their income removed they would struggle to service their massive debt pile and could quickly drift into financial difficulty. If their licensees had the option of a free-of-tie alternative, as proposed, then most tenants would take this. The pubCo would be entitled to increase the rent to reflect the licensees' benefit of not being tied. But the benefit to tenants, if purchasing beer as an individual, would be substantially less than the amount of margin which would be lost to the pubCos because of the weaker bargaining position of tenants. Therefore the increased rent to the pubCo would be substantially smaller than the tied margin which they currently receive. If the tenant's benefit, in being freed from the Tie, was reflected in increased rent, the tenant would stand still, financially and the landlord would lose, substantially. The benefit would actually be with the brewer, who could sell their beer at reduced discounts.

As the vitriol between the two rival groups continued to flow the BISC Committee (successor to the BEC), reported to government after the June 2011 deadline to complain that the voluntary code was not in place. The government report issued in November 2011 advised that it could see no justification for removal of the Tie or statutory regulation but that it expected the industry to provide a system of self-regulation.

At this, the campaign was intensified, in particular with 5,000 CAMRA members writing to their MPs. This prompted a parliamentary debate only two months later, on 11th January. This criticised the government's lack of action. The debate agreed that an independent review take place into the matter. This represented a rapid change of mood within the corridors of power.[4]

As a result a formal government public consultation was commenced in April 2013 with a deadline on 14th June. The issue focused on whether the relationship between pub owners and their tenants should be governed by a statutory code, with an independent adjudicator, and whether tenants would be entitled to a free-of-tie option on their leases. The document suggested that if this was to be adopted it would apply to any company that owned over 500 pubs, thus avoiding any impact on the family brewers and small pubCos. Consequently, these companies should have been prepared to step away from the dispute as their own estate would be free from interference. But they were not, and the family brewers, in particular, continued to express serious concerns about the impact on the viability of their breweries.

As the June 2013 deadline approached for the consultation period for the government to judge whether to introduce a statutory code the campaigning intensified further. The licensees' side galvanised into the 'Fair Deal for your Local' campaign and protested outside Parliament. It could now claim that an impressive ninety MPs had signed the early day motion demanding a statutory code. Toby Perkins, the Labour shadow pubs minister who attended in support, spoke about the 'forces of darkness' lined up against them. Perkins added that he hoped that the weight of public opinion would give the pubCos the message that time was up.[5]

The deadline given in the consultation for a government response expired in September 2013, with no decision emerging. As the months drifted by and speculation and tension increased it appeared that the government was doing some hard thinking. They had probably realised as a result of the submissions on the consultation just how high the stakes were. The big two pubCos are battling to stay on top of huge debt mountains. They are in a vulnerable position. If their financial model is undermined by the loss of the Tie, then they could be in trouble very quickly.

And if, in this nightmare scenario, they were forced to sell most or all of their pubs, perhaps 8,000 or more, then chaos could result. Whilst unfortunate comparisons could be made with MMC, the difference would be the lack of pubCos to provide a safety net to step in and purchase these pubs because the pubCo financial model would have just been destroyed by the legislation. So in the absence of this option, who would be interested in taking thousands of tenanted pubs off the hands of the big two pubCos?

A solution might have been to sell to existing tenants or lessees. But many of these would struggle to raise finance in current circumstances. Some of the later packages were acquired by the pubCos at over £500,000 per pub, above alternative unlicensed value in many cases. And almost certainly beyond the financial reach of most tenants to raise on mortgage. Many of the pubs would end up converted to residential or commercial use. Possibly, the pubCos might even sell large pub packages directly to property developers. If there were an outcry the pubCos (or their administrators) would simply point out that this course of action had been forced on them.

Whilst the above is the most extreme scenario many other damaging consequences were revealed when the various responses to the government's consultation were made public in late December 2013. Greene King advised that they would immediately sell or convert sufficient tenancies to get below the 500 pub limit, and that many others would do the same, creating chaos in the market with many of the pubs concerned becoming unlicensed. Spirit suggested that they would revert to upward-only rent reviews and threatened a legal challenge to various of their rights including the suggestion to ban their beer-flow monitoring equipment. Punch focused on the number of jobs which would be lost at its suppliers and objected to the suggestion that the Tie on pub gaming machines be removed. This was supported by a number of the major suppliers suggesting that if this was unregulated there would be chaos and a rise in illegal machines.

Shepherd Neame warned that removal of the Tie would 'destroy the basis of the traditional tenancy', and would almost certainly result in the closure of their brewery. Heineken's submission warned of unintended consequences but, in particular, criticised the proposed government interference as a managed decline of the industry, which would interfere with their ability to properly manage their pubs on a partnership arrangement. They also suggested that the 500 pub limit would create an artificial two-tier system.

Marstons referred to the likelihood of brewery closures, complained about the costs of the proposed statutory adjudicator who would deal with disputes and argued that its franchise agreement, because it was not based on rent, should be excluded from any new measures. JW Lees, the Manchester-based brewer, suggested that the guest beer proposals would be disastrous and affect its viability, as well as complaining about the effects of progressive beer tax. Trust Inns, a smaller pubCo with around 500 tenancies and leases, suggested that its future investment was on hold because of the uncertainty created. Wellington pub group, a uniquely free-of-tie operator, complained about the proposal to make upward-only rent reviews illegal, especially as they remain unchallenged in other sectors. They suggested that the entire package would be self-defeating because it would discourage investment in pubs and make the market worse off. And to round things off the OFT, Office of Fair Trading, warned the government against statutory intervention because upsetting the pubCo model might have a whole range of consequences which would not be in the public's interest.

A wide range of substantial, and experienced, operators within the trade, all opposed to any intervention, and significantly raising a very wide range of different concerns and issues. Plus the OFT, an objective government department advising caution because of the possible consequences. On top of this, the suggestion of legal challenges, which could run for years and leave the industry in damaging suspense.

The chaos uncertainty and disruption which could result from statutory intervention to give a free-of-tie option should be unthinkable to anyone, but particularly CAMRA and the large number of politicians who profess to love the pub and have its interests at heart.

CAMRA had followed their instincts to intervene on behalf of the little tenant against the despised pubCos. They had simplified the issue into a good-versus-evil contest, rather than looking at the possible consequences of pub disposals and brewing viability. The Beer Tie is the glue which holds the industry together. Without it our Regional and family brewers would be unsustainable, tenanted pubCos would disappear, and the chaotic switch to a largely freehouse market for non-managed pubs would result in many closures. Their demands for a referral to the Competition Commission and the statutory code was gambling with the whole future and stability of the tenanted pub market. CAMRA know how important the Tie is. When the EC reviewed it in the Nineties they spoke out strongly in its defence, in articles like 'Don't let the tie die' in the 1997 *Good Beer Guide*.

Whatever the reason for the delay, the government played for time. Having promised a decision by the end of the year, a statement finally emerged in December 2013 from Jo Swinson, Minister for Community Affairs, that the government did not want to rush into a decision, and that this was therefore delayed. She spoke of a huge number of responses, 1,100 written and 7,000 online, and a huge number of issues that had been raised.

A strong pointer to the likely outcome was given in January 2014 when the Labour opposition forced a debate on the subject. A vote to bring forward immediate legislation was defeated by 311 votes to 244.

The Conservative majority appeared to have realised the possible effects of conceding to this emotional and divisive campaign.

Perhaps the government was thinking of the investors and bondholders of the original pubCo securitisations. With something over £4 billion in debt, powerful investors must be concerned as to the impact on their money. They have remained very quiet during the lengthy dispute. But the government must be aware of them, and concerned that with such large sums involved, an unfavourable outcome might have a negative impact on the whole economy.

Whatever the outcome, when it finally emerges there can be no real winners. The relationship between the pubCos and their tenants has been damaged. That is inevitable, when campaigners and politicians have advised the tenants how poorly they have been treated, how they are being ripped off and that the politicians will intervene to sort it all out for them. And if the Tie remains, how many new tenants will wish to sign up to it and enter the industry in the future?

The tragedy of the affair is that the drinks industry faces a whole range of issues. Instead of standing together to face these, employing the substantial bank of goodwill which has developed in Parliament it is wasting its energies in a destructive and time-consuming internal war. For example, what benefits may have accrued across the industry, if the same time and energies had been devoted to a fully-justified, concerted campaign to reduce beer duty to levels in line with Europe?

PART NINE

Some Shafts Of Light

L ooked at as a continuum over the last sixty years, the period from the early Seventies to the late Eighties represented a rare break from the pattern of continual restructuring and turbulence within the licensed trade. That short period of stability can be regarded as an exception to the normal hurley-burley; a period when the big six brewers paused to consolidate and internally reorganise, whilst converting their tenancies to management.

Seen in this context a further bout of restructuring was probably well overdue by the start of the 1990s. The impact of the MMC ensured that when change did come for the big six it was dramatic and comprehensive. It also allowed the brewers to claim the moral high ground and blame the government for bullying them into a savage restructuring when it may have happened anyway, as a result of the declining beer market.

The brewery closures of the Nineties, the regional brewery battles and the churn of the pub estates can thus be seen as a return to the normality of takeovers, mergers and general upheaval. The UK beer industry appears to generate an inbuilt, unrelenting dynamism for change.

Although the ongoing churn has had many unfortunate repercussions in terms of closed breweries and pubs and the impact of this on individuals and the nation's heritage, there is at least an upside. The current shape of our drinks industry by ownership and type of outlet is varied and vibrant and provides a really wide and comprehensive range of pubs, bars and restaurants to meet almost any customer need. The freeing-up of the rigid structure of the market and thousands of pubs from the big six has made such opportunities readily available to anyone with the finance and conviction to try their luck.[1]

The current profile of the biggest pub estates at present shows a touch of nostalgia with a new big six. These are Enterprise and Punch, followed by the two former regional brewers Greene King and Marstons plus Heineken's former S&N leased estate, renamed Star Pubs and Bars and the pubCo, Admiral Taverns. On the managed side, Mitchells & Butlers are currently foremost with Wetherspoons, Spirit and Stonegate, also of major significance. Below these is an exotic pot pourri of different types of leisure group, branded pub operator, leased pubCo, smaller family brewers, and chains who measure their pub ownership in the tens and hundreds.

The future for the pubCos that operate large tenanted and leased estates will remain clouded until any government intervention has been resolved and any possible impact taken effect. Due to the pressure imposed on the tenancy system and the tied model, alternatives are being explored. Spirit are currently experimenting with turnover rents, offering discounted rates on some products, franchising and 'co-investment' to assist licencees. It is encouraging to see such innovation. Given the issues with the Tie a fresh approach may help to renew belief and confidence in the landlord-tenant relationship.

The profile of the two former Regional brewers is not unlike that of the survivors of the big six during the late Nineties. A high proportion of revenue derived from their managed divisions, falling brewing profitability and plans to reduce the leased estate and transfer pubs to management.[2] One hopes that the outcome is not the same.

The retail pub groups that operate in the managed house sector are focusing more on food, given its sparkling performance. Amongst these, Stonegate, Spirit and of course M&B are responsible for a range of strong and established brands. Generally, the high degree of experimentation with brands, which we witnessed in the early days, has passed and these companies now operate mature brands in an experienced and professional manner.

But innovation is always necessary. The appearance of new operators with new ideas and concepts is hopefully an indication that the industry is returning to full health. Notable examples are Drake and Morgan and Loungers.

Drake and Morgan's new licensed emporiums have been appearing in and around the city of London since the group was founded in 2008. They have now opened seven outlets with exotic names like The Happenstance, The Folly and The Anthologist. These names do some justice to the unique and luxurious cornucopia of consumption that have been created. Trading areas are large and, in most cases, on two levels, configured in an unorthodox and imaginative way, containing bars and areas for formal and informal dining. Escapism indeed for the City worker, and generating huge turnovers for the private founders.

Loungers is also expanding rapidly, in this case across the south and Midlands from their base in Bristol. Their operations are large cafe bars, which appear to be more faithful to the continental model than most of the genre, and which have been given non-pubby latin names like Tinto, Ocho and Brasco. Mood changes through the day but remains inviting and relaxed. The menu is imaginative and fun, with a monthly range of specials to keep it spiced up. A proper bar area serving a wide range of beers, ciders and spirits plus an imaginative and specialist corner dedicated to teas and coffees provide something for everyone.

Loungers are already running over thirty units and clearly have the potential to become much larger, having a brand that could work in almost any town. Drake and Morgan contrast with Loungers in style, market and geography. But they are both geared very effectively to their particular market and are proving highly successful as a result. Such focused creativity creates optimism for the future.

The pubs market has fragmented into three distinct styles of operation, whose characteristics are as marked as their prospects; branded bars, food-led pubs and wet-led pubs. The distinction is increasingly adopted industry-wide, for very good reason. Brands have always been very distinct from traditional pubs in appearance, turnover and ownership. Within the traditional pub sector food and non-food pubs may look the same, but their operating styles and prospects are heading in very different directions. The three sectors are examined below.

Not In Seriously Bad Elf

Old Leghumper, Hop Monster, Winnies Honey Heaven, Bolster's Blood, Beheaded, Betty Stoggs, Twisted Porter, Rucking Mole, Bumblethwacker, Nun's Ruin, Skullsplitter, Colonic Irrigation, Village Bike, Seriously Bad Elf and Old Engine Oil. Just a small sample of the many new brews on offer from the UK's latest cottage industry, microbrewing.

The good news is that beer consumption is slowly coming out of its long decline. But only the cask-conditioned bitter variety as produced by the domestic brewers. That is, the regional and family brewers, assisted by the 1,000 or so microbreweries squeezed into brew pubs, backstreets, farm buildings or industrial estates. Utility takes precedence over romance in many of these settings. Meanwhile, the rest of the market for the high-volume lagers, kegs and stouts is continuing its long, relentless contraction.

SIBA, the Society of Independent Brewers, hold court over their growing membership of microbrewers. The vibrancy and confidence of the sector is epitomised in SIBA's public face and announcements. The number of microbreweries now tops 1,000, which is double the number ten years ago. CAMRA have been quick to point out that Britain now has one brewery for every fifty pubs which is an impressive statistic. Along with the increase in the microbrewers is the increase in the number of brewpubs, which provide a particularly agreeable way of sampling local beer.

The good news for the sector is highlighted by SIBA's 2012-13 Cask

Report, showing that cask volumes had increased in 2011 for the first time in twenty years. Volumes were up 1.6%, along with the claim that the product was getting to a wider market. Further scope for optimism was provided in the 2013-14 Cask Report which showed that cask was now outselling keg within the on-trade. And with other products declining and cask volumes more or less steady, cask is commanding a steadily increasing proportion of overall sales.

Unlike the cider boom that we witnessed a few years back, supported by extensive advertising, real ale is asserting itself in a more broad-based, organic, but insistent manner. And with a current figure of over seven million adults who apparently have the taste, the product is becoming rapidly mainstream.

There are around twenty-seven surviving family brewers who provide a reassuring backbone to our domestic brewing industry. These bastions of timeless tradition provide some delightful local character in their old breweries scattered around the country. The family brewers continue to work diligently on the brewing and marketing of their products. Most also operate flourishing, albeit small, pub estates. Given the current market, they have opportunities to expand and generally their sales curves are moving upwards. Between them the family brewers own around 3,850 pubs, which is significant in its own right. But given the popularity of their beers and the strength of the free-trade operation of some, their influence and market penetration goes far beyond this.

At the other end of the spectrum, instead of the old big six we now have a big four in terms of brewing. And these four hold a 78% market share (as compared to the 76% of the big six in 1986 just prior to MMC). Every one of them is foreign-owned. Some of the names are still familiar; Heineken and Carlsberg, whilst Diagio is the exotic name for the new owner of Guinness.[3] The final member is the largest. Anheuser-Busch In-Bev is an old Belgian company, which is quoted on the New York stock exchange. It has an impressive range of products and a global reach.

If one studies the accounts for these companies, a similar picture is evident. Overall sales performance is good, with growth in developing countries, but Europe, affected by continuing uncertainty and government-led austerity measures, is generally declining a little each year. The falling numbers are derived from trade across Western Europe as a whole, not just in the UK. Whilst the tax regimes may be somewhat kinder elsewhere, social trends are at work in nearly all of Western Europe to remove drinkers from their seat in the *bierkeller* or *brasserie* and instead leave them sitting at home, probably drinking water or coffee. And as in England, these trends have been at work for a long time, well before smoking bans or the recent recession.[4]

The other change in the UK is not how much we buy and consume but where we do so. This is the lamentable story, certainly for the pub, of the take-home trade now having claimed almost a 50% share of the beer market by volume.[5] This represents a huge shift in behaviour. Effectively Britain has abandoned its uniquely intimate relationship with its pubs. If one studies figures for 1986 which were part of the MMC report, these indicate our 16% take-home consumption compared with Belgium and France at 57%, Germany at 60% and the USA at 80%. We must hope that the current take-home figure does not continue climbing upwards towards overseas levels. To ensure this, we all need to turn off the TV, get off the sofa and go down the local a little more often.

Despite the continuing decline in overall beer volumes the brewing sector appears to be relatively stable. The big international brewers still earn large profits in Britain. If there is restructuring at this level it will have limited impact on the UK market as, with the exception of Heineken, the other three major brewers own no pubs here. As an example of the strength of these international brewers it is worth quoting some statistics from the website of Heineken, the second biggest brewer in the world. Their workforce of 54,000 people worldwide operate 119 breweries across sixty-five countries and brew and distribute 170 different alcoholic products. As such, whilst one may not regard them with the same affection as Theakstons or Wadworths, they do exude a certain aura of permanence and stability.

It seems likely that the market share of these big four will continue to reduce slowly. What is more important to an increasing number of British drinkers is that cask-conditioned ale is enjoying such a renaissance. This will hopefully provide a solid platform on which our pubs can build their future.

Regimentation

There was a tremendous outcry against pub brands. CAMRA, traditionalists, pub licensees, the media and even MPs all decried the artificial and contrived atmosphere created, and the threat to our heritage. Irish pubs seemed to attract a particularly virulent reaction from the traditionalist's corner, but any modern pub brand was likely to receive the same savage disapproval.

CAMRA's *Good Beer Guides* used to have plenty to say on the subject. Brands were dismissed as being tasteless and short-term. Much of the contempt was misplaced in relation to their quality and durability.

They may not be to everyone's taste but, in some respects, they have helped to raise standards in the trade. They have also remained, contrary to the expectation of some, and remain successful. It is also worth remembering that the process was not confined to Britain. In the late Nineties there were thirty-one Irish pubs in Berlin, twenty-eight in Rome,[8] and similar numbers in other centres throughout Europe. Most of these continue as an established and popular part of the scene in these cities.

The numerous critics of the brands failed to look at them from the perspective of their customers; the families in Harvester and Brewers Fayre; the young women and office workers in All Bar One and Pitcher & Piano; youngsters on the pull in Yates' and Walkabout; old boys enjoying beer at £1 a pint in Wetherspoons. These people were delighted that branded pubs had arrived. They provided the customer with a choice of outlets that was lacking a decade or two earlier.

No-one is forcing real ale enthusiasts to be shoved around in a noisy disco bar, drinking out of plastic glasses. They have their own outlets. The fact that our towns and cities can now boast a comprehensive range of bars from Yates' to the Yew Tree gastropub suggests that a strong and diverse market exists. And the pub purists have slowly come to accept that they cannot dictate taste to the masses, and that the new bars, however objectionable to them, are serving a distinct need. It is noticeable that recent copies of the *Good Beer Guide* and other CAMRA publications have calmed down hugely in their attacks on pub brands. An interesting aspect of the debate is that Wetherspoons is a confirmed favourite of many real ale traditionalists. And yet it is as much a brand as O'Neills, Yates' or All Bar One.

The brands of the Nineties have also contributed to modern pub design. They opened the door to an exciting range of new environments in which pub-goers could drink and eat. To accommodate the brands many different and unusual properties were purchased and converted. Whitbread secured a number of parkland mansions to convert to Beefeater and Brewers Fayre, which provided an excellent setting for those brands. The public could enjoy, at their leisure, the interior of these, and other premises, carefully and sympathetically refurbished and restored.

The new brands were more professionally designed than the earlier themed pubs. Critics complained nonetheless about their artificiality. But the design of pubs has always been fanciful; their culture and character is borrowed from the world around them. Over the years we have experienced mock-Tudor, artificial rustic themes, pretend-Parisian in the cafe-bars, and imitation-Irish. Pubs and bars are part of the leisure industry and an integral aspect of this is escapism. Victorian pubs were equally guilty, by providing lavish bars and lounges amongst fetid and squalid housing in the centre of our large cities people could escape their awful surroundings for a few hours.

How long will individual brands last? Can they become as established and enduring as retail chains? Well actually, they have. On the pub-restaurant side, Beefeater and Chef & Brewer have now been around for almost thirty years. Some of the Nineties' brands like Slug and Lettuce and All Bar One are twenty or more years old, and now seem to be as much a part of the high street as Pizza Hut or Boots. As Wetherspoons approaches 1,000 units it is difficult to envisage it quietly fading away for many years to come.

The more critical question is what the impact has been upon the traditional pub. The fear during the Nineties boom was that the superpub would dominate the market, sweeping away all else. With the continuing attrition of traditional pubs, huge concern still remains. But few now regard branded bars as being one of the main causes of the decline. It is recognised that the two sectors have their own distinct markets and the two co-exist rather than compete.

The Nineties' branded circuits still remain, and continue to attract their target market in large numbers. But they have lost a little of their lustre, having matured and been around for so long. In the same way that they emerged and threatened the traditional pub they may in turn be challenged by a new wave.

This may well come from independent bars, designed and run by a new generation of free-trade operators fighting their way to prominence. At present the only widespread evidence of this movement is in the larger cities, in places like the inner suburbs of Manchester, and Shoreditch in London. These popular centres, and one-off bars emerging elsewhere are establishing themselves at the cutting-edge end of the market. Some of these new bars are substantial and are able to surpass the corporate brands for impact and atmosphere. They are also pitching for the late-night market. As the conventional night-club market continues to decline, the new bars are encroaching on this territory as they gain late licenses and turn up the volume. This threat to the brands also encompasses an increasing sentiment amongst discerning drinkers that they want to step away from the mainstream and the corporate and embrace individualism.

In terms of the corporate, Bass had established itself in the Nineties as the godfather of brands, spawning a wide range and constantly devising more. Its successor, Mitchells & Butlers, retained this approach. Following a 2010 strategic review it has reduced its range of brands and will concentrate more on food and develop bigger trading premises. It has returned to acquisitions to expand All Bar One, Browns, Harvester, Toby and Ember Inns.

Meanwhile Marston's, which has energetically built up its chain of new-build, destination pub-restaurants has announced that it was opening its first 'large format core model', whilst it also had an even larger 'Magnum model' half as big again to maximise returns and margins. Other operators seem to be following this lead with a desire to increase turnover by building larger versions of their brands. The 'superpub' mentality is still with us.

An unfortunate aspect of the growth of brands is that as they become widespread they reinforce the clone-town feel. The multiple retailers have been accused of imposing a standardised sterility on identical main shopping streets in our major towns. Increasingly such streets will harbour the same repetitive combination of branded bars as they sit alongside a familiar range of retailers, all competing for the best pitches.

Branding also raises concerns that it contributes to the polarisation of society. Pub marketing involves segmenting the market, breaking it down into distinct customer groups who behave in a predictable manner, and have stereotypical and identical needs and desires. Detailed studies will advise what these people eat, wear, spend and read. And of course how many times a week they go out to either eat or drink, and how much they will spend when they do so.

The brand owners will identify the groups that are growing in number and increasing their spend and target them. The key markets are the increasingly affluent and high-spending young, the business sector, females, the family market and to a lesser extent the grey market, of active and well-off pensioners, and students.

Some other groups are simply not wanted at all. Therefore in the brands revolution as well as the winners who have brands designed for them, other customer types are ignored and avoided. The consequent manipulation of people's behaviour may prove an ideal basis for operating brands successfully but such standardisation raises a concern as it reinforces the creeping wave of uniformity imposed upon society.

Pub Food;
From Ghastly To Gastro

F ood in pubs has blossomed from the curled-up sandwich of the Sixties, through the chicken in a basket and carvery eras of the Seventies and Eighties to the refined pub-restaurants and impressive gastro-pubs of today. Looking at the industry as a whole food represents the most fundamental change in the way that pubs trade.

In 2010 a Publican Market Report annual survey of 970 licensees indicated that an average of 52% of pubs' annual turnover came from food sales. This compares to just 7.7% of pub turnover in 1977. This figure had grown to 21% of overall pub turnover by 1986, an impressive increase in just ten years.[9] During this formative period many pub landlords had to make the huge transition from offering a few snacks as an occasional sideline to serving proper meals on a regular and serious basis.

One can appreciate the massive impact that this change in emphasis has had on individual pubs. For the first time ever pubs were selling overall a greater value of food than alcohol. And this is the average. For those pubs that specialise in food that percentage will of course be greater, pushing up towards 60% or even 70% of overall turnover. The implications in terms of kitchens and equipment, staff training and general attitudes have been very far-reaching.

Another report, from Key Note analysts in November 2009, had reported that pubs served 35.2% of all UK restaurant meals.[10] This demonstrates how far pubs have come in establishing themselves within the catering landscape, but it also illustrates how much more turnover there is to go at, as pubs become more adept at marketing themselves and gaining even more customers.

Whilst formal pub-restaurants leave no-one in any doubt as to their function, it may not be obvious that so many local pubs are now food-led. Externally little will have changed, except for possibly a rear extension to create additional space. In most cases there will be an unobtrusive external chalkboard or 'good food' sign. The presence of good food in a traditional pub is often understated. Even internally food pubs do what they can to preserve all the trappings of a traditional pub. Their customers still like the informal, historic surroundings of traditional pubs. If not, then logically most of those customers would patronise restaurants instead.

Closer analysis will reveal how much has changed. Firstly and most obviously, the majority of customers who use the pub will arrive, intending to eat. That immediately changes the customer profile. In come families, couples, groups of women and the comfortably-off retired. Out of the back door, the random ragtag mixture of pub locals will probably have been steadily disappearing as the new customers arrive and food becomes the priority.

If the food-pub is well operated it will still feel like a pub as one enters, with customers having the flexibility to sit or stand, or sit around the bar on traditional stools. But most of this is window dressing to retain a pub atmosphere. The vast majority of customers will sit at a table. And even though the placing of the tables may be informal and higgledy-piggledy and the tables and chairs may all be different, nearly all of the trading area is occupied by these tables.

Trade will show a distinct peak around lunchtime and, depending on the pub's style and location, the evening dinner period. Some food-led pubs will only cater at lunchtimes or may end food early evening. But these are increasingly the exception, because limiting the hours of food detracts from the pub's credibility as a catering establishment. In the new millenium the public expect food at any reasonable hour. And of course, if most of your turnover is driven by food, then why limit this?

If a food pub has a split of turnover which is perhaps 70% food and 30% wet, that is not to say that 30% of its trade is derived from old-fashioned standing-up drinkers. Much or possibly all of that 30% alcohol sales will be drinks taken either with or after a meal. Therefore, considered as a whole, virtually all the trade of a fully-developed food-led pub will be driven by its food offer. Or, looked at another way, few customers will visit simply for a beer, an astonishing situation for a pub really.

In terms of food, a trained chef is pretty much obligatory to be able to provide the quality that the customer now expects. And having got their chef, the pub will make full use of him by providing a good range of well-cooked main meals, plus the usual safe line-up of starters, and some beguiling and mouth-watering puddings to keep people ordering when they may think they had eaten enough. What is not on the menu is equally significant. Food-led pubs believe that it is damaging to their trade to provide snacks or even a basic sandwich. These provide an alternative which may reduce overall spend, and could also be eaten standing up, which is to be avoided because groups of people standing get in the way of serving food and give the wrong message. Sandwiches or other snacks are thus elaborated with salad and other extras to justify a higher price and served to the table with cutlery.

As the choice of food has become wider, and more sophisticated, so has the wine selection. Wine sales have become a significant part of the sales mix for many food pubs with an impressive range on offer. The use of chalkboards is ubiquitous, almost like a badge of authenticity. This pub has the knowledge; it belongs to that select club which can offer refined catering. As well as freshening up the choices from a printed menu, the chalkboard is also an indication that there is an ongoing creative and cultivated process at work within the premises.

Some of these boards can approach a work of art as well as a literary journey, with exotic dressings, foreign references and methods of serving amongst the trendy and oblique terms used.

The atmosphere in food pubs are distinct from 'wet-led' pubs. Some pubs, particularly in villages, manage to maintain a compromise between wet and dry trade where the nature of the regulars and the style of the premises allow the two activities to happily co-exist. But more boisterous 'vertical drinkers' create a problem. It is rare to find large groups of regulars in the conventional food pub. As well as occupying valuable space that can be laid out as tables for dining, their activities and just the presence of noisy locals may be disruptive to the diners' appreciation of their food. Pool tables and darts are space-hungry and encourage drinkers so they will have been removed. Diners, enjoying an expensive meal, do not expect to have a pool cue shoved in their ear, or the waiting staff delayed by noisy revellers blocking the route from the kitchen.

Therefore vertical drinking and food-led pubs do not readily co-exist. A successful balance can be achieved, particularly in larger operations like Wetherspoons where the two activities will tend to establish their own 'safe zones'. Almost every traditional pub now feels obliged to provide some sort of food, but the success of the exercise in drinkers' pubs depends on the pub's individual character, layout, and types of customer.

At the other end of the spectrum there are now many high-class gastronomic pubs, run by or employing top chefs and providing lavish 'pubby' surroundings in which to enjoy the quality food available. Some drinkers may feel that salmon croquettes, truffled celeriac and lime parfait is not the perfect accompaniment to their pint. But for those whose priority is food then an old historic pub interior seems to provide a convivial ambience for their fine dining.

Gastropubs still look like a pub, and normally provide a respectable choice of real ale and other drinks, but whether they remain a pub is often debatable. The number of restaurant reviews given to gastropubs suggests that food is fairly dominant in these. Not that many operators of gastropubs will be at all concerned, but ultimately the test as to whether their establishments remain a pub is whether customers feel comfortable in entering them simply to enjoy a pint.

Food is a double-edged sword. It has been the salvation of many pubs that have the necessary attributes and their prospects are, clearly, very good. They are in a favoured position. The Smoking Ban not only ensured that eating areas were smoke-free but also gave the message to 'pub ambivalents' that pubs are intended to provide an environment friendly to diners.

But many compromises have been made to the pub to allow food to claim such a dominant role. Whilst recognising that food is now an essential fact of life, some pub and real-ale enthusiasts must still sometimes long for the days when a pub simply sold beer.

Crafting A New Image

The propensity of the licensed trade to adapt has become evident in the last few years, with the emergence within the UK of craft brewing. This has picked up on the huge growth in the sector in America over the last few decades. The USA boasted 2,360 craft breweries in 2012, by which time the craft beer market had gained a 13.7% share of the US beer market by value. This was up from an 8.5% share in 2007, illustrating a spectacular growth. In 2011 the number of craft breweries grew by 12%.[11] These were now penetrating into areas of the country like the south and mid-west which had previously appeared impervious to the trend, and were noted for having much more conservative taste.

In the UK, the craft beer movement has been around for little more than five years. In that time we have witnessed a surge of new microbreweries and the emergence of a wide and tantalising range of new products supported by a whole new philosophy and class of drinker.

Much of that philosophy has grown from the promptings of Brewdog, high priests of the UK craft beer industry. Brewdog craft an interesting range of beers from their purpose-built brewery in the remoteness of Ellon, Aberdeenshire. From this outpost they have managed to generate a huge amount of publicity to promote their products and raise the profile of craft brewing. To do so they have fully exploited the internet. Their prolific use of the medium has worked so well because the aficionados of craft would appear to be highly active members of the internet chattering classes.

Brewdog's products include Dead Pony Club, 5am Saint, Punk IPA, Libertine Black Ale, Dogma, and Hardcore IPA. Sound like a list of typical cask ales? Well they might to some, but their makers would be horrified to hear such a suggestion. Apparently one of the traits of craft beers is that their names deliberately avoid the kind of sexual stereotyping and puns characteristic of many real ales.

More importantly there is one fundamental difference between real ale and most craft beer. The latter is largely drawn from the barrel by gas, in contravention of the gospel as espoused at every opportunity by CAMRA for the last forty years. Beyond this, and as a great deal of the internet debate would suggest, craft beers are somewhat difficult to define. They cover an incredibly wide range of brewing styles, ingredients and strengths. Typically, one of the fast-growing number of craft beer bars in our inner cities will have fifteen or more fonts, all offering very individual products and tastes. And strengths, with some beers offering 10% abv or more. The exciting thing for a beer drinker is that there is a whole new world of flavours and tastes out there to explore and experience.

But not for the absolute real ale devotee, because craft beer remains forbidden territory because of its fizz. For them, a visit to a craft beer outlet would be approaching an admission that one has a lager-drinking habit or a secret stash of Caffrey's for special occasions. CAMRA has raised the stakes by excluding craft beer from its big party of the year, the London Beer Festival, for the last three years. And the craft industry, or Brewdog to be precise, has responded with criticism of CAMRA and its narrow and dated attitudes. Unfortunately, CAMRA is in danger of appearing to be as out of touch with, and dismissive towards, new trends and the needs of consumers as the brewers were in the early Seventies when first challenged by CAMRA.

The craft industry appears to struggle to define its own product and how craft beer relates to real ale. But to distinguish between real ale devotees and the new breed of craft ale drinkers is easy. We all know the stereotypical image of the real ale trainspotter; from his male, white, middle-class background to his liberal outlook, his advancing years, and his beer-paunched and bearded appearance. This image is becoming as dated as the corduroys and sandals that he is supposed to be wearing. A visit to most beer festivals will reveal a selection of hardened enthusiasts mixing with a healthy slice of newcomers of all genres.

Most of the occupants of the new craft beer outlets, all focused on trendy inner-city locations, are more homogenous. They tend to be young, late 20s or 30s, well-dressed, urbane, eloquent and with a good female representation. In marketing speak, they have been tagged hipsters. People who avoid mainstream conventions and activities and are 'too cool for school'. The contrast between the two groups of drinkers may keep them, and their products, apart. A more practical reason for this is that it has become the norm for craft beer bars to offer a very wide range of product, including many 'guest' craft beers. With anything between twelve and twenty fonts and beer lines to accommodate a craft bar requires all the space available in and around the bar servery, and in the cellar. So, in many cases they have no room to squeeze any real ale in.

Brewdog have, in typical fashion, found another way to encourage grassroots participation in the expansion of their product and network. They highlight the opportunity to share in their growth by promoting their shares as a crowd-funded investment. Not only does this help to fund the ongoing expansion but it also gives people a stake in the process and an incentive to sample the product. And an opportunity to attend their AGM which is, apparently unlike any other AGM that one could imagine, relatively unburdened with financial formality.

In December 2013 Brewdog announced the result of their latest 'Equity for Punks' fundraising to continue their bar expansion. They had reached their target of £4.25m a month before the deadline. An average of £426 had been committed by almost 10,000 investors from twenty-two different countries.[12] The message was certainly spreading. Brewdog expressed their gratitude to the 'passionate and evangelic craft beer drinkers'. There are obvious parallels with Wetherspoons.

Despite the irony of Brewdog's location, craft beer has been an inner-city phenomenon thus far, a trendy venture into left-field urban dynamics, almost as much as the brewing of a new type of beer. Much of the action has been focused on London, or rather bohemian, inner-city London. The phenomenon is being powered by an explosion of microbreweries, similar in character to those which have been established over the last couple of decades by real ale devotees. The London borough of Hackney, in north-east London, can claim to be the epicentre with an impressive total of eight craft beer microbreweries thus far. Until now, the only statistics that the area has dominated have related to crime or deprivation, so this reflects on how the area is regenerating. Perhaps it also reinforces the reputation of the area, with Hoxton and Shoreditch at its southern gateway, as a refuge for hipsters.

The real ale market has grown slowly and steadily over the years. Whilst CAMRA membership has now passed 150,000, this has taken forty years to achieve. In those early years, real ale stubbornly remained a minority interest, as fashionable as blancmange. It can be argued that the slow spread in the popularity of real ale is attributable, at least in part, due to the image of the real ale drinker. The consumption of alcohol, more than most products, seems to be driven almost as much by the image of those who consume it as the product itself. As a result it was only like-minded people who, for many years, were receptive to cask ale. It has proved to be notably slow to catch on with young people and women.

Bitter is an acquired taste, and unlike say lager or cider requires a little perseverance before it becomes a positive experience and one gets the taste for it. Most real ale drinkers will probably recall that their first few pints of bitter were something of a challenge to down. So the entry requirements for a life of indulging one's real ale cravings can, initially, be quite demanding. Craft, with its range of products and flavours, may have more instant appeal. But, to real ale devotees and session drinkers, the fizz of most craft beers may limit its attraction and quaffability. More reasons why the two products may compete rather than complement?

Is craft beer the new rock and roll or just a lot of fizz and froth? It is changing and refreshing the image of beer and those who drink it, adding further vitality to the drinks industry. With its positive role models and more easily accessible flavours it could spread far more quickly than cask beer has done. But the current devotees of craft may savour their involvement because it is fringe and alternative, their personal domain. The prospect of having several craft bars in every town may limit its ability to go mainstream.

There is currently a huge interest in the brewing process, as evidenced by an avalanche of new books published on the subject over the last three or four years. Appreciating beer and its ingredients, and its manufacture, could perhaps rival cooking within the next decade. Craft beer is an integral part of this trend, and as such would seem to be much more than a fad. Over time, craft may have a substantial impact on our drinking habits. In the meantime we can only watch the craft explosion with fascination, and wonder where it will end.

A Hazardous Journey

The biggest structural change in the pub industry over the last fifty years is arguably not the tame surrender of the big six and the arrival of the pubCos, or branding and the way pubs look. It is a fundamental and irreversible change in the way we, pub customers, behave. Our pub use has altered in two critical ways. Firstly a high proportion of pub-goers now regard the pub as somewhere to eat rather than drink. And those of us who do still patronise the pub as drinkers visit less often and drink less when we do.

Picture the typical street-corner pub, snugly enclosed by surrounding terraced housing. It isn't difficult as, despite the number of closures, many still survive and remain a very common scene in the older band of housing just outside our town and city centres.

In the fifty or so years on which this book has concentrated, the pub in our picture has, externally, hardly changed. Perhaps it will have a small beer garden instead of a private yard. Internally, alterations may have been more intrusive with the likelihood of modern toilets, and the possibility of old saloons and snugs being obliterated in the name of progress, to create one big open trading area.

But the street-corner pub is essentially the same as it always has been. Meanwhile almost every other commercial entity in the area will have been transformed, modernised, or, most likely, replaced. And our own tastes and requirements have also drastically changed. Whilst most of us claim to love nostalgia, we don't all put that into practice when it comes to deciding where to devote our leisure time, and our leisure spend. As a result the traditional local is now way down the list, if it features at all, in the places where most people go for a night out. Many of the pubs remain, shrouded more in melancholy than nostalgia, guarding their street corners, but increasingly abandoned by their customers, still living within shouting distance all around them.

The working class generation, many of whom based its entire leisure week around the pub in the last century, has largely disappeared. It has certainly lost the habit of regular attendance at the local. Reinforced by rapid increases in beer and spirit prices and the temptation of cheaper drink from supermarkets, during a tough recession, the Smoking Ban was the final straw. A high proportion of these hardened pub-goers were people who could least afford to go out drinking regularly. Many probably continue the habit at home now, at half the price. As this group has dwindled, so their pubs have died. The community pub without a community just doesn't work. When past regulars return to their old haunt, if it is still trading, they would find that much of the familiar ambience, which was an essential element of the experience, had disappeared, along with their old drinking buddies.

In the current century, the attrition rate for bottom-end pubs has increased alarmingly. As concern has become widespread, more accurate and rapid measurement of the pub closures developed. And so regular updates on the weekly rate are issued, like news of casualties from a distant and bloody war. The casualties did not return in body bags but were left, stood in the centre of their villages, alongside our main roads and back streets standing silent and forlorn. They act as a reminder that a desperate economic battle is being waged all around us, every day, for survival.

And as in a war, we all become a little blasé at the casualty figures as they relentlessly pile up. From thirteen per week in the early years of the new century, the rate of pub closures stepped up to a figure in the twenties a few years later, when recession started to bite. Then, with the impact of the Smoking Ban, and recession deepening, the death rate increased alarmingly, almost doubling. Research for the BBPA in

January 2009 suggested that this soared to thirty-nine in the second half of 2008. The report blamed the government's incomprehensible policies and suggested that of each thirty-nine closures, on average nineteen were suburban community pubs, thirteen were rural pubs and eight were in town centres. Further analysis of the closures in 2011 showed that nearly 90% of the lost licences were drinkers' pubs.

Pub losses peaked at around fifty a week in 2010/2011, according to the leading monitor, that of CAMRA. This is an eye-watering 2,500 per annum, which is a loss of 5% of the stock of pubs or nearly one in twenty in a single year. Finally by 2013, the closure rate relented to less savage levels. All of this brutal weeding-out had, according to figures from the BBPA, reduced the number of drinkers' pubs to 30,968.[13]

The Fitch Pub Sector Review[14] issued in May 2012 concluded that for a variety of reasons, but most notably the Smoking Ban, many bottom-end pubs were now permanently unviable. Further studies piled on the pessimism. Research by Mintel released in April 2013 told us that 43% of pub-goers spent less in pubs and bars in the preceding twelve months compared with the year before it, whilst only 8% spent more.[15]

A report from the *Financial Times*[16] provided little solace in comparisons with Ireland where, after their smoking ban, over a thousand pubs had been lost, an horrendous attrition rate of one in eight pubs, leaving only around 7,000 pubs in the country. Beer volumes were felt to have fallen by around a third since the 2006 Smoking Ban there.

Around 70,000 pubs started the roller coaster ride fifty years ago, which has been the subject of this book. Only a little over two-thirds have survived to complete the journey thus far. The many reasons for the casualties have been well documented. The way things are, how many will survive the next fifty?

The sad paradox for regular pub-goers is that it was our type of pub which was in trouble. Drinkers pubs. Places which have all the qualities of a 'real pub'. Places where beer is what you drink, where you can sit at the bar, where the landlord still matters, and where, most significantly, an authentic pub atmosphere still exists. But for how much longer? It is a small consolation that food-led pubs and branded outlets, whose customers would be unlikely to show huge loyalty towards them, or concern at their loss, seem to be surviving fairly well.

There are of course many traditional drinkers' pubs which continue to defy the statistics, attracting a lively group of punters and trading with unbridled gusto. And a number of towns which, despite the general downturn in trade, appear to have some curious genetic make-up in their demographic profile to somehow ensure that almost all of their pubs continue to flourish.

And some operators who are demonstrating that, with sensible management, the traditional drinkers' pub still has a solid future. Amber Taverns operate eighty-six managed houses, largely northern community pubs trading at around £6,000 per week. The company's latest annual report[17] showed like-for-like sales up 2%, with the company looking for more sites.

Amber operate town centre pubs that are uncompromisingly drinkers' pubs, catering for a solid working-class clientele. The food offer is limited and a range of standard pub-issue lagers and keg beers dominate the bar counter. The pubs themselves are clean and contemporary-looking with solid modern furniture and decorations. Screens showing sport are prominent throughout

What is Amber's trick in achieving such solid performance within the struggling drinking man's pub sector? It would appear to be nothing too difficult or sophisticated. Just comfortable surroundings and efficient bar management within solid traditional town-centre pubs. What is unusual is that Amber are owned by LGV Capital, a very discerning and respected private equity investor which is part of Legal and General. And LGV saw sufficient potential to acquire Amber and then allow its management team to continue to manage. Amber are also succeeding because they are carefully buying pubs that work for them at the right price. They are not splashing cash to expand. The ongoing disposals by the pubCos suggest that the market should hold plenty of opportunities for Amber. One key element that the company highlights is that their pub managers are highly incentivised.

Perhaps part of the answer to the viability of pubs is elusively simple. Normal management works for the big branded operations with high turnover and staffing. Problems arise further down the managed house spectrum. In recent years, many of these pubs have been let on lease by the pubCos. But with the pubCo model currently threatened, the future might lie in a system where good-quality managers are incentivised and empowered sufficiently to run pubs on a longer-term basis than is normal and which encourages them to use their own initiative far more than has been the case. A radical new model that achieves a position somewhere between a tenancy and a managed house and which combines the best attributes of both. Could this possibly be achieved by some type of franchise, a system which is slowly gaining ground with some of the larger companies?

An interesting approach was taken by Beannchor, the largest hospitality operator in Northern Ireland with forty-six licensed premises, twenty-one of which are in Belfast. Many of these are in the Cathedral Quarter, meaning they tend to compete with each other. Owners the Wolsey family, inspired by service standards in a coffee shop that they visited, decided on a different approach when they opened the National Grande Café, the impressive former home of the Bank of Ireland.

To differentiate the new outlet and widen its trading hours they developed a patisserie with its own bakery alongside, provided a specialist artisan coffee and marketed the premises as a 'hybrid' operation, opening from 7am onwards. They employed social media via the internet to publicise the changes. The result has been impressive, generating substantial daytime activity and food sales with coffee alone at £5,000 per week. Encouraged by this, they have also retargeted two other nearby bars, Whites 1630 which now provides food by day and a serious music programme at night and The Dirty Onion, which adopts a modern take on the traditional Irish pub.

At the time of the National opening Bill Wolsey claimed;

"Pubs are now going through a very difficult time, but they need to adapt and be much more relevant to people."[18]

What is common to most high-turnover bars now is substantial trading space. This provides several benefits. Most obviously, space means money. It allows operators to maximise turnover at peak periods because there is room for everyone. Secondly it means comfort. Plenty of tables and seating, in a range of positions, so that everyone can have one. Finally, as Wetherspoons have long discovered, it provides an element of private space for customers to create their own environment. And to choose between different parts of the premises to reflect their own mood; either a quiet corner or at the buzzing centre of the action, or something inbetween.

Space is increasingly a key point of differentiation between traditional pubs and modern bars or even a chain of unbranded town pubs such as those run by Amber Taverns. A small traditional pub is an intimate affair. Space is limited and one is often squeezed in amongst strangers. A conversation can easily be overheard and will often be shared throughout the bar. One unified atmosphere will often prevail, tending to envelop the entire bar.

Pub regulars love this atmosphere and regard it as an essential part of the pleasure of spending time in pubs. But many others do not. Society in general is becoming less gregarious and outgoing. The one is company, two is a crowd, attitude which underlies the endemic rise of the single-person household, and the demise of the extended family. Of course most people do like to mix and socialise at times. But only when they choose to, and with people of similar age and background. Hence the rise of branded bars.

In June 2013 CGA strategy drew on the latest economic and market data to predict that the on-trade share of the alcohol market by value would grow a little but despite this the market would reduce by a horrendous 7,704 pubs within the next five years. It added ominously that establishments that failed to take advantage of the new consumer trends would be particularly vulnerable.[19]

In this context consumer trends means only one thing: food. For many pubs this isn't helpful. Either ignore the advice and perish or heed the advice, risk damaging one's remaining wet trade and go to the wall somewhat sooner. According to the PMA market report 24.3% of pubs don't serve food. For another 15%, food accounts for under 10% of turnover. Commercial madness or licensees' resistance to change? No, primarily because their pubs' characteristics in internal layout, style or location and customer profile mean that food simply doesn't work.[20]

These drinkers' pubs which cannot look to food as their salvation and are equally unsuited to other common trade-builders like satellite sport, real ale, live music, or providing regular entertainment need to revert to the basic qualities that define a good pub; friendly and efficient service, decent beer, and a winning atmosphere. Landlords must remain dedicated and committed, do everything necessary to attract customers and earn their loyalty, and exploit their genuine pub atmosphere with all the benefits that this can bring.

Sadly, for many, this will not be enough.

After-Hours;
Final Thoughts

In March 2011 Andrew Pring, a senior figure within the trade, and a measured voice of reason, suggested that 25% of pubs don't deliver on service standards or professionalism and that there are still too many pubs for the market to sustain.[21]

It is always difficult for a pub-lover to accept that we have an excess of pubs. But the number that are continuing to close adds credence to the claim. And perhaps there are still 25% of pubs which are not run in line with modern convention or expectations.

However, those 25% of pubs happen to be the type of pub which I like. Whilst I can appreciate the modern and trendy, and the well-ordered, basic drinkers' pubs are what I grew up with and still enjoy. These will be the antithesis to the modern branded bar where staff have to be coached as to how they greet their 'guests'; instead the barman and barmaid are as idiosyncratic as their customers and respected for it, where the carpet is worn, and outdated posters hang on walls. Such pubs and their landlords are survivors from a previous age. They are certainly not what the modern consumer has in mind when he is looking for somewhere to take the family or business contacts for a nice meal.

The experience one will get in a branded bar or an efficient well-run pub is predictable and carefully managed. The modern consumer wants to be confident in his choice of licensed outlet. To know what will be on the menu, and that the prices are affordable and the beer is drinkable and the carpet has been hoovered, and that he and his party won't be sitting next to a group of punk rockers, or an old man who hasn't shaved since Christmas Day. And that is what many people want and need from a pub; predictability, comfort and safety.

For the rest of us who delight in individuality there is the esoteric and often scruffy drinkers' pub. It is a marvellous experience to wander randomly around an unfamiliar town and duck into pubs that take your fancy because they are historic, or quirky or noisy, or tranquil, or welcoming or even extremely basic and grubby. The most essential element of the traditional pub offer is that it is open to all, young and old, rich and poor, fashionable or otherwise. It is this unique melding of different groups under one roof that almost defines a traditional pub's appeal and atmosphere. But for how much longer? Such pubs would now only appear to be suitable for a shrinking minority of people.

The process of real pubs dying is desperately sad and unfortunate. Each and every one of the thousands of pubs fighting for survival right now are more than a mere number, a licence entered in the register, an old building with a few rotting signs attached. The faded lounges decorated in yesterday's styles and weathered and worn public bars pay testimony to the years of drinking and revelry, argument and debate, mateship and rivalry, thought and contemplation that characterise the intimate histories of every pub up and down the land. And the characters who made them what they were; the heavy drinkers and deep thinkers, the jokers and the smokers, the darts players and the soothsayers, dolled-up young tarts and beer-bellied old farts. It is this rich and varied tapestry of people that has conferred on public houses their unique place in British society. And it is this same human element which gives rise to the sense of loss when pubs, even the most out-moded, badly-run and plain ugly, are forced to close.

The Ultimate Guide
To Pub Brands

T his who's who of pub brands, past and present, is an endeavour to include all pub, pub-restaurant, bar and other industry-related operations that have developed as or have become a recognisable brand or theme. They stretch to 149 in number.

A brand is a concept or operation that has standardised features of design, product and service, and is widespread enough and sufficiently established that there is general recognition of it as a brand by the public. Such a strict interpretation has not been adopted here and concepts that have only reached a modest number and some outlets with only a broad theming have been included.

Whilst there is a desire to be comprehensive, there will inevitably be some operations which have evaded the net. The comments applied to each brand are subjective and are simply a personal view. Readers, and indeed anyone else, are as entitled to their opinion as the author.

The good, the bad and the ugly of the branding world is presented in alphabetical order. It will be apparent that with the continuing changes in the market, many of these brands are no longer with us.

A BAR 2 FAR PubCo Ascot Inns' infant brand that operated, somewhat unusually, as a cafe by day and a pre-club bar at night.
ACADEMY Brave but misguided attempt by Bass to harness the youth market with a late-night music bar of distinctive contemporary

design. A handful were opened, mainly on leisure parks, but the type of trade involved proved to be a difficult area for a non-specialist like Bass to handle and they soon closed or sold these units.

GE ALDWINKLES Only a few of these saw the light of day and perhaps, Regent would claim, were ever meant to. Gave the impression of living on former glories, having lain dormant under a layer of dust for many years and recently reopened before anyone was really prepared.

ALE AND PIE HOUSE Chain of traditional-looking pubs, typically in converted banks and similar premises operated by Fuller's in prominent situations in and around central London and now well-established. They specialise in good old-fashioned food, and of course meat pies.

ALE CAFE An endeavour by Greene King to have a slice of the action on the high street. Quite lavishly designed, large premises attempting to be all things to all people. A reasonable attempt at a quality, all-purpose brand but a concept that Greene King were seemingly never quite at one with.

ALL BAR ONE Bass used to modestly inform us that this is an exceedingly good place. And few amongst its prime market of city types and trendy females would disagree. Long trestle tables, back fittings full of rows of wine bottles and minimalist design, with large clocks and blackboards, provide an environment that one would achieve by converting the local primary school to a wine bar. The safely neutral atmosphere proved to be ideal for the local *cognoscenti* to create a chattering and exuberant ambience.

The open-glass frontage is regarded as a fundamental design feature, the essential key to female friendliness, allowing customers to appraise the atmosphere inside before entering. On the negative side, the hard minimalist décor created a reverberating tin can sensation when busy, but this has been addressed with more soft furnishings.

The availability of substantial food at all times ensures that All

Bar One maintains credibility as a cafe-bar, and a relative air of gentility on busy evenings when the majority of its competitors and imitators can become more raucous. An early arrival in the branding game, its durability has ensured that it has grown substantially.

ARENA One of a number of concepts inherited by Bass when it joined with Punch to acquire the Allied Domecq managed estate. For a short while when the high street market was struggling, M&B became very committed to alternatives such as Ember Inns and Arena. The latter was a little surprising given its community market but in 2002 its flavour of the month status was apparent in this statement from then-Six Continents Chief Exec. Tim Clarke;

"I think Arena has been a really exciting development. It gives a very high quality of entertainment in large pubs in residential areas and they're doing very well indeed. They remain very much community houses but give a more contemporary offer."[1]

Within a few years the operation had returned to obscurity.

ARTISTS FAYRE Peculiar name for Morland's out-of-town pub-restaurant chain, mostly in pleasant Thames Valley locations and otherwise unremarkable. Greene King as the new owners converted these to their own brands.

BALLS BROTHERS These were a selection of high-quality basement bars and restaurants in and around the city of London. There was no theming involved, just pleasant traditional surroundings. Now owned by Novus, which appears to involve something of a change in direction.

BAR BUDDA Chain of young persons' bars across central Scotland, run by Dark Star Scotland which went into administration in 2009.

BAR COAST Brief flirtation by Bass with the new wave of cafe-bars. Bland, minimalist interior with little to distinguish it from others of the genre. To its designers, the key was to differentiate it from heavy traditional pub interiors which encourage the 'pub ambivalents' like women and upmarket shoppers. In practice, it tended to attract a younger market who wanted to be seen to be frequenting the right places. The problem was that as soon as 'Coast' was not perceived to be the right place to be, there were few other reasons to go there. And thus no reasons for Bass to continue investing in it.

BAR ESSENTIAL A handful of sites developed in a typical stylised cafe-bar manner by the Cardiff brewer Brains around their South Wales heartland. Brains remain but the brand has had its day.

BAR EXCELLENCE Fairly obvious and reasonably effective copy of All Bar One, part of Eldridge Pope's determined drive to become a retail force. Unfortunately when Eldridge Pope disappeared the brand had no champion to keep it alive.

BAROOSH Stylish and comfortable town-centre modern cafe-bar. Operated by McMullens in around eight towns across the northern Home Counties. Serious food offer that endeavours to be a little innovative.

BAR OZ Perhaps S&N felt that the Australians, like the Irish, had an ingrained and popular beer culture, making this ideal material to take over as the Irish mania receded. The result was Bar Oz, a blatant satire of Australiana complete with toilets marked Blokes and Sheilas, surfboards, fries served in a billy can, stuffed kangaroos and chilled Australian beer in place of anything English. The numbers of pubs suffering this brutally undignified and not very popular treatment remained mercifully low.

BARRACUDA South African-themed, high street bar run by Barracuda, of course. Concentrated on sports screens and food with a slight South African feel.

BAR RISA Commenced as Regent Inns' interpretation of a cafe-bar and often combined with Jongleurs. Has developed under Intertain, which took over from Regent after it went into administration, into a major late-night venue.

BAR ROOM BAR Chain of bars which were briefly independent under the eponymous Bar Room Bar Group. When this went into receivership in 2009 it was rescued by former owners Orchid Group. The contemporary bars specialise in standard pub food by day, and then gradually ramp up the music during the evening.

BAR 38 This was a Scottish & Newcastle endeavour to be cutting edge and trendy. A premium brand for prime city centre sites. Unlike Rat and Parrot, it was very design-conscious which unfortunately meant that it was very popular for a year or two and then declined when fashions moved on. Not many were developed and, since the sale of the S&N retail estate, one or two have survived in independent ownership.

BE AT ONE Now up to around twenty units, mostly in and around central London. This is a totally dedicated cocktail bar attracting a bright young crowd. The locations of some of these in pubby-type buildings rather than within nightclubs or fancy hotels are a little incongruous for a cocktail bar but the brand is popular and provides some genuine choice in a fun and friendly way.

BEEFEATER (currently Beefeater Grill). Has been a dominant feature of the suburban pub-restaurant scene since 1974 when it was founded by Whitbread. Since then has become synonymous with out-of-town dining and reached about 300 units at its peak during the Nineties. But there have been a few ups and downs in its fortunes, with Whitbread seeming to lose confidence in the old brand at times.

Problems followed the BSE crisis, and focused on safety fears over red meat and trends towards healthy living. With Whitbread's propensity to experiment and introduce new restaurant concepts, observers wondered whether it was being starved of investment during the Nineties. An extensive relaunch followed the BSE crisis whilst a review weeded out 50 unsuitable operations for disposal. Then in 2006 Whitbread decided that sites not linked to a Premier Inn didn't trade so well. A huge clear-out of Beefeaters and Brewers Fayres followed, with 239 of these sold to M&B. In its new format, having had its wings clipped, it numbers around 140 outlets.

Beefeater remains firmly devoted to a steak-based menu and the old warhorse continues to survive as it approaches its 40th birthday.

BEL AND THE DRAGON Chain of five bar-restaurants developed in attractive old buildings in wealthy towns around Surrey and Berkshire.

BELUSHI'S Bar operated by Beds and Bars, known for its St Christopher chain of hostels across Britain and Europe. The bars are geared to the requirements of young backpackers who frequent the hostels and, when they get going, provide a lively fun environment.

BENNIGAN'S Not to be confused with Brannigan's the music bar, this is a franchised American theme restaurant, of no originality, briefly and expensively imported by Bass from the States. Very similar to TGI's in appearance, but with a dominant green instead of red stripe. Bass didn't cover themselves in glory in this market. Back in the mid-Eighties when Whitbread commenced rolling out TGI's and Allied opened its first Calendars, Bass was up there with Jeffersons, operating in two sites in Birmingham and north-east London. Instead of matching the growth of its competitors the brand stood still whilst Bass became distracted by T.J.s, another of the genre which never quite took off, and after a further long pause, plumped for the inferior Bennigans.

TJ BERNARDS Sounding more like a travelling circus than a pub chain, this was the S&N answer to Nicholson's, the business-orientated London chain. Branding was minimal, giving these pleasant town-centre pubs all the trappings of an individual traditional pub, with a decent food offer. Reached about sixty units at its peak.

BERNI INNS The pioneer of the branded restaurant. Established in the Bristol area from 1955 onwards by brothers Frank and Aldo Berni, and based on American-style restaurants. Offered a restricted steak, gammon or plaice and chips menu with a few obvious starters and sweets on a value basis, and standard décor. Purchased by

Grand Met in 1970 when it had grown to well over 100 units and then by Whitbread in 1990, by which time it felt extremely dated and was largely used for conversion to Beefeater.

BIG HAND MO'S Destination fun pub of variable style and limited quality typically inhabiting a bleak stretch of the inner ring road. S&N should not have allowed this brand to escape beyond the 1980s.

BIERODROME Growing chain of bars in London, based on Belgian beer and cuisine. If you haven't yet sampled these yet then you should, without delay. Belgian beers are excellent, providing an impressive range of strong flavours, whilst the food rarely fails to please. The Bierodrome chain now covers many of the trendy inner London suburbs and are suitably congenial, providing separate eating and dining areas.

BIG STEAK Masterminded by Allied Breweries, this started life as a brash advertising promotion using huge banners draped over the front of pubs. Suddenly Big Steak pubs were leaping out from unsuspecting roadside pubs everywhere. If space allowed, Wacky Warehouses were added to allow the kids to run riot whilst Mum and Dad consumed their eight-pounders with indifference and béarnaise sauce. The operation had few common distinguishing features other than the ubiquitous signs, and proved to be variable in operational standards, undermining its status as a brand. Some of the Big Steak licensees looked as if they would struggle to serve a ham sandwich. The Punch takeover of the Allied Breweries pub estate signalled the overdue end of the line for Big Steak. Many of the sites were good enough for Bass to grab as their share of the package and convert to their own brands, commonly Ember Inns.

BLOB SHOP Great name for alternative, very basic, pub chain founded by Yates plc. Only got to a few operations. The outlet in Liverpool still survives, now run, along with its former parent by Stonegate.

BOARDWALK Modern high street chameleon bar developed by London brewer Fullers, hoping to serve the business market by day and a young trendy market at night. By 2001, when they were up to six strong, Fullers realised that this wasn't their thing and killed the brand.

BRANNIGAN'S Developed by First Leisure, which passed the operation of fourteen outlets to Mustard Entertainment in 2001 following a management buyout. Two years later Mustard were in trouble and multi-millionaire leisure operator Trevor Hemmings stepped in. Brannigan's became the responsibility of Herald Inns which reduced the chain to eleven outlets. By the end of the decade this group was also struggling, which signalled the end for Brannigan's.

Which was a shame because in their short and troubled existence they had provided a safe and fun environment for many young drinkers. The bars tended to occupy a cavernous space and put on a good range of music, entertainment and dancing to pull in the crowds at night, all supplemented by a dining area. The music focused on famous names from the past or retro nights, i.e. Seventies or Eighties. The standard signage at one time intriguingly promised *cavorting* in addition to the more predictable activities.

BREWERS FAYRE One of Whitbread's original holy trinity of restaurants (along with Beefeater and TGI's) which they retained when the pub estate got the chop. Grew phenomenally during the Nineties on the back of Whitbread's supreme confidence in their food brands and knowledge of the roadside market. This made it the most numerous brand reaching around the 400 mark.

By then, Whitbread started tinkering with style and brands and created Brewsters. And then came the huge decision in 2006 to dispose of all those units which weren't alongside a Premier Inn hotel. The survivors are now decorated in a restrained traditional style, with an all-purpose menu and a bland safe atmosphere to cater for pub ambivalents.

BREWSTERS External signage promised 'Pub, food and fun factory'. Spin-off from Brewers Fayre after Whitbread decided to use the Brewers Fayre label for non-family operations. Mostly with 'Charlie Chalk's fun factory' internal play areas and ghastly signage attached. Didn't last long before Whitbread started meddling again when they realised that it was its worst-performing brand, possibly because of all the noisy children! The whole estate was then lumped back into Brewers Fayre until the next reshuffle of brands and units.

BROWNS Restaurant founded back in 1973 by entrepreneur Jeremy Mogford in Brighton. Mogford then allowed himself a further twenty-five years to lovingly expand the chain into an impressive range of buildings in Bristol, Oxford, Cambridge and London with a cult status to match. In 1998, in stepped Bass with a large cheque to claim the brand for itself and roll out the 'neo-colonial theme' in carefully selected prime sites in the major centres, accelerating the growth of the chain just a little in the process. Still expanding and largely managing to maintain Browns' high standards and some of the vibrant atmosphere of the original.

CAFE ROUGE Bought in the summer of 1996 for £133 million from Cafe Pelican, the purchase gave Whitbread the opportunity to establish the type of dominance that they had established in out-of-town pub-restaurant food on the High Street. The seventy-five branches of Cafe Rouge were expanded enthusiastically in preference to the other two brands acquired in the deal, Mama Amalfi Italian restaurants and Dome cafe-bars. However either the returns were not sufficient, or the novelty of running French-style brasseries wore off after only six years when the chain was sold to Tragus, a restaurant group.

CALENDARS Launched with much razzmatazz by Allied Breweries as a one-off in Watford in the mid-Eighties this was intended as a prototype to challenge the success of TGI's. Allied realised they had a marketable brand to compete with and started to roll it out. However numbers were always limited and the brand lost its way due to reorganisations and the distractions of the Nineties. Internally, design was absolutely standardised, to the last reproduction Indian canoe and New York road sign hanging from the ceiling. In some locations the central bar area proved to be popular with young 'vertical' drinkers.

CAPE Barracuda brand, aimed at circuit drinkers by night but also intended as a cafe-bar during the day to help pay the rent, which could be substantial in the prime locations targeted for it. Intended to be 'smart, colonial and cosmopolitan', but such subtleties could be a little overwhelmed when packed with a boisterous crowd at night. A little variable in size and standards and, given the recent demise of Barracuda, having a somewhat uncertain future.

CASA Designer cafe-bar overrun with pastel shades and sculptured furniture. Featured several distinct areas from cocktail bar to serious dining area. Developed by Whitbread but as soon as this estate became independent under Laurel, its pretentious days were over. Casa was also subject to a bizarre experiment when it was reported that the brand was to be given twice-yearly makeovers to hang on to customers bored with the same décor. It was suggested that the idea was encouraged by the popularity of the TV programme *Changing Rooms*. The innovation appeared to do little to enhance the popularity or fortunes of Casa.

CHEF & BREWER One of the first pub-restaurants founded in the innovative atmosphere that grew up around Grand Met whilst it had an interest in the beer industry back in the late 1970s. Traditional in fit-out, generally relying on the character of the buildings it occupied, it proved to be enduring and popular. Retained by Grand Met when nearly everything else was lumped into Inntrepreneur. The sale of the Chef & Brewer estate of managed houses to S&N indicated the final goodbye to the trade for Grand Met. Adopted by S&N as its flagship brand out of town and was gradually growing with conversions when S&N sold their estate to Spirit. The change of ownership didn't appear to matter.

Chef & Brewer is so well-established, and such a natural fit, that it seems to run itself.

CHICAGO ROCK CAFE The original model, founded by Luminar Leisure, looked like a diner with stripy blinds and check tablecloths. But food turnover for most outlets was fairly limited, even at lunchtime. And as the rampant nighttime trade predominated the food became a total sideshow. As Luminar's flagship this grew to around sixty units with its 'formula' tending to work best in smaller towns where the competition wasn't too sophisticated. The survival battles of Luminar in recent years caused the sale of many units, some for conversion to Wetherspoons. Now some of the chain survive, still trading to the same market.

CITY LIMITS Originally a bar-diner in north-east London but S&N purloined the name for its family entertainment brand for which it showed great enthusiasm briefly.

COUNTRY CARVERY More carvery than country, this S&N operation chugged along for a number of years offering an 'alternative' pub-restaurant menu without making any great impression in the wider marketplace.

CROWN CARVERIES Creative use of sites acquired by M&B in various packages and moulded into family-friendly value eating houses where suitable demographic markets were identified, presumably sufficiently distinct from the Toby brand it also runs. The chain currently has a strength of something approaching the hundred mark.

DAVE AND BUSTER'S Not a bar but a family entertainment centre, providing a combination of games areas, ten-pin bowling and restaurant. A concept introduced from America with great hype by Bass. Apparently massively popular in the States, its failure here ensures that we don't have to accept every fad which arrives from across the Atlantic. Dave and Buster's peaked at two operations and Bass quickly realised that it was high time to distance themselves from this latest sensation.

DE ALTO Attractive Mediterranean restaurant developed by S&N.

DOME Originally developed by Courage, this cafe-bar was an individual success, creating a very credible Bohemian atmosphere, not least due to general neglect. The local beautiful people loyally adorned the brand but subsequent owners Forte and then Whitbread couldn't confidently embrace this market and the chain languished with little more than a handful of units. The flickering flame was finally and sadly extinguished by Laurel when it took over.

DROUTHY NEEBORS Pub concept of Scottish brewer Bellhaven, a kind of Scottish 'Irish bar' with plenty of atmosphere and a decent food offer, with a Scottish angle. The indications are that new owners Greene King are showing the Neebors the door. The name comes from a Burns poem, incidentally.

DRUMMONDS The Bass version of the cafe-bar which competed in the original themed bar contests of the 1980s. Unimaginative and in many cases so unconvincing that punters largely ignored the food and continued to use it as a pub. Bass, suitably deterred, gave up and abandoned the idea. Bass/M&B have learnt a lot more about both branding and catering since then.

EATING INN Low-key brand name for chains of pub-restaurants acquired by Greene King across the north and Scotland in attractive country locations, and numbering about twenty-five.

EAT YOUR HEART OUT Four-strong chain of gastropubs across the Home Counties which went into administration in 2009. Perhaps, if customers were guided by the name, the lack of portion control was a key factor in the demise of the chain.

EDWARDS Yet another of the extensive collection of Bass brands. Edwards was a tribute to Yates's, an attempt to provide large versatile premises which can be everything to every man; from breakfast and coffee in the morning, through lunch and afternoon cakes to the five o'clock swill and finally, from mid-evening, the music turned to full volume to pull in the young circuit drinkers.

Too ambitious a concept to cope with such dramatic changes of identity, with the inevitable result.

EERIE BARS Not so much a brand as a broad theming along the horror/gothic route, at one time with eight affiliated operations. Scottish & Newcastle made this spooky domain their own with such delights as Bram Stoker in Chelsea, the Pit & Pendulum in Nottingham and Jekyll and Hyde. Gothic arches, dark corners and heavy chains formed the mainstay of the decor. The concept was a bit of fun but too quirky to survive long in the hard-nosed world of Sober October.

ELBOW ROOM Whilst pool is the centrepiece of this Nineties brand, separate bars and a dancefloor might also be featured, in a style far superior to the average Mr Q's. If pool bars are to flourish then a mass-market version of Elbow Room may be the future.

EMBER INNS Relatively recent creation in the last days of Bass, featuring fireplaces and a front-room ambience with leather armchairs, traditional food and beer, whilst discouraging children. The brand encourages one to feel at home. Obviously there are enough people who wish to go out but feel like they have not, as the brand continues to expand. Fortunately the awful 'pillar' pub signs with a glowing fireplace at the top are now less common.

EXCHANGE BARS Grew out of New England diners, a development by Tetleys when it was a semi-autonomous part of Allied Breweries in the Yorkshire area. Allied then rolled it out nationally as Exchange Bars, each having its own unique American appendage, ie Monteray Exchange, Vermont Exchange etc. Developed into an enjoyable and profitable operation, but which suffered at some sites because of its separate bar/restaurant approach. The local lads partying boisterously in one bar was not always conducive to dining next door. Allied knew the solution to this; sell the whole lot and start again with Big Steak. Morland stepped in to purchase and soon after Greene King inherited the brand when they bought Morland. Unfortunately they found the operation not to their liking and the

Exchanges were no more, with most of the sites subsequently being passed on to Whitbread for conversion to its various restaurants.

FAT CAT CAFÉ BARS Sadly went into administration in April 2013 after nearly twenty years of expansion to reach about ten units across North Wales and the Midlands.

FAYRE AND SQUARE Pretty standard destination pub-restaurant with fairly wide and good value menu. Operated by Spirit and now up to around 150 units.

FESTIVAL ALE HOUSE Concept to which seventy or so suitable-looking pubs were subjected by Allied in their brand-frenzy period of the early Nineties. Whilst other houses were being turned into Scruffy Murphys, Mr Q's, Firkin or Big Steak, the lucky ones were being given a traditional makeover. The decor was woody and inoffensive but the operation was never quite authentic enough or committed to real ale in the manner of Hogshead, to which it seemed to be a tribute of.

FINE LINE Carefully nurtured by Fullers and focused on The City, these are a modern variant on the traditional pub with more emphasis on food. The operation works well under Fullers' watchful control.

FINNEGAN'S WAKE Well-named Irish bar clone, developed half-heartedly by S&N and then abandoned when the inspiration of Bar Oz came along.

FIRESIDE INNS Eldridge Pope's out-of-town brand, designed for cosy drive-to country pubs with a good food selection. More a collection of similar pubs than a replicated chain.

FIRKIN Created in 1979 by David Bruce, an ex-brewery man who, disenchanted with the politics and constraints of big company life decided to provide his own interpretation of what a good pub should be. And the first wave of genuine Firkins were highly popular and a breath of fresh air. Each had a house name along the theme of 'Flounder and Firkin', 'Fox and Firkin' etc. and a very traditional woody interior. The beers were brewed in a microbrewery on the premises and were memorable for their originality in taste and name. Dogbolter, a distinctive, potent mix, was revered in drinking circles. A sing-song was even added to the routine at those outlets with a piano in the corner. Beer buffs and those who enjoyed something different were enchanted.

Bruce decided to move on in 1988 and sold out to Midsummer Leisure, turning his hand next to converting narrow boats for the disabled. Midsummer became European Leisure, who then sold to Stakis Leisure in 1990. Allied Domecq stepped in a year later, committed to growing the brand substantially. Over the next ten years they showed steadfast dedication to this task, building up to over 170 outlets, mainly conversions from existing Allied pubs. To a degree they remained faithful to the original format, retaining the distinctive Firkin signage and recreating the irreverent feel of the original chain. But with the brand rolled out on the conveyor belt at an alarming rate, the original atmosphere of Firkin was totally devalued. The massed ranks of fruit machines and large open spaces gave Firkin an unrefined feel, bereft of its original charm. The suggestive and corny signs brashly thrown up on every bit of wall not already occupied by a fruit machine or game attracted a predictably young and boisterous audience. The charm of the original group of Firkins was not something that was suited to mass production.

With the sale of Allied's pub estate to Punch, the brand's days were numbered. The majority of sites, over 121 in number, were taken by Bass who were obliged and committed to convert to their own brands. Meanwhile, Punch, which retained the brand name and about sixty of the Firkins, was very quick to abandon the few surviving brew-sites amongst these. Operating just one or two of these may have earnt the pubCo the unwanted label of brewer and some draconian MMC restrictions as a consequence.

Firkin can also claim to be one of the leading international brands. There are chains of Firkin pubs that observe the same naming convention as the original in Canada and the USA and one or two others in both Australia and the Netherlands. It appears that in all these places Firkins are regarded as 'English-themed pubs'.

FIRST AND LAST Another city-centre businessmen's establishment, with a particular focus on decent bar food. Yet another from the Bass brand factory in Cape Hill, Birmingham.

FLARES Big entertainment pubs on nighttime circuits developed by Bass and shrouded in Seventies irony, music and frequently revellers in appropriate fancy dress. Surprisingly popular and now run by Stonegate.

FOR YOUR EYES ONLY Originally a one-off developed in the unlikely environs of Park Royal Industrial estate, in north-west London. Surrey Free Inns acquired this as part of a small package and initially rolled it out, taking numbers up to four. It classified the operation as tableside dancing venues – the closest that the mainstream pub industry has come to adopting girly bars. The operation made the tremendous leap from Park Royal to Mayfair, suggesting lofty ambitions, but soon after SFI realised the implications of involvement in this sector and sold the operation off.

GOOSE AND GRANITE Obscure name for an obvious theme; the brewers coming to the conclusion during the Nineties that if they couldn't beat Wetherspoons, then they would join them. Or rather in typical industry fashion, plagiarise. Bass created the fiction of the 'Just So Pub company' to roll out the Goose and Granite. The brand never became very substantial and drifted into oblivion following reorganisation.

GROANING BOARD Informal pub-restaurant developed in a handful of roadhouses by Regent Inns in their early days, offering hearty fayre with much enthusiasm and, one suspects, limited profit.

HA! HA! BAR & CANTEEN Unusual name for what Yates intended to be an innovative concept. Designer Amanda Wilmott, also responsible for All Bar One, was heavily involved, claiming that the inspiration was lifestyle issues. Add more than a few touches of All Bar One, and Yates felt confident that they had a winner. Never became very substantial and was then acquired, ironically, by M&B as part of their 'brand-focusing' strategy. And indeed, some of the sites acquired have become All Bar Ones.

HARD ROCK CAFE Restaurant privately developed in Piccadilly, London in the early Seventies and became an institution, especially due to the rock memorabilia all over the walls. Then bought by Rank, who expanded the brand all round the world.

HARVESTER Originally developed by Courage in the Eighties, who converted most of their good roadside sites for the purpose. Courage sold out to Trust House Forte who milked the operation for all it was worth whilst putting back little in the way of refurbishment or development. Meanwhile Bass had been striving for years to come up with a major steak house brand to compete with Whitbread. So it suited both parties in 1996 when Bass paid out £170 million for the seventy-five or so sites, almost all in the south. Bass then tapped into its own vast empire for new sites to accommodate further growth. Harvester was originally very rustic in a no-holds-barred, pitchfork-in-your-face type of way. If you like farmyard memorabilia and traditional favourites this was the place for you. Food was a little expensive, although the famous 'early bird' early evening price offers more than compensated. The farmyard bric-a-brac feel has now largely disappeared apart from the dominant green colouring but expansion continues up to over 200 outlets. Demonstrates an enduring popularity, due in the past to effective TV advertising.

HARVEY FLOORBANGERS Young persons' haunt, being one of the many Regent Inns operations that have long since disappeared.

HENRY'S Early cafe-bar style, young persons' bar developed in some impressive sites around the country. Whitbread then lost interest with the chain and sold it to Greenall's which then passed it on to

S&N in 2000. Unlike Muswells, its old rival, the chain has remained, partly due to its generous size and the survivors, in prime night-circuit, positions are now re-styled and have a trendy feel.

HENRY J. BEAN'S Cult status bar that started in Kings Rd, Chelsea but has since expanded to a few other sites. Originally operated by small leisure company My Kinda Town, this was big in Americana but now concentrates on food by day and pumping up the atmosphere later.

HENRY'S TABLE Inherited from Boddingtons and therefore orphaned twice with its passing to Greenalls and then S&N. As a result it became prime material for rebranding.

HOBGOBLIN Intriguing and unorthadox bars developed by the diminutive Wychwood Brewery of Oxfordshire, which approached thirty outlets across the south. The connotations of the brand tended to attract an alternative following.

HOGSHEAD Whitbread was never quite as formidable in-town as out but Hogshead proved to be a success, rising to over 150 trading outlets until Whitbread included the chain in its grand pub clearance sale. Hogshead was a real real ale brand. Design was predictably traditional, with lots of exposed timber. To give the brand credibility, Whitbread presented an impressive range of real ales free of the constraints of loyalty to their own products. Hogshead also ran a number of real ale festivals to promote trade.

After transfer to Laurel performance declined and by 2002 the company trialled a new 'more customer-friendly' format with conventional décor and floorwalkers to serve customers at their tables. But the trial was taking away from the original concept and didn't make sense. The market had changed and independent real ale pubs were now much more widespread, which begged the obvious question as to why real ale aficionados would frequent a pubCo chain when they could have the real thing, or a Wetherspoons at a much lower price. The result was the end of Hogshead.

HOMESPREADS The S&N family pub, often with its Funky Forest children's play area. This, like many of the former Company's operations, represented a safe middle way, apparently devised after careful observation of what the opposition had done.

HOOTERS A bar-restaurant brand with extensive coverage in North America and South Africa whose appeal is derived from a range of burgers and similar offerings served in a loud raunchy atmosphere by buxom, under-dressed waitresses. Claims to be 'delightfully tacky yet unrefined'. An assault on the British market recently commenced with Nottingham and then suddenly died away. Appeals to an obvious market, whilst the reaction from feminists is equally predictable.

HUNGRY HORSE Developed by the intrepid Michael Cannon as part of the Magic Pub Co which was sold to Greene King. In 1994, at the time of purchase of 282 pubs from S&N, some of which formed the nucleus of Hungry Horse, Cannon commented; 'food sales in these pubs are 50% below the national average at 8% of turnover. This is an area we will attack'.[2]

This is the community version of Harvester, located in accessible areas within towns, and thus aimed at a different market to destination pub-restaurants. Full of bright colours and large platefuls of wholesome, cheap food. Performance has been good and the brand is steadily expanding.

INNKEEPER'S FAYRE Family pub developed by Bass during the early Nineties. Suggestive of Brewers Fayre in name, logo and style.

ISOBAR Minimalist interior and large format. Morland's idea here was to provide a wide range of bottled beers from around the world. Nice idea that failed to catch on and the number of units never reached more than a handful before the demise of the brand's sponsor.

JEFFERSONS Defied the rule that a small brand in a large organisation will not survive and retain its standards. See Bennigan's for background. Occupied the same sort of building which is standard for TGI's and its cousins and worked to a similar menu. But unlike these Jefferson's had a more stylish interior devoid of masses of bric-a-brac.

JIM THOMPSON'S Impressive chain of Oriental restaurants, with strong and effective colonial theme, many in converted roadside pubs. Developed by Noble House's Tony Carson. Interesting menu, authentic-looking design and furnishings, and an innovative approach with bric-a-brac on sale made this a welcome arrival on the scene.

JOHN BARRAS S&N's standardised community brand. Started during the Nineties, and largely based on conversions from the existing estate. The resulting style was that of an estate pub trying to behave like a Wetherspoons. In some cases something was lost in the process.

But the operation has been refined over the years and has created its own identity as a modern urban local with sports screens, good value food and entertainment. Now under the control of Spirit and has continued to expand to a strength of over 250 which suggests that performance is more than satisfactory.

JONGLEURS Comedy clubs developed by Regent Inns, who often combined them with Bar Risa. Not a mainstream bar but clearly a welcome facility within town centres.

JUMPIN' JAKS Live entertainment bar developed by Rank, mainly on leisure parks. Grew to nine sites that offered a weekly routine of live music, duelling pianos, line dancing and whatever else came into vogue, along with some contrived anarchy to keep punters amused. Rank Entertainment was purchased by Northern Leisure in 1999 which then sold on to Luminar a year later. Luminar's problems in the new millenium meant that the brand was closed but one or two of the sites have battled on as independent nightclubs.

KINGS FAYRE Greene King's original family pub-restaurant, eclipsed by Hungry Horse. Large ambitious sites, efficiently developed, but perhaps lacking, at the time, the control of an experienced catering operator.

LITTON TREE Unexceptional young persons bar, modelled broadly on Yates's and aiming for a similarly young market. Main brand of Surrey Free Inns (SFI) until the group acquired Slug and Lettuce. Now in the reliable hands of Stonegate.

LIVING ROOM Another Stonegate brand, providing formal dining and a swish cocktail bar in the main UK cities.

LLOYDS NUMBER 1 Generally large, distinguished buildings with high ceilings and elegant stonework. Developed in large centres of the Midlands and north by Wolverhampton & Dudley. Good lunchtime food and evening music helped to ensure success. When the company got into trouble in the Nineties, Wetherspoons swooped with an £8 million cheque to buy the ten outlets and acquire its first real alternative brand to the bog-standard Wetherspoons. The units have since been ring-fenced by the Watford-based company and retain their separate identity.

LOUNGERS Recently founded and rapidly expanding concept created by a new independent group. The brand is a cafe-bar, developed in town centres and prominent suburban parades, largely in vacant retail space, of which, there is of course, plenty available. The operation feels relatively faithful to one's image of a French brasserie but very extensive in area. Ambience is carefully controlled and effective whilst the food offer is comprehensive and imaginative. Watch this brand expand!

MALTSTERS TABLE Uninspired Allied attempt at the pub-restaurant, abandoned when Big Steak burst energetically onto the scene. Not helped by having a contrived and awkward name.

MAMA AMALFI Nice name, pleasant concept and good food but once it came under Whitbread's control as part of the sale by Pelican group the writing was on the marble-effect walls.

MR Q's Allied interpretation of Open House with sports screens, pool tables and questionable decor. During the early nineties Allied seemed to take a leaf out of Grand Met's imaginary 'pub-operating manual'. All in-town pubs apparently had to become either a Mr Q's, a Big Steak, Scruffy Murphys, a Festival Ale House or a Firkin. The policy did result in some square pegs being forced into a variety of shaped holes. Punch, in claiming the proud inheritance of this brand, revamped it as Q's.

MILESTONE TAVERNS AND RESTAURANTS General all-purpose destination pub-restaurants operated by Marstons, including some attractive sites. Now well-established, having been set up by W&D some years ago.

MILLER'S KITCHEN Pleasant enough traditional family pub-restaurant. The chain of ninety or so was developed by Greenall's. When taken over by S&N, suitable sites were converted to Chef and Brewer.

MILLHOUSE INNS Eponymous chain of generally rural and small town pub-restaurants notable for their fine settings, run by company of that name. Grew to eighty units and purchased by Punch in 2006 for £2m per site.

MISSOULA "Missoula is best known for its style, sophistication and great music." So say the owners of this small chain, Stonegate. All this, and proper food from breakfast to evening. A contemporary version of a long line of cafe-bars which ramp up the action at night.

MOLLOY'S Yet another of Stonegate's brands, Molloy's is their own version of the Irish-themed bar. Unlike the O'Neill's operation, Molloy's would appear to be specialising on value Irish food along with live sports and entertainment. Nine of the O'Neill's which were part of the package acquired from M&B are to be converted to Molloy's, so we may see more of this brand.

MOOD Chain of eight late-night bars run by Herald Inns and Bars, alongside Brannigan's. The operation, along with tenanted pubCo Trust Inns was owned by leisure entrepreneur Trevor Hemmings.

MUSWELLS The original continental cafe-bar chain developed by Allied during the Eighties, and therefore a pioneer of in-town branding. Nice atmosphere and a good tex-mex menu. Very popular in some circles but limited, mainly by small sites. Its demise owed more to circumstances than shortcomings in the operation.

NEWT & CUCUMBER Chris Hutt formed Unicorn Inns with just one pub in 1985 and expanded to a mixed estate of high street and destination food pubs. Newt & Cucumber was its flagship brand, created from unexceptional town centre pubs, that were operated carefully in order to appeal to a number of market sectors during the day, and circuit drinkers at night. After an intense bidding battle with Regent Inns, Morland secured Unicorn for around £13m in 1996. But they didn't have long to enjoy their new acquisition as in 1999 Greene King took over Morland. The brand did not long survive the change in ownership.

NICHOLSON'S Not really a brand. What this collection of forty or so premium London pubs have in common is a traditional style and common signage. Managed for many years by Taylor Walker, the operating company of Allied Breweries, Nicholson's claims many prime London trading locations and some very attractive and historic interiors. Mostly aimed at the business market. Acquired by Bass as part of the Punch purchase of Allied's pubs and retained since by M&B, despite Nicholson's non-food focus because of the sheer quality of the estate.

OLD ENGLISH INNS Purchased from the company of that name in 2002 by Greene King. The estate was not a brand but a collection of delightful old hotels and inns.

OLD MONK After a period working for the brewers and subsequently assisting his brother in the expansion of Wetherspoons, Jerry Martin decided to do his own thing. Why not start a pub chain? The result was the Old Monk. Concentrated in and around central London, the clientele was a mixture of city business types and Wetherspoons all-sorts. Many of the units were in basements, design and atmosphere owed much to the influence of the brewery and Wetherspoons days. The Old Monk company, which grew to twenty-four units, included eight Springbok bars, aimed at South African rugby types rather than animal lovers. Unfortunately, in the tough trading conditions of 2002 the chain went into receivership. Many of the units were acquired by Barracuda. Afterwards Jerry retained the Springbok bars, trading them as 'Bush Pig Bars' for another two years until this operation also went to the wall.

OLD ORLEANS These units were developed in a mixture of buildings, most of which managed to convey a 'southern bayou feel' with a suitable background atmosphere. The food operation was normally dominant, and was distinguished by a somewhat narrow range of ribs and similar southern-states Cajun-type cuisine. Developed by Grand Met this was acquired by S&N as part of the 1994 Chef & Brewer package. S&N stayed loyal to the brand for a number of years, adding further outlets to expand the chain. But by 2002 under pressure to make changes, twelve of the units were sold off individually. The others went to Punch a year later with the rest of the S&N pub estate and these twenty-six were sold to Regent Inns in 2006 for £26m. But with Regent's own administration, the brand was coming towards the end of the line which sadly arrived in 2011.

O'NEILL'S Bass were not the first to develop Irish bars when they exploded onto the scene in 1995. The Ulster 'peace dividend' that flourished at the time created an Irish feel-good factor which added impetus to their roll-out. O'Neill's rapidly became the market leader, peaking at around a hundred units.

Irish bars have taken the brunt of the 'brand rage' exhibited by real ale types. Blatantly artificial interiors were dominated by wood, old stoves and bric-a-brac, all plastered with references to the Emerald Isle. Another typical feature was partitioning to create intimate and enticing snugs. The 'authentic' atmosphere was enhanced by Irish music and predominantly Irish staff. Perhaps the critics of Irish bars were particularly offended by the manufactured 'craic' created by staff and floorwalkers. O'Neill's' future may be limited now that M&B has passed control to Stonegate.

ORANGE TREE Founded by Luminar Leisure in 2001 as part of MD Steven Thomas's plan to segment the market and ensure that his company had a hand in each portion. But before he had a chance to fully roll out his grand strategy the high street market collapsed. The Orange Tree was designed to take on Wetherspoons in the high street but, after only a handful had opened, meltdown arrived for a number of companies operating in this market. Luminar were hit by the heavy discounting that followed and the decline of the nightclub market, which was their principal activity. As a result Luminar had to concentrate on basics and Project Orange was dropped.

PARISA BARS Unusual concept of cafe-bar that incorporated a wine shop. The twenty-four largely northern units were purchased by Surrey Free Inns in 2001 and most were soon rebranded.

PITCHER & PIANO Imposing locations and stylish interiors for the sophisticated and trendy office worker, complete with Chesterfields and palm trees. However, on a busy evening session, when the drink-fuelled crowds create a very boisterous atmosphere the veneer of quality rubs off a little. Developed independently from 1986 and purchased by the original Marston's in 1996 and then passed on to Wolverhampton & Dudley (which then became Marstons), this has been their in-town operation since and grew to twenty-plus units.

PJ PEPPERS Whitbread's successor to Henry's in the cafe-bar market. Bland, formulaic and in its original guise surprisingly lacking in conviction in its food offer. The lack of internal character was a shame as the brand gained some impressive buildings which, when subsequently converted to other uses, could provide a spectacular setting.

PORTERHOUSE Predictable steak house designed by Allied to compete with Beefeater, and at one time reaching about eighty units, almost all conversions. Stepped aside, on the arrival of Big Steak.

PURPLE TURTLE An individual operation, limited to a few secondary sites in Reading, Oxford and London, but deserving of mention because of their popularity with the student/grunge market and the tremendous name. Not for the faint-hearted at times.

QUE PASA Chain of high street young persons' venues, offering tapas food most of the day and turning up the volume at night. Founded by Michael Cannon, veteran pub dealer and brand builder. Cannon purchased the ailing Eldridge Pope in 2005 and did some rebranding of the heavily themed estate. Specifically the Slurping Toad chain became Que Pasa. Cannon did not have long to appreciate his handiwork as he quickly turned the estate around with a sale to Marstons (formerly W&D) in 2007.

QUINCEY'S Greenall's version of the large American diner. Pretty standard effort that the new owners S&N thankfully felt no compulsion to expand further.

RAT AND CARROT Fun pub developed by Greene King, presumably in one of their weaker moments. Predictable style with a surfeit of brash signage, much on a vegetable and rodent theme, and lots of amusement machines and bric-a-brac. The rat has long since consumed the carrot and retired from the trade.

RAT AND PARROT For a number of years, S&N's flagship town centre brand. Few distinguishing features but endeavoured to be cafe-bar by day, evolving into a young persons' venue. By the end of the Nineties the brand was tired, and soon all that was left was a dead parrot.

REVOLUTION VODKA BARS Inventive Leisure have now expanded to over sixty sites, proving that there is plenty of life left in the young persons' high street market. Modern, refined-looking operation, aimed at the bright young things out on the town.

RHYTHM ROOM Recent concept from Luminar, the Chicago Rockers. Restaurant and bar downstairs with dancing above, in period style.

ROAST INNS Yet another of Whitbread's pub-restaurants that competed with and then was overpowered by the unrelenting growth of Brewers Fayre.

SCREAM The full title is 'It's a scream' which is happily ambiguous given the Munsch brand logo and the party atmosphere regularly engendered. An idea which has worked far better than anyone could have imagined. A wide range of buildings have been converted as Screams whilst some suitable existing pubs have been added to the collection. Interiors are basic and hard-wearing, beers and the basic food offer are ideally-pitched. Add loud music, sympathetic management and a wide range of games, including giant versions of Jenga and Connect-4, and you have a formula that works. Students are the core customer; unlike other customer groups, they move on regularly, thus supplying a fresh and captive audience each year. Meanwhile other young drinkers are also attracted. Founded in 1995 by Bass and, as a result of M&B's food-based strategy, was sold in 2010 and is now in the care of Stonegate.

SCRUFFY MURPHY'S Allied were, debatably, the first Irish bar on the scene. They concentrated on a traditional style, with a trademark old pushbike parked outside each. Pleasant effort and a good museum piece visually, but lacking the atmosphere and 'fun' of more managed environments like O'Neill's. Turnovers were not substantial and Allied soon lost confidence and were content to stand aside and let Bass and others dominate.

SEAMUS O'DONNELL'S Yet another of the Irish family but with a slight difference. This was developed by Discovery, a pubCo who concentrated on squeezing in a great deal of Irish bric-a-brac. Despite the Enterprise takeover, the brand has survived and a number of pubs so branded continue to operate as tenanted or leased pubs.

SHOELESS JOE'S Large sports bars with late licence, which peaked at four units across London. The size of the units drew a large following and an impressive atmosphere for large sporting occasions. Named after similar bars the other side of the pond and the legendary US baseball player Shoeless Joe Jackson.

SLUG AND LETTUCE A real veteran of the scene, the original was created in Islington in 1984. Developed by Grosvenor, an independent pub group who took care to obtain sites in the best locations, carefully manicured their décor and trading style and nurtured a reputation as a trendy upmarket operation. This process can't have been helped by the whimsical name, more suggestive of a fun pub, and this is more the impression one gets on a weekend evening. Now run by Stonegate, who are ensuring that the operation provides a serious food offer with a dedicated dining area.

SLURPING TOAD Distastefully named, this followed the pattern of many 'chameleon' brands with large stylish premises lavishly fitted out to encourage dining by day with the computer-controlled music system gearing up the music during the course of the evening, to a DJ and video wall later on. Developed in primary locations within provincial towns within striking distance of Eldridge Pope's Dorchester base. Unfortunately all this effort was wasted when Michael Cannon grabbed control of the company and converted the Toads to his own pet brand, Que Pasa.

SMILING SAM'S Joint venture between Allied and Namco, the machine company with a huge amount of investment thrown at it. Developed on a few leisure parks and was extremely adventurous, creating a totally alien environment for most pub-goers, much closer to an amusement arcade. The operation was never perceived as a success and has been long since shelved.

SMITH AND JONES Town-centre bar developed by Barracuda in a style reminiscent of Wetherspoons, but with a strong food bias. Reached 150 units in its glory days. But with the owners being restructured as Bramwell Pub Company, which then went into administration a year later, the brand has an uncertain future.

SPORTS BAR AND GRILL Interesting mix of restaurant and bar,

liberally served by sports screens. So far limited to four outlets, all at London stations.

SPORTS CAFÉ Opened in 1995 in Haymarket London to much publicity. Featured constant sport on 120 TV sets and four super-screens in the premises, alongside bars and restaurants crowded with sport memorabilia. There were plans to expand to five around the country but this never happened, and the original unfortunately closed in 2013.

SQUARE/ SQUARE BALLOON Dominated by a giant rotating cube of video screens in an atrium between multi-level bars, this operation had tremendous presence. Won the battle with Yates's to be the kingpin of the Nineties circuit for those who enjoy thumping music and rumbustious overcrowding. Evolved from some ordinary young persons' bars under Greenall's. With the subsequent sales of pub packages this monster did not survive.

STEAM ROCK CAFE Fun pub developed by Inn Leisure during the Eighties, including one or two memorable sites with the likes of railway carriages dropped into town centre sites. Subsequently inherited by Devenish, then Greenall's and then S&N.

TABLE TABLE With their array of restaurant brands, Whitbread were perhaps running short of ideas for new names. The surroundings of Table Table are more contemporary than Brewers Fayre and the brand now has over 100 units. Could change at any time, as the parent company continues its regular 'refinement' of brands and styles.

TAP AND SPILE Traditional beer haunt developed in modest town centre pubs by Pubmaster and now run by Punch. The brand has continued to operate in its new ownership.

TAYBARN Started in 2007 by Whitbread along with the tag 'the ultimate eatery'. The major point of distinction from its other restaurants is the all-you-can-eat buffet format with a wide choice of traditional and continental cuisine. A corporate run all-in-one food court.

TGI's The ultimate American-themed restaurant has outclassed and outlasted the opposition. TGI's has poll position in many towns and a solid reputation within the American diner market. What has kept it ahead since its establishment in 1986 is its maintenance of excellent standards of training, and service. TGI's staff are an elite, and are well rewarded for being so. The high prices and enduring popularity of the brand combined, with this professional approach, enabled Whitbread to maintain such standards. Whitbread held the UK franchise for the brand from Carlson, the American hotel and leisure corporation, and in 2007 Whitbread decided that despite TGI's' reputation it didn't fit the company's needs any longer. The forty-five-strong brand was sold to a JV, including Carlson restaurants.

TIGER TIGER More of a nightclub than a bar, Novus Leisure have now rolled out nine of these impressive and lavish complexes in major city centres, complete with multiple dance floors, bars and restaurants.

TOBY CARVERY A natural survivor, seemingly from the dreaded era of fizz and formica, of Toby Jugs and Party Sevens. Operates as a pub-restaurant at the economy end of the scale and with a functioning bar area geared towards a community-type market. This brand remained as an institution in the industrial heartlands of Bass country, but surprisingly has now migrated to more challenging markets further south, where it is nonetheless establishing itself with value diners and pub ambivalents.

TOM COBLEIGH Developed by the entrepreneurial Derek Mapp and then purchased by Rank. Nearly all Tom Cobleighs were new builds, so design and layout were largely standardised. Sites were mainly edge of town centre or facing the ring road aiming at a family audience on the Brewers Fayre model. Signage was a little dated and off-putting. Sold off by Rank in 1999 to Electra, a venture capitalist that increased the brand to seventy-five fairly rapidly and then sold to Spirit in 2003 for conversion to other bar-diner brands.

TUT N SHIVE A very brave but extremely misguided idea. Imagine Heath Robinson built a pub. The doors are crooked, the ceiling is covered with corrugated iron, strange devices whirl in corners and chairs hang from the ceiling. Paintwork is bare or poorly applied. You get the idea. Extremely hard to imagine in a corporate environment. In Whitbread's own words the brand was 'a traditional alehouse with various wacky themes and attractions.' When the novelty wore off it's also hard to imagine who would want to return.

VIA FOSSA Gothic-style bar set up by Greenall's and quickly taken over by S&N who perhaps saw some synergy with their Eerie bars.

VINTAGE INNS Originally called Fork and Pitcher, this has been one of Bass's enduring concepts, and, because of its relatively low-key approach, one of its best-kept secrets. Vintage Inns trade on 'the illusion of seclusion', flourishing in locations that appear to be leafy and rural but are conveniently located for access from main roads and nearby towns. The pubs are very traditional, taking full advantage of the character buildings they occupy. Key features of design are flagstone floors with loose rugs, real wood fires and individual tables and chairs. Food is traditional English with wholesome pies being a favourite, and ample proportions being a feature.

Customers in many of these pub-restaurants look as if they have been hand-picked. Either over-fifties or business people, with perhaps a few quiet and respectful locals in the evenings. Many customers are not aware that they are in a branded pub. The grey market is particularly targeted for the brand as marketing man has decided that the wealthy retired wish to spend much of their free time taking short drives into the countryside to be followed by a meal in a pleasant but accessible country pub. In marked contrast to the steak-house market there is no brand advertising and nothing to suggest that these outlets are not a high quality free house. The main giveaway is the humorous swing-signs. The brand has been much imitated by others, but if this is your thing a visit is recommended.

WALKABOUT The concept started off in life bearing the name Outback. As one might imagine, Australian-themed. One can 'walkabout' in over thirty locations now enjoying a rip-roaring atmosphere. Intertain have been running these since it emerged from the Regent Inns administration in 2009. Regent started the brand in the Nineties, as a sports bar rather than a giant copy of Bar Oz, and it has always been a mainstay of the circuit. The bric-a-brac and theming is largely under control, having been sensibly toned down from the original. Some sites are very extensive and, especially since recent refurbishments, are achieving some impressive turnovers.

WAXY O'CONNORS The original Waxy's was developed on the fringes of London's Chinatown in the peak of the Nineties branding boom. As soon as one descends into the intimate and labyrinthine confusion of levels and recesses, punctuated by an artificial tree and gothic imagery, it is clear that Waxy's is not the average circuit pub. Waxy's pulled in the crowds then and has continued to do so in spectacular fashion since.

Waxy's is referred to as an Irish pub, and it may have an Irish name, sell a lot of Guinness and contain a great deal of gaelic symbols and carvings within its furniture and extravagant fittings, but it does not feel overtly Irish. With its gothic arches and mystery of its symbols and hidden corners it feels almost ecclesiastical, a Sagrada Familia for the licensed trade. And they come to worship in large numbers.

Waxy's is the inspiration of Peter Salussolia, the immensely experienced head of Glendola Leisure. Glendola operate a small but distinguished group of operations that includes the huge World's End at Camden and the Rainforest Café near Picadilly Circus in central London. Whilst so many high street operators have over-stretched themselves with ambitious and rapid expansions and have paid the price, Glendola have sensibly and diligently focused on their existing pubs and been happy to accept a low profile. But when the time was right, Waxy's has grown. Now the brand numbers three, with operations in Manchester and Glasgow, carefully designed to match the original in scale and atmosphere.

There has also been talk of Waxy's being exported overseas, so whilst the expansion may be at a considered pace, it is an operation that would appear to have a big future.

WAYSIDE INNS An attractive chain that Whitbread quietly built up from among its managed estate for pubs that were not up to Beefeater or Brewers Fayre standard in terms of size or trading potential. Not overtly branded, these functioned as pleasant country pubs, usually with a good standard of food. Because they were a pub rather than a restaurant, these were all included in the 3,000 Laurel pub package and since then Wayside Inns have ceased to operate as a group.

JD WETHERSPOONS The ultimate pub brand, with an impressive national coverage and extensive brand recognition. See page 136 to 143 for more detailed comment.

WIG AND PEN Circuit pub, developed by Morlands.

YATES This brand has the most ancient heritage of any. Seventy or more years ago Yates Wine Lodges were firmly rooted in an era of old ladies escaping from their northern drudgery to drink sherry in mock gin palaces.

More recently, the brand embraced the young trendy scene with great enthusiasm, and in return young circuit drinkers converged on Yates's, typically forming long queues to gain access at weekends. They would enter an environment which still acknowledged the Victorian roots of the brand, with flock wallpaper and a riot of brightly-coloured signs, seeming to belong more to a fairground ride than the 'best meeting place in town'. Loud music, short skirts, large bouncers and a frenetic pace were essential trademarks. In the Nineties the brand expanded in as exuberant a fashion as its customers, up to 120 units or more and hurrying to join the party on almost every serious drinking circuit in the country. And not content with this, Yates developed the Ha! Ha! Canteen brand to rival All Bar One and opened the quirky Blob shop.

But then as the millenium party faded, harsh reality kicked in. We learned that Yates had a new management team and then were in merger discussions, and finally were selling a few units here and there. In keeping with the new feeling of austerity, the lavish décor was replaced by more discrete plainer backgrounds. And the Wine Lodge appendage was dropped. But this could not turn the tide, and in 2004 the original owning families Dickson and Yates succumbed to a management buyout. Again, this did not stabilise the position and the next year the company became part of Laurel Pub Co.

Following more financial instability during the credit crisis, Laurel also disappeared and Yates is now a modest constituent part of the Stonegate empire. Under Stonegate, the approach to the evening market is unchanged. A determination to exploit their town centre premises throughout the day sees the same area that was throbbing with noise and excitement at night scrubbed down and polished the next morning, so that it is wearing a smile as it offers coffee and croissants to the office workers now walking past on their way to work.

Definitions, Acronyms And Abbreviations Used Within The Book

ALMR
Association of Licensed Multiple Retailers
(represents mainly retail pub groups)

BBPA
British Beer and Pub Association

BLRA
Brewers and Licensed Retailers Association
(the BLRA succeeded the Brewers Society when some of the big six stopped brewing. It then decided in 2001 to change to BBPA to better reflect the changing nature of the Industry.

BII
British Institute of Innkeeping
(the professional body for individuals within the licensed trade)

Beer Orders
The regulations introduced after the 1989 MMC inquiry.

Beer Tie
Normal situation in pub leases and tenancies that obliges the tenant to purchase products of his brewer landlord, or products nominated by his pubCo landlord under supply agreements.

Big six
The big six brewers who dominated the trade during the 1970s and 80s; Allied Breweries, Bass, Courage, Grand Met, Scottish & Newcastle and Whitbread.

Brand
Branded pub or bar i.e. Wetherspoons, Beefeater, All Bar One, Slug and Lettuce etc.

CAMRA
Campaign for Real Ale

Craft beer
Modern-style beers, defined by small-scale production.

FSB
Federation of Small Businesses

Grand Met
Grand Metropolitan, the hotel group that purchased Watneys and Trumans

IFBB
Independent Family Brewers of Britain (started in Nineties as splinter group from Brewers Society. Mainly, but not all of the small family brewers)

IPC
Independent Pub Confederation (new umbrella group representing FairPint, ALMR and CAMRA)

Lease
Modern alternative to the pub tenancy

LVA
Licensed Victuallers Association (body for licensees in one area)

Managed House
Pub run directly by the owning company.

M&B
Mitchell & Butlers (successor to Bass Taverns)

MMC
Monopolies and Mergers Commission. But also used extensively in the book as shorthand for the episode of the critical MMC inquiry and report of 1989 into the licensed trade and the beer orders which followed it and its impact upon the pub trade.

pubCo
New wave of companies that have emerged since MMC by purchase of large packages of pubs. Mainly but not exclusively own and manage tenanted and leased pubs.

Regionals
Regional brewers. From the late Nineties onwards, this term came to be used for the two surviving regionals Marstons and Greene King.

Retail pub group
Companies like Regent Inns, Surrey Free Inns, Wetherspoons, Barracuda and Yates who operate only managed houses, normally branded.

S&N
Scottish & Newcastle

SIBA
Society of Independent Brewers, formed in 1980 as the Small Independent Brewers. Membership is open to any brewer but is dominated by the small microbreweries.

Superpubs
A term adopted by the media in describing large, generally town centre branded chain pubs. The analogy is with supermarkets and their impact on the retail trade.

Tenancy
Situation where the owner of a pub lets it to a tenant in return for an annual rental. Different to a leased pub but often used as shorthand for both tenanted and leased pubs when considered as a whole.

The Tie
Shorthand for the Beer Tie.

Traditional pubs
Most pubs that are not branded or themed.

'Wet' and 'dry'-led
Terms used within the trade for pubs geared towards either beer and alcohol sales, or food.

W&D
Wolverhampton & Dudley Brewery

Appendix One

The Family Of Brewers;
Pubs And Breweries Owned At 1986 Before MMC

	PUBS OWNED	MAIN BREWERY (S)
Big Six		
ALLIED BREWERIES	6,600	Burton, Leeds, Romford
BASS TAVERNS	7,190	Cape Hill
COURAGE (ELDERS)	5,000	Reading, Tadcaster
GRAND MET	6,300	Mortlake
SCOTTISH & NEWCASTLE	1,700 (2,300 by 1989)	Edinburgh, Newcastle
WHITBREAD	6,500	Magor, Preston
Regionals		
BELHAVEN	260	Dunbar, East Lothian
BODDINGTONS	518	Strangeways, Manchester
DEVENISH (Inn Leisure)	332	Redruth
GREENALL'S	1,626	Warrington, Birmingham
GREENE KING	766	Bury St. Edmunds
HOME ALES	450	Arnold, Nottingham
MANSFIELD	306	Mansfield
MARSTON'S (original company)	853	Burton
MATTHEW BROWN	500	Blackburn
FREDERICK ROBINSON	378	Stockport, Ulverstone
DANIEL THWAITES	379	Blackburn
VAUX	577	Sunderland, Sheffield
WOLVERHAMPTON & DUDLEY	750	Wolverhampton, Dudley
Family Brewers		
ADNAMS	65	Southwold
ARKELLS	69	Swindon

GEORGE BATEMAN	85	Wainfleet, Lincs
BATHAM & HOLDENS	8/18	West Midlands
BRAINS	123	Cardiff
BRAKSPEAR	117	Henley
BURTONWOOD	271	Burtonwood, near Warrington
ELDRIDGE POPE	183	Dorchester
ELGOOD & SONS	52	Wisbech
EVERARDS	139	Narborough, Leics
FELINFOEL	72	Llanelli
FULLERS	150	Chiswick
GEORGE GALES	97	Horndean, near Portsmouth
GIBBS MEW	75	Salisbury
HALL & WOODHOUSE	146	Blandford Forum, Dorset
HARDY & HANSON	205	Kimberley, Notts
JOSEPH HOLT	93	Manchester
HOOK NORTON	35	Chipping Norton
HYDES	49	Manchester
JENNINGS	78	Cockermouth
KING & BARNES	65	Horsham, West Sussex
JW LEES	143	Middleton, Manchester
MACLAY	28	Alloa
MCMULLEN	162	Hertford
MITCHELLS	52	Lancaster
MORLAND	206	Abingdon
MORRELLS	134	Oxford
PALMERS	67	Bridport
RIDLEY'S	65	Chelmsford
ST AUSTELL	131	St Austell
SHEPHERD NEAME	249	Faversham, Kent
SAM SMITH'S	264	Tadcaster
TIMOTHY TAYLOR & CO	29	Keighley
WADWORTH	151	Devizes
CHARLES WELLS	282	Bedford
YOUNG'S	149	Wandsworth

Appendix Two;

The Family Of Brewers; Pubs And Breweries; Changes Since MMC

	DATE OF; COMPANY CLOSURE*	CLOSURE/SALE OF BREWERY(S)
Big Six		
ALLIED BREWERIES	1999	1996 (Carlsburg – Tetley)
BASS TAVERNS	now M&B	2001 (Interbrew)
COURAGE (ELDERS)	1995	1995 (S&N)
GRAND MET	1994	1991 (Courage)
SCOTTISH & NEWCASTLE	2008 (Heinekin)	2008 (Heinekin)
WHITBREAD	2001**	2000 (Interbrew)
Regionals		
BELHAVEN	2005 (Greene King)	
BODDINGTONS	1995 (Greenall's)	1989 (Whitbread)
DEVENISH (Inn Leisure)	1993 (Greenall's)	2004
GREENALL'S	1999 (S&N)	1991
GREENE KING		
HOME ALES	1986 (S&N)	1996
MANSFIELD	1999 (W&D)	2002
MARSTON'S (original company)	1999 (W&D)	
MATTHEW BROWN	1987 (S&N)	1991
FREDERICK ROBINSON		
DANIEL THWAITES		
VAUX	2000 (Swallow-Whitbread)	
WOLVERHAMPTON & DUDLEY	2007 (renamed Marston's)	
Family Brewers		
ADNAMS		
ARKELLS		

GEORGE BATEMAN		
BATHAM & HOLDENS		
BRAINS		
BRAKSPEAR		2002 (Refresh UK)
BURTONWOOD	2005 (Marston's)	2003 (Contract brewg)
ELDRIDGE POPE	2007 (Marston's)	2003 (Thomas Hardy)
ELGOOD & SONS		
EVERARDS		
FELINFOEL		
FULLERS		
GEORGE GALES	2005 (Fullers)	2006
GIBBS MEW	1998 (Enterprise)	
HALL & WOODHOUSE		
HARDY & HANSON	2006 (Greene King)	2006
JOSEPH HOLT		
HOOK NORTON		
HYDES		
JENNINGS	2005 (Marston's)	
KING & BARNES	2000 (Hall & Woodhouse)	2000
JW LEES		
MACLAY		1999
MCMULLEN		
MITCHELLS		1999 (Thwaites)
MORLAND	2000 (Greene King)	2000
MORRELLS	1998 (Michael Cannon)	1998
PALMERS		
RIDLEY'S	2005 (Greene King)	2005
ST AUSTELL		
SHEPHERD NEAME		
SAM SMITH'S		
TIMOTHY TAYLOR & CO		
WADWORTHS		
CHARLES WELLS		
YOUNG'S	2006 (now Wells-Youngs)	

The date in the first column is either when the company was taken over, closed or merged, OR changed its method of operation and ended any substantial involvement within the licensed trade. The named company is the acquiring company.

The date in the second column is when that company's main brewery closed. If there is a name in brackets after the date then the brewery/beer brands were bought by that company.

* Not always the formal date of closure, but when the company effectively left the trade by ceasing to operate its brewery(s) and pubs.
** Whitbread still operate their restaurants but for practical purposes they are no longer participants in the licensed trade.

References And Notes

General

All MMC material and quotes from politicians reproduced by kind permission of the National Archives.

Part 1   The Halcyon Years

1   See table below.
2   Chartered Surveyor Weekly; 12/12/1985 Breweries over a barrel on valuations. Barry Gillham.
3   Mutch, Alistair, *Strategic and Organisational Change; from production to retailing in UK brewing 1950-1990* (2006). Routledge. 1967 figure of 77%. (Source 1989 MMC report)
4,5 The source of the beer consumption statistics and historical background on takeovers and Victorian investment bubble is *The English Pub; A History by Peter Haydon* (Robert Hale Ltd), 1995. By kind permission of Peter Haydon.
6   Area managers were also referred to as regional managers or business development managers or BDMs for short. They had a critical role in representing their brewery to its tenants, maintaining the relationship between the two and promoting company products. Their equivalent for managed estates would look after significantly fewer pubs, typically fifteen to twenty and were effectively the manager of the pub manager.
7   For tenants of the big six, wines and spirits were normally supplied

by a subsidiary or linked supplier. Most of these brewers had purchased or created such companies for this purpose.

8   During the 1970s or 1980s the total cost for an 'ingoing tenant' would be little more than around £5,000 or perhaps £10,000 for a large pub (in 1970's money).

9   Mutch, Alistair, *Strategic and Organisational Change; from production to retailing in UK brewing 1950-1990* (2006). Routledge.

10 Also known as segmentation, or market segmentation.

11 John Young, 1971, source unknown.

12 Hutt C., *The Death of the English Pub*, Arrow Books, 1973. With kind permission of Chris Hutt.

Part 2   The Heavy Hand of Government

1   All information in this section from *The Supply of Beer 1989,* MMC Report, HMSO.

2   All quotes from Estates Times *Licensed Premises* survey 19/5/1989

3   Keyworth T, Lawton Smith H and Yarrow G, 1994 *The Effects of Regulation in the UK Beer Market.* Regulatory Policy Research Centre, Oxford University.

4   Assignable leases create a capital value for the pub landlord as the remaining lease period can be sold to another licensee. This is a major point of differentiation to the traditional pub tenancy.

5   The Competition Commission (CC) replaced the MMC on 1st April 1999.

6   *The Independent,* 27/5/1994, 'S&N deal restores Cannon to pub trade'.

7   Source The Supply of Beer, Office of Fair Trading Report, December 2000 (Table 7, appendix E67).

Part 3   Branded!

1   *Sunday Times* 25/9/1994

2   Bruce Masters still holds his record. Having started his pub visits

in 1960, as of 19/1/2012 he had visited an impressive 44,736 pubs. Source guinessworldrecords.com

3   *The Times*, 17/10/1996

4   *Independent on Sunday* 27/8/95 Is it a shop? Is it a cinema? No it's a superpub.

5   *Inn Touch*, Bass Company magazine Oct/Nov 1996.

6   *Evening Standard* 2/4/1997 'Look what they've done to my pub Ma'.

7   *Evening Standard* 2/4/1997 'Look what they've done to my pub Ma'.

8   *Independent on Sunday* 27/8/95 'Is it a shop? Is it a cinema? No it's a superpub'.

9   *Estates Gazette*, 8/6/2002 'On thin ice'

10 *Independent on Sunday* 27/8/95 Is it a shop? Is it a cinema? No it's a superpub

11 *The Times* 27/8/97   Roman Bath fights a losing battle to keep superpub hordes from the gates

12 *Estates Gazette* 12/9/98 Leisure centre

13 *Leisure Week* 6-19 November 1998 'York licensing laws spark uproar'.

14 *London Evening Standard* 30/11/1998 'Covent Garden bans vertical drinkers'.

15 *Estates Gazette*, 22/7/2000 'Westminster puts the lights out'.

16 *Independent on Sunday* 27/8/1995 'Is it a shop? Is it a cinema? No it's a superpub'.

Part 4 Market Mayhem

1   Key Note Market Report, April 2001

2   *Morning Advertiser* 9/2/94

3   *Morning Advertiser* 8/1/94

4   *Licensed and Leisure Property* April 1995 Investing in revolution

5   *Morning Advertiser* 24/9/93

6   *The Times*, April 14, 1994

7   *Morning Advertiser* 28/9 and 4/10 1993

8   Average total capital expenditure by big six brewers between 1982 and 1985 on their managed houses, £74,400 on their tenancies £11,200 (source Supply of Beer, MMC 1989)

9   With kind permission of Adnams plc

10   Hutt C., *The Death of the English Pub,* Arrow Books, 1973.

11   *Western Morning News* 7&8/8/1995 'Rural institutions at risk as breweries insist on change'.

12   *Guardian* 11/7/2000 'Minister bitter over pub signs of the times'.

13   *Leisure Week*, 10-23 August, 2000 'Independents to fight big brands'.

14   The Town and Country Planning (use class) order 1987 classes pubs as an A4 use. It then permits A4 uses to convert to A3, food & restaurant use, A2 town centre bank and office use and A1 retail without planning permission.

15   *Big Hospitality* 7/2/2014. 'Supermarket Sweep; CAMRA research shows that 208 pubs have become supermarkets in the previous 2 years'.

16   *The Express*, 3/3/1997 'That's the way to do it, brewers are told'.

Part 5   Ripples From The Revolution

1,2 Mutch, Alistair, *Strategic and Organisational Change; from production to retailing in UK brewing 1950-1990* (2006). Routledge

3   The 'rescue' of Boddingtons by Whitbread is an illustration of how the Whitbread 'umbrella' developed. These were a variety of smaller brewers in whom Whitbread invested, generally for paternal reasons, and particularly in the era of Colonel Whitbread who, by all accounts, was motivated by the best intentions. Unfortunately this influence, and shareholding, was used subsequently to gain control of many of those brewers, supposedly under Whitbread's protective guidance.

4   Davenports and Simpkiss of Birmingham and Shipstones of Nottingham, Wem Brewery, Wrekin Brewery.

5   Premier became the name and supplied many of the outlets which

were merged with Whitbread's lodge operation to become what is now the ubiquitous Premier Inns.

6   Quote by kind permission of Peter Haydon.

7   *Daily Telegraph*, 21/3/2001 'How Whitbread got to be small(er) beer'.

8   *The Independent*, 26/8/1996 'Bass buys Carlsberg-Tetley for £200m'.

9   *Morning Advertiser,* 8/7/13 Roger Protz; 'Truman takes the (yeast) strain'.

10 University of Leeds; virtuallabs@leeds; where do brewers get their yeast from?

11 Samuel Smith, Greenall's and Devenish were most prominent.

12 *Daily Telegraph*, Business news 20/9/97 'An Orwellian vision pays off for the pub iconoclast'.

13 CAMRA newsletter, March 1997

14 *Daily Telegraph* 27/1/1996 'It's the pub; but not as we know it'.

15 *Leisure and Hospitality Business* magazine 31/5/2001 'Pub deals to remain profitable for City financiers'.

16 *Property Week* 10/5/2002 'Happy hour in the City'.

Part 6   Sober October

1   www.wilson-drinks-report.com

2   *Local Government Chronicle* 29/11/2010

3   *Morning Advertiser*, 22/1/2009 'Sunset industry danger warns BII boss'.

4   *Caterer and Hotelkeeper* 19/7/2012 'Average British pub pays £65,500 a year in beer taxes'.

5   Hansard on-line 27/2/1976 Licensing (amendment) No 2 Bill

6   The six o'clock swill is the slang term given to the practice of swilling beer quickly and excessively caused by the restrictive hours adopted across much of Australia until the 1950s and 1960s (repeal varied from state to state)

7   Fleurets Rental Survey, June 2001

8   www.retail-week.com/topics/policy/shop-vacancy, 4/9/2012 Vacancy rate stands at 14.6%

9   Centre for Retail Research; retail futures 2018 report 28/5/2013

10 *Guardian* 6/7/1995

11 *Morning Advertiser* 5/5/2005 'JDW delays conversion of pubs to non-smoking'.

12 *Morning Advertiser* 3/7/2012 'Smoking ban; majority of licencees want smoking legislation amended for pubs'.

13 *Local Government Chronicle* 24/7/1998 'Task-Force calls time on Outdated Licensing Laws'.

14 *Evening Standard* 2/5/2001 '24-hour pubs to end yob culture'.

15 Department for Culture, Media and Sport, 8/11/2007

16 BBC News website 21/7/1998 'Open all hours'.

17 *Journal of Social Science and Medicine* 2/12/2013 'Violence rates unaffected by twenty-four-hour licensing laws'.

18 BBPA 25/11/10

19 www.crp-news.com, 21/09/2009 'Massive decline in arrests for drunkenness helps take the stigma out of bingeing'.

20 *Telegraph* 6/4/2010 'Owners of bars and clubs face six months in jail if they allow "all you can drink" deals.'

21 *Estates Gazette*, 17/1/2004 'Westminster humiliated'.

22 www.dalstonist.co.uk Special Policy Area

Part 7 Starting A New Life

1 The background information for some of the pub histories was gained from The Lost Pubs Project, a web-based record of closed pubs throughout the country. This is an invaluable memorial to our many closed pubs. Over 24,000 pubs are listed with over 11,000 photographs. Clearly a lot of work has gone into this and thanks are due to the organisers and all contributors. For details in your area visit www.closedpubs.co.uk

2 *Cemetery Junction in Reading* is a 2010 film directed by Ricky Gervais and Stephen Merchant. It documents coming of age in 1970s Reading. Ricky Gervais grew up in the area around Cemetery Junction in Reading.

Part 8   The Beer Tie Untied

1   *Morning Advertiser* 26/4/2001 'Pub trade split by clash of cultures'.

2   In an extensive survey, The Complete Pub Picture, Reader Survey, printed on 11/8/2005, conducted by the *Morning Advertiser* of 2,000 licensees only 36% of all landlords saw their business development manager (BDM) more regularly than once every six months. That figure dropped to 32% and 22% in the case of Enterprise and Punch tenants. 28% of all tenants rated their BDM less than satisfactory. There was a high correlation between the regularity of seeing their BDM and the rating of his performance.

3   *www.enterpriseinns.com/Investors/.../Documents/Annual-Report-2013.pdf*

4   In July 2012 research by CGA showed that 71% of pubCo lessees and tenants would sign with their landlord again, a 10% increase on the result from a year earlier. A peculiar verdict by lessees in the context of the battle raging on their behalf. *Morning Advertiser* 28/6/2012 'Pub Companies satisfy 10% more tenants'.

5   *Morning Advertiser* 6/6/2013 'Statutory Code; pubcos under fire at Fair Deal for your local Westminster Rally'.

Part 9   Some Shafts Of Light

1   To provide a breakdown of the current size of the various sectors of the trade, the Institute of Public Policy Research (IPPR) provided figures in 2009 which were quoted in the government response to the BISC Consultation. The figures showed that in that year there were 55,530 pubs in the UK. Of these 28,800 were tenanted or leased, 8,500 were managed and 18,230 were free houses. Of the managed and tenanted groups about 25% were owned by brewers and 75% by pubCos.

2   Greene King's full-year numbers in June 2013 were, as ever, fairly robust. We learned that its retail division now provided 72% of its revenue and that it planned to increase its number of managed

houses from 993 to 1,100 with more purchases and some conversions from tenancy. It claimed that food, wine and coffee were the key to future growth. The retail activity seems to be supporting the rest of the company as the brewing side was showing a fall in profitability of 7-8% whilst 108 units had been sold from the tenanted sector and there were plans to dispose of a further 125 in the coming year to reduce that estate to 1,200 units. There were plans to transfer as many as 10-15% of these to management.

3 Diagio was formed in 1997 when Guinness merged with Grand Metropolitan, by then a distiller of vodka and Johnnie Walker amongst many other products.

4 One of the most alarming falls for instance is in wine consumption in France. During the 1960s French adults drank an average of 160 litres of wine per year, over 200 bottles, or about four per week. This had fallen to around fifty-seven litres per head by 2010, roughly a two-third drop. Considered another way, in 1980 51% of the French drank wine almost every day. Thirty years later this figure was at a third of this level and both tap water and bottled water were consumed in larger quantities at mealtimes. Source BBC online news 25/3/2013

5 On-trade 52.6%, off-trade 47.4% as confirmed by BBPA Feb 2014.

6 Bryson, B, *Notes From A Small Island,* Harper Collins, 1995.

7 *Daily Express,* 4/3/1997; 'Out with the inn crowd'.

8 *The Times,* 31/8/96.

9 *The Telegraph,* 13/8/2010 (2010 Market Report, *The Publican*) 'Pubs are for drinking, not dining, in'.

10 *Caterer & Hotelkeeper* 20/11/2009 'Pub food continues to grow despite recession'.

11 State of the craft beer industry 2013, Demeter Group Investment Bank.

12 23/12/2013 BBC online news, 'Scottish beer-maker Brewdog hits funding target'.

13 CGA strategy on behalf of CAMRA.

14 bighospitality.co.uk 4/5/2012 'Continued divergence between managed and tenanted sector'.
15 *Morning Advertiser,* 26/4/2013 - Mintel; British Lifestyles 2013.
16 *Financial Times,* 8/1/2012 'Closing time beckons for irish pubs'.
17 bighospitality.co.uk 16/9/2013 'Amber Taverns ramps up expansion plans'.
18 Belfasttelegraph.co.uk 6/3/2014 'Belfast National Grand Café bar banking on round the clock trade'.
19 *Morning Advertiser,* 14/6/13; CGA strategy report
20 *The Publican's Morning Advertiser,* 27/2/2014, 'Pub market report'.
21 *The Publican's Morning Advertiser,* 23/3/2011, 'The UK has too many pubs.'

The Ultimate Guide to Pub Brands

1 *Morning Advertiser,* 30/5/2002 '6C fans flames of Ember growth'.
2 *The Independent,* 27/5/1994, 'S&N Deal restores Cannon to pub trade'.

Appendix 1 and 2

Sources; various company histories, MMC report, Independent Family Brewers of Britain website. (IFBB.)

Select Bibliography

The Death of the English Pub, Chris Hutt, (Arrow Books), 1973.
The English Pub; A History, Peter Haydon, (Robert Hale Ltd), 1995.
Man walks into a pub, a sociable history of beer, Pete Brown, (MacMillan), 2003.
The Search for the perfect pub, Paul Moody and Robin Turner, (Orion), 2013.

Acknowledgements

To Liam for his invaluable contribution, both in a literary and licensed respect. To Lyn for putting up with me, and some moments of deep insight, to Paul for his input and promptings over the years, and Dave G for his views on regular occasions, and guiding me into the industry in the first place. To Ken for sterling work with computers on many occasions, and to Ricky for his creative input. To Giorgio for his thoughts and encouragement from afar.

To John Longden for being so generous with his time and advice, to Nick Bish for some valuable input, and an embarrassing spelling lesson! and to Andrew Pring, a firm pub supporter, for his help and support in the past, and more recently.

To everyone at Troubador who has assisted with advice, or in producing the book and helped to make this a pleasant experience. In particular I wish to mention Naomi, Lauren, Sarah, Terry and Rachel.

To four books in particular; *The English Pub*, by Peter Haydon, a fantastic read and the source of much of the historic background on early pub history. *The Death of the English Pub*, from many years ago, *The Search for the Perfect Pint* and *Man Walks into a Pub* have all influenced me but, more than this, convinced me that I was heading in the right direction.

To all the journals, newspapers and websites from which I have drawn information, but in particular, the *Publican's Morning Advertiser*, a stalwart presence over the years, maintaining a balanced and incisive view of all matters to do with the trade.

To Chris Hutt, Peter Haydon and The National Archives for their kind approval in authorising me to use their work. To BBPA for providing me with some key statistics.

To all the many characters I have worked with in the trade. And finally, not least, to everyone else who I have enjoyed a pint with over the years.